ESTMAR COLLEGE LIBRARY

D0078237

SHAKESPEARE'S
MATURE
TRAGEDIES

SHAKESPEARE'S

MATURE

TRAGEDIES

by Bernard McElroy

PRINCETON UNIVERSITY PRESS

PRINCETON, NEW JERSEY

822.33
Sm

PR
2983
.M317

Copyright © 1973 by Princeton University Press
LC: 72-5389
ISBN: 0-691-06247-1
ALL RIGHTS RESERVED. No part of this book
may be reproduced in any form or by any electronic
or mechanical means including information storage
and retrieval systems without permission
in writing from the publisher.

This book has been set in Linotype Times Roman

Printed in the United States of America
by Princeton University Press,
Princeton, New Jersey

89923

But there where I have garnered up my heart,
Where either I must live or bear no life,
The fountain from the which my current runs
Or else dries up—to be discarded thence. . . .

Othello
(IV.ii.57-60)

ACKNOWLEDGMENTS

IT IS A PLEASURE, first of all, to express my gratitude to Professor Anthony Caputi, who has been a wise critic and staunch well-wisher of this study since its inception several years ago. He patiently read the very long and none too tidy initial drafts, and came up with pages and pages of good suggestions. I also wish to thank Professors Barry B. Adams, Paul Hummert, H. Scott McMillin, and Norman Rabkin, all of whom read the manuscript in whole or in part at various stages of its development, and offered helpful advice or encouragement. It would make a very long list indeed were I to try to thank individually all the friends and colleagues who spent so many hours with me, listening, talking, and sometimes arguing about these plays. I hope they realize how much their friendship and generosity are appreciated. Such, too, is my gratitude to the fine teachers with whom it is my good fortune to have studied.

In the course of writing this book, I have used the libraries of Cornell University, Loyola University of Chicago, Northwestern University, and Columbia University, as well as the Public Library of the City of New York and the Newberry Library in Chicago. A timely grant from Loyola's Committee on Faculty Research assisted in preparing the final manuscript.

Since this study was essentially complete in draft form in 1970, material which appeared after 1969 has not influenced its development. Nevertheless, I have tried, by means of last-minute additions to the notes, to acknowledge at least a few of the parallels between my thinking and the work that has been published in the past several years. Shakespearean scholarship is, of course, a bottomless pit, and there are bound to be many parallels and perhaps even instances of unconscious indebtedness which I have failed to specify in

ACKNOWLEDGMENTS

the notes. For any such omissions I make a blanket apology here and now.

Textual references are to *The Complete Pelican Shakespeare*, Alfred Harbage, general editor (Baltimore: Penguin, 1969).

Bernard Mc Elroy, Rome, 1973

CONTENTS

SHAKESPEARE'S
MATURE
TRAGEDIES

ONE

"AND THAT'S TRUE TOO":
THE WORLD OF SHAKESPEAREAN TRAGEDY

FOR ALL their diversity in tone and subject matter, Shakespeare's four mature tragedies, *Hamlet, Othello, King Lear,* and *Macbeth,* all embody at least one essential experience in common, the collapse of the subjective world of the tragic hero. By this I mean that the world-picture of each of the title characters is undermined at a fundamental level; his most basic assumptions about who he is and what reality is are rendered untenable, and he must struggle to reconstruct his total vision upon some new basis. Though the process is somewhat different in each play, the essential experience is central to all four. With his subjective world in ruins, the hero undergoes a period of extreme disorientation, a dislodgment which in Lear's case precipitates total psychic dissolution. From the low-point of such mental chaos, each must struggle to impose cohesion upon his personal world, and, in the interim, each faces the same basic problem, how to endure what is, for him, simply unendurable.

But it makes no sense to study the tragic hero's apprehension of the world without also studying the world apprehended; and, indeed, each of these plays does delineate a "world," a highly distinct, self-contained version of reality. Life in the *Hamlet*-world is quite different from life as lived by any real group of individuals, but it is no less different from life as lived in the world of *King Lear,* and the difference encompasses not only the general quality of existence but also the fundamental problems which reality, as envisioned in each of the two plays, poses for the heroes. The worlds delineated by *Othello* and *Macbeth* are equally distinctive. Therefore, my approach in the following studies will be to

3

comment upon the world delineated by each of the tragedies, and then to trace in the action the relationship between the world of the play—the macrocosm—and the subjective world of the hero—the microcosm.

When we speak of "the world of a play," we, of course, are using a metaphor, one that crops up with increasing frequency in the criticism of recent decades. Though this metaphor is used often, it is seldom used precisely; Maynard Mack has done more than anyone to clarify what the term can mean: "Great plays, as we know, do present us with something that can be called a world . . . a world like our own in being made up of people, actions, situations, thoughts, feelings, and much more, but unlike our own in being perfectly, or almost perfectly, significant and coherent. In a play's world, each part implies the other parts, and each lives, each means, with the life and meaning of the rest."[1] Through selectivity and emphasis, a playwright sets forth a self-contained definition of reality within his play, a world which proposes for itself the principles by which life operates within its matrix. Qualities or aspects of life which are relevant to the view of reality depicted are intensified by patterned repetition of incidents, problems and preoccupations of characters, recurrent imagery, and thematic structure, while those aspects of life irrelevant to the particular version of reality being offered are diminished or eliminated entirely. For instance, the *Hamlet*-world operates primarily by intrigue and deception, while the *Lear*-world operates mainly by naked power and violent energy in open confrontation. This is not to say that there is no violence in *Hamlet* or no intrigue

---

[1] "The World of *Hamlet*," in *Tragic Themes in Western Literature*, ed. Cleanth Brooks (New Haven: Yale Univ. Press, 1955), p. 30. See also A. C. Bradley, *Shakespearean Tragedy* (1904; rpt. London: Macmillan, 1952), p. 333; G. Wilson Knight, *The Wheel of Fire* (London: Oxford Univ. Press, 1930), pp. 3-7; Geoffrey Bickersteth, "The Golden World of *King Lear*," *Proc. of the British Acad.*, 32 (1946), 147; and Robert Speaight, *Nature in Shakespearean Tragedy* (London: Hollis and Carter, 1955), pp. 4-5.

in *King Lear*, the question is one of dramatic emphasis. In *Hamlet*, deception and perplexity are the most salient features of life, are, in fact, a *way* of life, while violence is refined to its most secret and sophisticated forms—poison, a forged death warrant, a rigged fencing match. In *King Lear*, on the other hand, Edmund's intrigues are depicted so perfunctorily that many critics raise objections to their probability, while violence reaches such extreme brutality that the same critics find it all but intolerable. Shakespeare could, of course, have made Claudius as bloody as Macbeth or Edmund as subtle as Iago. That he did not do so should in itself draw our attention to the quality of life he was emphasizing in each of the play-worlds. The characteristic problem of life in the *Hamlet*-world is how the truth on all levels is to be discovered, while the characteristic problem in the *Lear*-world is how the truth is to be endured.

Actions and patterns of actions, characters and their preoccupations, thematic selection and emphasis, patterns of imagery, prevailing or failing metaphysical systems, setting conceived of as a mode or way of life—these are the main constituents of the world of a play, and the list no doubt could be lengthened. In works of the greatest power and unity of conception, these elements coalesce to produce a varied but internally consistent, self-contained image of reality in which certain qualities or aspects of universal human experience are intensified. A more exact definition of the "world" of a play is probably not possible, for the term is, as I said, a metaphor. However, it is an apt and necessary metaphor for a play which embodies a vision of life so incisive and so fully realized that the drama is able to create its own definition of reality, and to propose for itself the principles by which life operates within its matrix.

That *Macbeth* takes place in a world which is quite different from that of *Hamlet* we need only our experience of the plays to attest. Yet, since the time of Coleridge and Hazlitt, there has been a persistent feeling that the four mature tragedies are not only related to each other in a way that they are

5

not to the early tragedies, historical tragedies, and Roman tragedies, but also that the four of them together, far more than any one of them individually, constitute Shakespeare's fullest realization of the tragic possibilities of life.[2] For Coleridge, the great unifying principle of drama, with specific reference to Shakespearean tragedy, was "that ever-varying balance or balancing of images, notions, or feelings (for I avoid the vague word, idea) conceived as in opposition to each other; in short, the perception of identity and contrariety."[3] It was he among English critics who first drew attention to the conflict of images, notions, or feelings as the prime conflict in Shakespearean tragedy, exceeding in importance the conflicts of personality or purposes in the plot.[4] Almost a century later, A. C. Bradley, under the influence of Hegelian dialectics, expanded an idea similar to (and indebted to) Coleridge's into a general theory of Shakespearean tragedy (pp. 5-39). Modern critics have generally renounced (and in many cases *de*nounced) Bradley's methods and

[2] Though the tendency to group the four plays together is well established, there is by no means unanimity on the subject. Derek Traversi, in *An Approach to Shakespeare*, 2nd ed. (1938; rpt. London: Sands, 1957), lists *Hamlet* with *Troilus and Cressida* and *Measure for Measure* as "problem plays," and groups the other three as "mature tragedies." L. C. Knights, in *"King Lear* and the Great Tragedies," *The Age of Shakespeare*, ed. Boris Ford, A Guide to English Literature (1955; rpt. Baltimore, Penguin, 1962), pp. 228-256, groups *King Lear, Macbeth, Antony and Cleopatra*, and *Coriolanus* as the "great tragedies." Willard Farnham, in *Shakespeare's Tragic Frontiers* (Berkeley and Los Angeles: Univ. of California Press, 1963), groups *Macbeth* with *Timon of Athens, Coriolanus*, and *Antony and Cleopatra* as the "final tragedies," dealing with a deeply flawed hero, while Francis Fergusson, in *Shakespeare, The Pattern in His Carpet* (New York: Delacorte, 1970), pp. 165-175, separates "the lonely world of *Othello*" from the other three which he considers tragedies of monarchy.

[3] *Coleridge's Shakespearean Criticism*, ed. Thomas Raysor (Cambridge, Mass.: Harvard Univ. Press, 1930), I, 205.

[4] Schlegel made a similar suggestion in Lecture 23: *Lectures on Dramatic Art and Literature*, trans. John Black (London: G. Bell, 1883), p. 368.

6

conclusions, but still the feeling persists that a single vision
of reality does underlie all four mature tragedies, and so the
search for common denominators goes on.

One of the most ambitious and stimulating of such searches
was undertaken by Norman Rabkin in his book, *Shakespeare
and the Common Understanding*,[5] in which he borrows from
quantum mechanics the concept of complementarity as set
forth by Robert Oppenheimer and Niels Bohr. Basically this
concept holds that two things which logically should contradict each other or cancel each other out can exist side by
side, both being perfectly true. Rabkin's summary of the
operation of a similar perception in Shakespeare is, I feel
certain, the most illuminating and provocative comment on
the canon in recent years. "Shakespeare tends to structure
his imitations in terms of polar opposites. . . . Generally the
opposition is rather between two complexes of related elements than simply between two single ideals. Always the
dramatic structure sets up the opposed elements as equally
valid, equally desirable, and equally destructive, so that the
choice that the play forces the reader to make becomes
impossible" (p. 12). The opposition is always basic and
total: "Each value, or set of values, is a total way of seeing
which excludes the other. There can be no compromise"
(p. 7). Thus complementarity is quite different from the
Hegelian thesis-antithesis-resolution in that there is no final
merging into oneness, no relaxation of dialectical tension.
Both thesis and antithesis remain fully distinct, both are
equally persuasive, and each has equal demands to make for
adherence. Above all, complementarity is not an ideology
and still less a "statement" which a play "makes." It is a
mode of perception which "enables the plays to create illusory worlds which, like the world we feel about us, make
sense in ways that consistently elude our power to articulate
them rationally and yet seem to represent the truth better
than rational articulation. Shakespeare's habitual approach

[5] New York: Free Press, 1967.

makes his plays definitive embodiments of our knowledge that we live in a world which though it makes sense to our intuitive consciousness cannot be reduced to sense, and which though palpably coherent is always more complicated than the best of our analytic descriptions can say" (p. 13).

Rabkin's study of the canon is replete with examples of complementarity as a mode of vision in Shakespeare, but there is a striking instance which he does not cite, one which shows with particular clarity the complementarity value systems of the mature tragedies. It occurs in Act v, scene ii, of *King Lear*. Since losing his eyes, Gloucester has been vacillating between suicide and patient endurance, just as Lear has been torn between patience and apocalyptic rage. Edgar has painstakingly urged his father to accept his intolerable lot, and leads him to the shade of a tree to await the outcome of the battle between Cordelia's forces and those of her sisters. For a moment there is a glimmer of hope that Edgar will return from the field to bring his father comfort, but that hope is, of course, instantly dashed when Lear and Cordelia are defeated and taken. Gloucester immediately backslides into his former despair, and, refusing to save himself by flight, asserts, "A man may rot even here" (v.ii.8). Edgar once again urges patient resignation:

> What, in ill thoughts again? Men must endure
> Their going hence, even as their coming hither;
> Ripeness is all. Come on.
>
> (9-11)

This speech is surely one of the most frequently commented upon in the play, and critics who would offer an optimistic reading of the tragedy are especially fond of it as Shakespeare's definitive pronouncement. Far more worthy of comment, I think, is Gloucester's astonishing reply: "And that's true too" (11). If Gloucester had simply said, "That is true," or "That is not true," the reply would be unremarkable; it would merely mean that Gloucester had made up his mind. But he is asserting that "a man may rot even here" and "men must endure their going hence" can both exert irrefutable claims for belief and adherence. Upon the question of a fundamental value, endurance, a major issue of the play, both alternatives offered by the dramatic situation make equal sense or equal nonsense. Both lay equal claim to validity. Significantly enough, "And that's true too" is the last line we hear from Gloucester.

The two diametrically opposed alternatives are based upon two diametrically opposed ideas of what man is, what the gods are, and what life itself is. The situation in which two mutually exclusive views exert inexorable claims is not unique to the Gloucester subplot, but is the prevalent condition of the *Lear*-world. Moreover, it is not unique to the *Lear*-world (though perhaps more clearly and forcefully present in this play than in others), but is an important aspect of tragic experience in the other mature tragedies as well. Final intellectual resolution is impossible beyond the paradoxical "And that's true too"; such resolution as the character ultimately finds is based upon emotional or intuitive adherence to one side or the other, or more often, as in Gloucester's case, is brought about by death which finally resolves all when the heart is too weak "the conflict to support." The complementary viewpoint is found again and again throughout all four of the mature tragedies, and constitutes, I believe, the common foundation of all four tragic worlds.

In his examination of specific Shakespearean works, Rabkin finds that, although complementarity is a mode of perception basic to them all, the issues involved in complementary tension are different in each individual play or poem. Here I disagree with him, at least as far as the four mature tragedies are concerned. In recent years it has been very widely recognized that Shakespeare lived in an era of intellectual, religious, and social transition, and that the conflicts and tensions which tore Western Europe apart in the sixteenth and seventeenth centuries are everywhere reflected in his works.[6] Fundamentally, these disputes centered on the break-

---

[6] See esp. Theodore Spencer, *Shakespeare and the Nature of Man*

down of the theocentric, hierarchically ordered universe of the Middle Ages, and the rise of the new skepticism, empiricism, and individualism of the late Renaissance. The medieval world-view was still very much alive in the minds of men, but its fundamental assumptions were being questioned or attacked outright by new discoveries in astronomy, by the renewed interest in pre-Christian philosophy, and by the writings of such contemporary intellectuals as Machiavelli, Montaigne, and Bruno.

Basically, mature Shakespearean tragedy is built around a few of the fundamental tensions generated by the conflict between opposed world-views. The issues involved do not take the form of questions, still less of theories, but rather of diametrically opposed possibilities about the nature of reality, about man's relation to the world and the cosmos, about the value of his actions and the limitations of his capabilities. The dialectical tension between those opposites permeates the thematic structure of all four plays. An outline of the opposed world-views might be set up as follows:

The universe is a moral order and operates by a natural law inherent in itself toward an end that, because it is natural, is desirable and good.	The universe is morally neutral, moves blindly, indifferent to events which transpire within it, and is without ultimate object.
Man's estate in nature is a special one, of a higher order than that of the beasts, but subordinate in turn to a higher natural or supernatural order. Thus man is noble because of his humanity, but required to live within the limits of his place in the hierarchy.	In an unstructured universe, man is simply another animal of the earth, having neither a special destiny nor moral sanction upon his actions. He is a free agent who may and does live by his appetites and his will, limited only by what he is willing to dare.

(1942; rpt. New York: Macmillan, 1958), p. 50. Also Irving Ribner, *Patterns in Shakespearean Tragedy* (New York: Barnes and Noble, 1960), p. 8. A very different view is eloquently expressed by Alfred Harbage, *Shakespeare and the Rival Traditions* (1952: rpt. New York: Barnes and Noble, 1968), pp. xii-xvi, 133-158.

Values arise naturally from the nobility of man's nature. Since they are in accord with natural law, they are absolute values, intrinsically good in themselves. The most important are love and honesty, which in turn breed further values such as honor, loyalty, compassion, generosity, etc. The opposites of these values, hate and deceitfulness, are absolutely and intrinsically evil, as are the anti-values they breed, cruelty, hard-heartedness, ingratitude, hypocrisy, selfishness, etc.

Since the nobility of man is a ludicrous self-deception, so are the values that arise from it. Man is ruled only by appetite and will. Love is lust, and honesty is folly. The only standard of values is what one desires for one's own purposes.

The basic institutions of society are in accord with natural law and hence the bonds of family and monarchy are sacrosanct. Any violation of them is a violation of nature itself.

Since man is free, societal bonds are arbitrary and artificial. Only a fool allows them to interfere with his self-interest.

Individual identity is permanently fixed by a man's place and function in the natural order. His identity is knowable by himself and by others.

Individual identity is an artificial construct created by social conventions and by assertion of one's own concept of what one would like to be. Those who realize this may create and reshape their own identity in freedom by ruthless self-assertion. Those who do not realize this may have their identity smashed by the destruction of the artificial tissue of which it is composed.

Since nature is orderly and purposeful, one may arrive at valid conclusions by examining it.

Since nature is neutral and man has been given no special lights by which to understand its mysteries, absolute truth and values based upon absolute truth are unattainable. Those who think they have, or can have, a firm grasp on reality by means of its appearances delude themselves.

11

The problem of suffering is primarily ethical. It often proceeds from a violation of nature and hence is both retributive and restorative in function.	Suffering is wanton, random, and utterly without moral purpose.
Death, though mysterious and terrifying, is part of the natural and supernatural order and must therefore be accepted patiently. When so accepted it may be a release from earthly suffering and injustice. The quality of a man's conduct in the face of death is a reflection of the life he has led. However, since a man's life is not exclusively in his own hands, it must be led and ended in strict accordance with natural law.	Death is the crowning absurdity of life, reducing to nothing all pretensions of nobility or accomplishment. Since an individual life is of no great worth, death may be imposed casually. Like everything else about individual man, his life is entirely in his own hands, subject to his own will.

Not all of these conflicts are necessarily present in each of the plays, and the degree of emphasis given to any one of them varies from play to play. What is common to all four of the mature tragedies is the tension between one or more sets of these paired opposites. The dialectic is rendered differently, however, in each of the dramas. In *Hamlet*, for instance, the dialectic takes place almost exclusively in the mind of the hero, whose most fundamental character trait is a propensity for seeing reality from several different vantage points at once. As I shall argue in the next chapter, Hamlet's mind is complementary, that is, he is quite capable of believing simultaneously two things which logically should cancel each other out. This unique quality of mind largely accounts for the many contradictions and internal inconsistencies which render him such a fascinating and endlessly debatable character. In *Othello*, on the other hand, the dialectic is dramatized by two characters, Iago and Desdemona, each of whom sees the world in terms that exclude the other. Between

12

these two poles moves the hero, who places total faith first in one version of reality, then in the other, and finally moves in agony back to belief in the first. In *King Lear*, the world of the play is itself complementary, that is, Gloucester's statement, "And that's true too," is a perfectly valid and correct observation about the universe depicted by the play. *Macbeth* is another case entirely: dialectical tension is generated between the ideas of reality held by the two principal characters at the beginning of the play. Early in the action, however, the hero commits himself irrevocably to the view of nature and man set forth by his wife. Yet he does so without ever being able to abandon his inner adherence to the opposite view, and, hence, for the remainder of the play is forced to judge himself and his deeds by a set of values from which his own actions have estranged him. "All that is within him does condemn / Itself for being there" (v.ii.24-25).

Obviously, in these four plays the hero is not necessarily the champion of an ordered universe, nor is the villain in all cases the spokesman of moral chaos. In *Hamlet*, for instance, it is Claudius who has a solid belief in the orthodox, moral universe pictured by medieval Christianity. He is acutely conscious of having violated its laws, but he never suggests, as do Edmund and Iago, that his actions simply cannot be judged by its irrelevant values. Hamlet, on the other hand, launches an attack upon the most basic assumptions of a purposeful moral order, and, if in the end he comes to terms with it, he does so only after having given it a thorough shaking up. Lear, too, in the terrible lucidity of his madness delivers a most scathing and uncompromising indictment of the traditional order and the hypocritical assumptions upon which it rests. Moreover, even when the assault against the ordered universe is launched by a self-centered, nihilistic villain, his assertions carry, within the world of the play, a certain unsettling credibility. Maud Bodkin is one of many critics who have pointed out that Iago's view of life cannot be totally discredited and that his intrigues are based "not

13

merely, as Bradley remarks, on falsehoods, but also on partial truths of human nature that the romantic vision ignores."[7]

To assert all of the foregoing is not to propose that Shakespeare's plays are elaborate debating matches between opposed systems of philosophy. Shakespeare's principal interest as a dramatist apparently lay not in the issues themselves but in the *tension* between them. The mature tragedies are not really about issues at all, but about characters who must face those issues within a particular dramatic context. Each of the heroes is depicted as having to take actions or formulate attitudes which depend largely upon which side of the opposed views he finally espouses. Thus, part of the hero's dilemma is to assume one view or the other and then to live with the ramifications of that assumption. And this brings us to the second major point of consideration.

I propose to examine the relationship between the world of the play and the subjective, perceived world of the hero. I have gone as far as I can for the moment in investigating the common ground of the four play-worlds; I shall examine each in detail in the succeeding chapters. The time has come to examine the ways in which Shakespeare depicts the subjective cosmos of his characters, especially that of the tragic heroes, and once again to attempt to isolate and define common denominators.

I am about to embark on the first of many forays into the realm of Shakespearean characterization, and, considering the critical brouhaha that has surrounded "character study" in recent years, a few prefatory words are perhaps in order. Throughout the first half of this century, there was a sweeping critical reaction against the type of criticism which approached the plays of Shakespeare, especially the tragedies, primarily through analysis of character and motive, and against the most eminent practitioner of that technique, A. C. Bradley.[8] It is not my intention to mount a defense of

[7] Maud Bodkin, *Archetypal Patterns in Poetry* (London: Oxford Univ. Press, 1934), p. 222.

[8] See esp. L. C. Knights, *How Many Children Had Lady Macbeth?*

Bradley, a critic about whom I have mixed opinions, and still less to advocate a return to his methods. The revolt against Bradley and the technique he epitomized was necessary and healthy, but, as with any battle that has been won, it need no longer be fought. The time has come, is, in fact, long overdue, to put Bradley in his proper historical perspective as the outstanding interpreter of Shakespeare for his age in much the same way as Dr. Johnson and Coleridge were for theirs. The trouble is that, in the course of dissenting from Bradley's particular approach and conclusions, too many critics have stated or implied that any approach to the plays through character study is distorted and harmful because it ignores the overall design of the work by treating a fictional creation as a flesh and blood human being. To state or even imply this is, I believe, simply to drive out one error by inviting in another. Like imagery, characterization is part of a process of artistic selection, and, in works of unified conception and execution, is as integral a part of the overall design as poetry, plot, or theme. Character must be studied not as a separate entity admired for its own sake, but rather as a viable avenue of approach to an understanding of the drama as a unified whole, "as a function of the idea that gives its form to the play," in the words of Peter Alexander.[9] If a slight shift in semantics can free us from old but still active and bothersome ghosts, what I propose to study is not "character" but "characterization," the selective process by which the creation of fictional people is made to serve the comprehensive artistic design of the work.

That the process, in Shakespeare's case, was highly selective is, I believe, indisputable.[10] Why, for instance, does

---

(Cambridge, Eng.: Minority Press, 1933). Also Lily Bess Campbell, *Shakespeare's Tragic Heroes* (1930: rpt. New York: Barnes and Noble, 1952), pp. 241-287.

[9] *Hamlet, Father and Son* (Oxford: Clarendon Press, 1955), p. 159.

[10] The most comprehensive study of Shakespeare's selectivity in characterization and the relationship between character and theme

15

Shakespeare tell us so much of Hamlet's experience outside
the immediate environment of the court, but almost nothing
of Lear's or Macbeth's? Why is there such a vast discrepancy
between what Iago says he feels and what he apparently does
feel? How can a character as foolish as Othello, as rash as
Lear, or as bloody as Macbeth inspire the awe that they do?
I shall be asking these and similar questions not to discover
what kind of "man" Hamlet or Iago is, but to examine why
they are depicted in the way that they are. It seems to me that
the central focus of Shakespearean tragedy is the experience
of the tragic hero. That this is not the totality of Shakespearean tragedy is obvious; but it is no less obvious, I think, that
the center of interest in *Hamlet, Othello, King Lear,* and
Macbeth is what the title character does, learns, experiences,
and endures.[11] An understanding of this, far from isolating
character from the context of the play as a whole, can shed
light upon every aspect of the drama.

Though the tragedies that befall Hamlet, Othello, Lear,
and Macbeth are different in kind, and even the degree of the
hero's conscious culpability in precipitating disaster varies
from play to play, one striking aspect of tragic experience in
all four plays is that tragic suffering is invariably mental
suffering. Among the four protagonists, only Lear suffers
extraordinary physical discomfort, and at the height of it he

---

is Brents Stirling's *Unity in Shakespearean Tragedy* (New York:
Columbia Univ. Press, 1956). See also G. B. Harrison, *Shakespeare's
Tragedies* (London: Routledge, 1951), pp. 24-26; D. G. James, *The
Dream of Learning* (Oxford: Clarendon Press, 1951), pp. 99-100;
F. P. Wilson, *Elizabethan and Jacobean* (Oxford: Clarendon Press,
1945), p. 122; Virgil Whitaker, *The Mirror Up to Nature* (San
Marino, Calif.: Huntington Library, 1965), pp. 157-165; Judah
Stampfer, *The Tragic Engagement* (New York: Funk and Wagnalls,
1968), pp. 6-16; Ribner, *Patterns in Shakespearean Tragedy*, pp. 8-9.

[11] Peter Mercer, in *"Othello* and the Form of Heroic Tragedy,"
Critical Quarterly, 11 (1969), 45-50, provocatively discusses a deep
ambivalence of feeling which some recent critics display toward the
very nature of heroic tragedy.

informs us that his physical agony is actually a blessing since it distracts him from the far worse anguish in his mind. This trait common to all four dramas strongly suggests that the most significant qualities shared by Shakespearean tragic heroes are not emotional propensities, nor tragic flaws such as pride or passion, nor a warped personality which is drawn irresistibly in one direction, but rather habits of mind with which all four have been endowed, ways of seeing and thinking with which Shakespeare has invested them. If, as I am arguing, the destruction of the personal world at the level of its basic assumptions is a central aspect of tragic experience in Shakespeare, then the tragedy which befalls the hero is predicated upon the way in which he views the world and the effect which that world-view has upon his actions. I believe it is possible to isolate five principal qualities of mind which the mature tragic heroes share in common.

The first of these is a tendency to universalize, to see instinctively in specific acts or situations the broadest implications about the nature of reality as a whole. Since the time of Coleridge, this trait has been commonly recognized in Hamlet. "Hamlet's generalizing mind is everywhere emphasized," a modern critic tells us; "his thought invariably leaps out to embrace the world as a whole, he talks of infinite space, his rhetoric includes the stars."[12] Yet, this trait, though most pronounced in Hamlet, is not restricted to him alone; it is, in fact, the common property of Shakespeare's tragic figures from the Ovidian narratives onward. To see how the tendency to universalize operates in Othello, we need only examine the Moor's soliloquy in Act III, scene iii, after Iago has planted the seeds of doubt. Othello starts from his specific situation, his marriage, but by the middle of the speech it is not his marriage alone but marriage in general which is amiss. He has broadened the implications of his particular situation in a most Hamlet-like manner to see marriage as an invitation to deception and cuckoldry:

[12] Spencer, *Shakespeare and the Nature of Man*, p. 96.

17

> O curse of marriage,
> That we can call these delicate creatures ours,
> And not their appetites!
>
> (III.iii.268-270)

By the end of the speech, it is not marriage alone which is tainted; rather, cuckoldry is but one facet of a malignant fate that singles out the best and most noble for the cruelest sufferings:

> Yet 'tis the plague of great ones;
> Prerogatived are they less than the base.
> 'Tis destiny unshunnable, like death.
> Even then this forkèd plague is fated to us
> When we do quicken.
>
> (273-277)

Finally, in the last lines the tension which will become his major preoccupation is galvanized. "If she be false, O, then heaven mocks itself! / I'll not believe't" (278-279). It is with this problem that he will struggle most bitterly in Act IV, identifying his own disastrous course with the cause of heaven.

Lear's mind ranges over even wider cosmic territory. The shocks administered by his daughters undermine the concept of nature which lay behind his irascible actions at the beginning of the play. He first directs his furious tirades at them as individuals, but, when neither heaven nor nature takes his part, he turns his anger upon humanity in general. When the flood of his rage subsides, he is faced with questions he had never had to ask before, and they are invariably general questions of the most universal scope and implications: "Is man no more than this?" (III.iv.97). "Is there any cause in nature that makes these hard hearts?" (III.vi.75). In the depths of madness he finds one set of answers to these questions, and they are invariably general answers. The specific daughters have been replaced by abstractions representative not only of ingratitude but of ubiquitous evil in all humanity

18

and its institutions: yond simpering dame, yond justice, the great image of authority, a scurvy politician.

In *Macbeth* the case is somewhat different because we are dealing here not with a character who is trying to salvage an ordered universe but one who is, from the first, wilfully attempting to destroy it. But the tendency to draw universal conclusions from particular experience remains constant. Even before the murder, Macbeth vividly realizes that regicide has universal implications which stretch far beyond the deed itself, and, once the crime is committed, those implications are by no means lost on him; in fact, they are the principal element in the torture of the mind which he must endure. Finally, when he reaches the bedrock of despair, it is not merely his own individual life that has fallen into the sear, the yellow leaf, but life itself, all life, which is a tale told by an idiot.

Of course, a tendency to universalize is not confined to the tragic heroes; it is a favorite device of characterization, which Shakespeare selected with increasing frequency and skill, enabling him to fuse theme and character. Iago, for instance, does not simply tell fibs. He constructs a whole world-view of general beliefs and speaks from his convictions. The comprehensiveness and cogency of his version of reality largely account for the chilling credibility of so much of what he has to say about human behavior. The same is true of other characters, good and bad, major and minor, throughout the canon. Rabkin makes an important point when he observes: "Nestor and Polonius, Claudius and Edmund are capable of telling us things we ought to know in ways that make it impossible to forget them. It is perhaps the most familiar mark of Shakespeare's complementary sensibility that he recognizes how from any subjective position there is a kind of truth; each man's world makes sense to him, and all his intelligence serves what he is—even if he is a scoundrel" (p. 69).

By having his heroes universalize their situations, Shakespeare gains two advantages without which his kind of trage-

19

dy would be well-nigh impossible. First, he confers upon them an intellectual scope and power which vastly increase their self-awareness and size as men. Second, he broadens the horizons of his own plays, making it possible to deal in the most universal ideas and issues without being heavy-handed or sententious. It is largely through this character trait in the hero that Shakespeare achieves the effortless coalescence of the universal and the particular which is one of the hallmarks of his tragedy. But the hero's tendency to generalize is not simply a device for giving the plays universality. The same character trait becomes an important factor in each of the individual tragic experiences. By the time each of the heroes is embarked upon a tragic course, he is predicating his potentially disastrous actions not primarily on the specific circumstances of his situation, but upon a generalized concept of the human condition and the nature of reality. Each man's world does indeed make sense to him, and his actions are predicated upon his world-view much more than upon "motives" in the Bradleyan sense of the term.

Another quality of mind with which Shakespeare invests all four of his tragic heroes is an extraordinary sense of self-awareness.[13] The title characters of these four plays spend far more time thinking about themselves, scrutinizing themselves, and talking about themselves than do the subordinate characters. Hamlet, for instance, is intensely interested in himself as a person, while Claudius is interested in himself primarily as a king. All four heroes are presented with situations in which they must make some radical reappraisal of themselves, and their heightened sense of self-awareness makes it impossible for them to shirk this obligation, however painful the conclusion to which it leads them. The same self-awareness also renders them uniquely well suited to explore the most profound and subtle problems of self-identity.

[13] See Robert Heilman, *Shakespearean Tragedy and the Drama of Disaster* (Vancouver: Univ. of British Columbia Press, 1960), p. 25; also the same author's *Tragedy and Melodrama* (Seattle: Univ. of Washington Press, 1968), pp. 14-18, 239-251.

This is not at all to impute to them a shallow egotism, nor to suggest that self-preoccupation is a "tragic flaw" which precipitates their disasters. We can clarify this by examining one of the salient differences between Othello and Iago. The Moor's very first speech indicates the awareness he has of his own worth and position, and we learn that it was by talking of himself that he won the love of Desdemona. But far from being the shallow egotism some critics have seen in the character, this self-awareness remains with him long after it has ceased to be a source of pride or self-satisfaction and serves only to make him acutely aware of his own misery.[14] It finally becomes the principal source of torment for him when he discovers his disastrous error. Up to the moment of his death, Othello is still attempting to form some evaluation of himself, for, even in such circumstances, he is always present to himself as an object for scrutiny.

Iago, on the other hand, is a true egotist, in spite of the fact that he talks far less about himself than does the Moor. In fact, it is the very absence of self-scrutiny and evaluation that differentiates the egotism of Iago from the self-awareness of Othello. The Ancient's major speeches are about a world of knaves and fools, a world-picture that is attractive to him precisely because he can see himself as preeminent in it. Though loquacious in the extreme when operating in a manner he thinks successful, he, unlike Othello, has nothing to say when his world collapses around him. "From this time forth I never will speak word" (v.ii.304). Iago in defeat is of no interest to himself or to us, for the limits of his mind have been exhausted. He has no conclusions to draw from his failure and no reappraisals to make of the Iago he had earlier thought himself to be.

We are told in the first act of *King Lear* that the old monarch "hath ever but slenderly known himself" (I.i.293). True enough, but, from the first moment of his entrance, we are struck by the degree to which he is aware of himself as the

[14] In Chapter Three, I take exception with the Eliot-Leavis-Heilman axis on the interpretation of Othello's character.

21

pinnacle of a hierarchical natural order, as king and father, grandly fetching forth dukes and kings, dispensing kingdoms, demanding absolute obedience from daughters and vassals alike. As with Othello, this sense of self-awareness makes him able to comprehend fully his misfortunes and to formulate a new concept of himself, a concept which goes through agonized metamorphoses.

A heightened sense of self-awareness is the most important single factor in Macbeth's tragedy. Unlike Lear, the Thane of Glamis knows himself all too well from the very beginning; he is aware of the dark stirrings within himself and the carnage which they can unleash. As he wades further and further into blood, his self-awareness, like a waking nightmare, reveals pitilessly to him what he has become: "I have supped full with horrors" (v.v.13).

That Hamlet is extraordinarily self-aware is so obvious, so widely agreed upon, that it does not require even token demonstration here. His heightened self-awareness is examined in detail in the next chapter.

The third mental quality which the Shakespearean tragic heroes share flows out of the two I have just been discussing: each of the heroes is conscious of himself not only as an individual, but also as a part of a broad structure which includes the rest of humanity and some higher system of nature. Each of them feels an inner compulsion to have his actions in consonance with the true nature of reality, yet at the same time, each of them instinctively sets himself up as a critic and judge of the widely held concept of reality that prevails at the beginning of the drama. This inevitably leads to a tremendous inner tension between the need to relate to an absolute and the doubt or skepticism about the validity of the absolutes presumed to exist. From this quality of mind arise the subordinate problems of truth versus seeming truth, patience in adversity versus rebellion, endurance versus suicide, and the worth or worthlessness of action. The dialectical organization of the plays is of prime importance in shaping the mental attitude and the actions of the hero. The tension

22

between opposed possibilities takes a different form in the mind of each hero, but it is common to all of them.

For Hamlet, the dilemma is the difficulty of forming absolute values based upon absolute truth in a world where absolute truth is inaccessible. Like several other characters in the play, he spends most of his time trying to get past appearances so that he can formulate a reliable estimate of the truth that lies behind them. As he makes his successive discoveries about the real nature of those around him, he is overwhelmed by an obsessive conviction that all apparent virtue is merely paint to disguise ubiquitous corruption and futility. To make things even more difficult, the inscrutability of the supernatural order precludes the possibility of external beacons to steer by. The upshot of such elusiveness is to make endlessly debatable the worth of an action designed to produce a "good" result. Hamlet is given his task in no uncertain terms; he must put an end to an intolerable situation, the incumbency of Claudius on the throne and in the royal bedchamber. In other words, he must deal with a specific evil; but by the time he has been given this command, he is obsessed with the general presence of evil masquerading as good. What he feels compelled to write down in his tables is not that his uncle is a murderer, but that "one may smile, and smile, and be a villain" (I.v.108). Punishing Claudius in such a situation is as irrelevant to Hamlet's inner needs as punishing Cassio is to the inner needs of Othello. Like the Moor, he is driven by the need to strike at the general, greater evil rather than the specific one. Before punishment can be meted out, the tissue of lies which mocks heaven and man by disguising evil as good must be torn away. Throughout the first three acts of the play, Hamlet devotes all his energy to unmasking evil, stripping off its disguise and forcing it to be seen in its true ugliness and corruption. He postpones killing Claudius not from ennui or moral debilitation, but because he wishes his actions to be founded upon absolute values, absolute truth, the attainment of which is impossible in the *Hamlet*-world.

Like Hamlet, Othello finally comes to see himself as a scourge and minister acting on behalf of heaven. In his own eyes, he is not simply punishing an offence committed against himself, but redressing a fault against heaven and nature: "Heaven stops the nose at it, and the moon winks" (IV.ii.77). Desdemona must die not because she has betrayed him, but "else she'll betray more men" (V.ii.6). But the tragedies of the two characters are exactly opposite; Hamlet postpones acting until he is sure heaven is on his side, while Othello assumes at once that heaven is on his side and errs disastrously. His tragedy is consummated when he must face the fact that "This deed of thine is no more worthy heaven / Than thou wast worthy her" (V.ii.161-162).

Lear provides yet another variation of the pattern. He presumes, not that he is acting in consonance with nature, but that nature will act in consonance with him. At every juncture of the first three acts, when he asserts his irascible will he calls upon nature not only to endorse his action but to be accomplice in it. Nature, far from rallying to his cause, becomes one of his principal tormentors. His conception of natural order in shambles, he attempts to relate himself to his new perception of things by becoming the naked, forked animal he sees in Tom O'Bedlam. In the second half of the play, Lear views life from a succession of different perspectives, and constantly strives to shape his own conduct to the world he sees—whether it be a grotesque parody of his own kingdom or a golden world of tranquility and love.

Macbeth also feels an intense need to act in consonance with a broad scheme of values, but, like the other heroes, he is divided in his own mind about what the true nature of reality is. Specifically, he must decide between two plausible notions of what it is to be a man. The nobility and honor with which he is endowed in the opening scenes are predicated upon a willingness to live within limits. Opposed to that situation is the possibility that man's greatness lies in what he dares to do, in his willingness to cast off all limitations, sacred and humane. Macbeth's tragedy occurs not simply because he

24

opts for the latter possibility, but because, having committed himself to it body and soul, he is never able to blot out his belief in the former. Thus he experiences a numbing sense of loss, an intolerable self-loathing, and a nightmare awareness of what is left when his former values have been foresaken. It is this experience that makes him a tragic hero rather than merely an interesting criminal like Iago, Edmund, or Richard III. When he says:

> I have lived long enough. My way of life
> Is fall'n into the sear, the yellow leaf,
> And that which should accompany old age,
> As honor, love, obedience, troops of friends,
> I must not look to have;
>
> (v.iii.22-26)

he is judging himself by those values he had abandoned irrevocably by killing Duncan, but which he has never been able to expunge from his mind as concepts of worth.

Since Shakespeare's tragic heroes are self-aware and universalize their experience, attempting to relate their actions to universal norms, they all share yet a further mental trait, an ethical sense which sees hypocrisy and the misrepresentation of truth as abominable crimes, perhaps the most hateful of all possible crimes. The omnipresence of the seeming-being problem in every nook and cranny of the canon makes it obvious that it was one of Shakespeare's prime concerns as an artist. In his four mature tragedies, he endowed each of the heroes with an almost obsessive hatred of hypocrisy, especially when it involves evil masquerading as good. I have already glanced at this aspect of *Hamlet*; indeed, it is the subject of the hero's first major speech: "Seems, madam? Nay, it is" (I.ii.76 ff.). In *Othello*, the most hideous aspect of Desdemona's supposed sin in her husband's eyes is that she appears so beautiful and innocent. "She's the worse for all this," prompts Iago, and Othello vehemently concurs: "O, a thousand thousand times!" (IV.i.188-189). In his agonized penultimate confrontation with her, he asks, "Was this fair paper, this most goodly book, / Made to write 'whore' upon?" (IV. ii.71-72).

Lear begins by rewarding hypocrisy and penalizing honesty, but, after he has endured his terrible education, his loathing of the disguised malefactor exceeds even Hamlet's:

> Hide thee, thou bloody hand,
> Thou perjured, and thou simular of virtue
> That art incestuous. Catiff, to pieces shake,
> That under covert and convenient seeming
> Has practiced on man's life.
>
> (III.ii.53-57)

In madness he denounces his imaginary subjects for the same basic crime, misrepresenting themselves: the woman who appears chaste but is lascivious, the judge who is much at one with the thief he condemns, the beadle who lusts for the whore he is chastising, the scurvy politician who seems to see the things he does not.

When Macbeth decides to kill Duncan, he says: "Away, and mock the time with fairest show; / False face must hide what the false heart doth know" (I.vii.81-82). Like the rest of his ravens, this one comes home to roost; the need to employ hypocrisy becomes one of the most loathsome aspects of life for him:

> Unsafe the while, that we must lave
> Our honors in these flattering streams
> And make our faces vizards to our hearts,
> Disguising what they are.
>
> (III.ii.32-35)

He is, of course, constitutionally incapable of being a hypocrite, and his attempt at the banquet to honor the man he has murdered ends in disaster.

By incorporating into each of his tragic heroes this hatred of false seeming, Shakespeare is once again able to direct the overall pattern of his work into the thematic channels that interested him most and to achieve unity between theme and

26

character. This brings us to the final and, for purposes of this study, most important mental quality which the four heroes share in common: a vulnerability to having their view of reality and of themselves undermined at the level of its basic assumptions.

I have said that the poet creates the world in which his tragedy takes place, and that this world, a poetic construct, is unique to that particular tragedy, though grounded upon a basic, dialectical foundation common to all four dramas. The hero is depicted as having a subjective view of the world in which he exists, and that view is usually based upon a few assumptions that are as natural to the character as his heartbeat, that are so basic, in fact, that he does not, in the ordinary course of things, question them.[15] All values to which the hero subscribes and by which he judges himself and others flow naturally from his subjective world-picture. Early in the play, the assumptions upon which the hero's subjective world is built are attacked, either by the words of another character who holds a different view (as in *Othello* and *Macbeth*) or by a development of events for which the hero is totally unprepared (as in *Hamlet* and *King Lear*). In each case, the attack is basic and total, undermining the "two plus two equals four" of the hero's idea of life, the world, and the universe. In each case, the world-view opposed to the hero's is its diametrical opposite. And in each case, the hero is susceptible to the attack because of the way in which his view is built entirely upon one or two principles or assumptions, and because of his tendency to see his own fortunes in cosmic terms.

Under such an attack, the hero's subjective world is utterly demolished, and he is left either torn by several equally possible concepts of reality or else plunged into a chaotic

[15] Alfred North Whitehead has described "the assumptions which appear so obvious that people do not know they are assuming them because no other way of putting things has ever occurred to them." Quoted in W. H. Toppen, *Conscience in Shakespeare's* Macbeth (Groningen: Wolters, 1962), p. x.

abyss in which all values, including his own identity, are without meaning. This portion of the drama is marked by abrupt changes in mood on the part of the hero as he is torn between conflicting possibilities about himself, those around him, the world, the proper course of action, and the manner in which to endure his situation. At this point, each of the four heroes faces the same basic problem, how to endure what is, for him, simply unendurable, how to reimpose upon the world an order or meaning which it must have if it is to be endurable, but which, for one reason or another, it has lost. This problem is the great unifying theme of mature Shakespearean tragedy. In the earlier works such as *Romeo and Juliet* or *Richard III*, the protagonists try to alter the circumstances of reality; in the mature works they try to impose a vision upon its very substance. They demand that the world conform to what they desire it to be, and, when it refuses, they attack furiously, procuring their own destruction. It is not possible to explore this process even tentatively, however, by means of the capsule demonstrations I have been using in this chapter. The time has come to turn to each of the plays in detail.

28

TWO

HAMLET: THE MIND'S EYE

THE world of *Hamlet* is divided into three parts. The most prominent is the court of Elsinore, to which all the major characters belong in one capacity or another and where most of the action is set. But with conspicuous frequency, Shakespeare reminds us of the existence of a world outside that court, a world which also has its function in the tragedy. Persons of various types arrive from it and others depart for it bound on various missions. It has its universities to which Laertes returns and to which Hamlet is not permitted to return, and from which Horatio, Rosencrantz, and Guildenstern arrive. It has its players who are full of news about hard times in the city, its dissident subjects, its armies, its vassal states, its pirates, and its gravediggers. Just enough of it is dramatized to stress the separateness and insularity of Claudius' circle. Indeed, it is only when the wider world asserts itself, as in Fortinbras' threatened invasion or Laertes' abortive revolt, that we are aware that the inbred, claustrophobic court presumably presides over a kingdom. The third sphere of the *Hamlet*-world is the highly problematic metaphysical realm, which is never far from the mind of the hero and which, in the person of the Ghost, physically intrudes upon the action.

But what interests us most about the *Hamlet*-world is not its geography but its qualities. In his article, "The World of *Hamlet*," Maynard Mack perceptively defines what he considers the most important qualities of the imaginative fabric Shakespeare has woven for the world of his play: mysteriousness, the relationship between seeming and being, and mortality, to include the slings and arrows of outrageous fortune and the shocks that flesh is heir to (pp. 32-46). I agree with

29

Mack's conclusions, but I would propose a somewhat different set of qualities which will, I believe, be better suited to
the purposes of this study. I would define the most important
qualities of the *Hamlet*-world as perilousness, elusiveness,
and the presence everywhere of decay. These qualities are
present in one form or another in each of the three spheres or
loci of the *Hamlet*-world, and the presence in each reinforces
and colors the presence in the other two.

All of Shakespeare's mature tragedies take place in an
aura of violence and danger, but in none of the others does
the ground seem to be quite so slippery and treacherous for
all characters as in the *Hamlet*-world. Nowhere, not even in
Macbeth, has a more nervous, uneasy group been collected
on a stage, and the prevailing sense of insecurity is amply
justified. The slightest miscalculation can be fatal; to let
one's guard down for even a moment is to find oneself
marshalled to knavery. If the world of *Hamlet* seems less
violent than that of *Lear*, *Othello*, or *Macbeth*, it is only
because at Elsinore the practitioners of violence are more
subtle in its application. In the more isolated or primitive
atmospheres of the other plays, the means of violence are very
brutal and physical; at Claudius' court, violence is usually
more polite, the favorite instrument being poison—poison
poured into the ears of sleepers, poison smeared on the tips of
foils, poison pearls dropped into cups, poison so deadly that
even a scratch means certain death. Even the more physical
manifestations of violence are invariably covert—secret death
warrants, altered secret death warrants, a friendly fencing
match, a stealthy approach behind the back of a man at
prayer, or a sudden stroke through a curtain at something
unseen. The world of *Hamlet* is more refined than the world
of *Macbeth* but, for all that, no less lethal.

The prevailing aura of peril is not confined to fear of
physical violence, but extends to the metaphysical sphere of
the play, a sphere defined largely in terms of the horrors it
may contain. From the Ghost's first reference to "sulph'rous

30

and tormenting flames" to Laertes' argument with the churlish Priest, the afterlife is habitually thought of as the place where men are damned, not saved. It is significant that most references to religion concern death and the violent terrors that may lie beyond it. In the *Hamlet*-world, death is not only the ultimate metaphysical phenomenon; it comes close to being the *only* metaphysical phenomenon.

To live in constant danger would be harrowing under any circumstances, but the characters in this play must act at their peril in a world where the true facts are maddeningly and mockingly elusive. I prefer the term "elusive" to Mack's "mysterious" to describe the *Hamlet*-world, because the former term implies the constant, at times desperate, attempts to get behind the uncertainties and deceptions, and arrive at some assessment of reality. For the first three acts, every major male character spends most of his time and energy trying to determine the real facts of the situation and what those around him are up to. As C. S. Lewis put it: "The characters are all watching one another, forming theories about one another, listening, contriving, full of anxiety."[1] Nowhere else in Shakespeare are so many characters seen groping so unsurely, spurred on by conflicting possibilities, dark suspicions, and a sense of imminent peril. The first line of the play is a tense question shouted into the darkness: "Who's there?" In many ways it is the pivotal question of the entire first half of the drama, since so many of these characters are trying to find out who is really there behind the mask of appearance.[2] Each suspects the other of somehow misrepresenting himself, and usually the suspicion proves correct. In the climactic closet scene, it is a mistake on Hamlet's part about "who's there" that trips the mechanism of disaster.

[1] "Hamlet: The Prince or the Poem," *Proc. of the British Acad.*, 28 (1942), 149.

[2] Harry Levin, in *The Question of* Hamlet (New York: Oxford Univ. Press, 1959), pp. 20-21, comments on the significance of the line.

Throughout the first scene, a rapid fire staccato of such questions establishes what Mack has described as the inter-rogative mode of the play.[3]

At question is not only the veracity of the Ghost, the cause of Hamlet's peculiar behavior, and the stratagems of Claudius and his henchmen, but also a wide range of religious and philosophical questions pondered by the hero and, to a lesser extent, by some of the other characters. Predictably, the results, even at the end of the play, are tentative and pro-visional; there is more in heaven and earth than is dreamt of in any of their philosophies. The surest sign, however, of metaphysical confusion is the singular state of organized religion in the *Hamlet*-world. Critics have been at some pains to make theological sense out of the situation at Elsinore, but their speculations, like those of the hero, have been flawed and inconclusive.[4] Various scholars have argued that the court is Catholic, while others have demonstrated that it can only be Protestant. But if it is Protestant, what are we to make of a purgatorial ghost in a system which had largely rejected belief in purgatory and held that all purported spectres were instruments of the devil? Indeed, what did Shakespeare intend his mostly Protestant audience to make of a papist shade? But if, on the other hand, the court is Catholic, why is no mention made of a dispensation for the marriage of Claudius and Gertrude, and what has Hamlet

[3] "The World of *Hamlet*," pp. 33-34. Levin notes that the word "question" is used seventeen times, far more often than in any other Shakespearean play (*The Question of* Hamlet, p. 20).

[4] See John Dover Wilson, *What Happens in* Hamlet (Cambridge, Eng.: Cambridge Univ. Press, 1935), pp. 60-78; also Eleanor Prosser, *Hamlet and Revenge* (Stanford: Stanford Univ. Press, 1967), pp. 102-122; Roy Battenhouse, *Shakespearean Tragedy: Its Art and Its Christian Premises* (Bloomington: Univ. of Indiana Press, 1969), pp. 237-244. Cf. Nigel Alexander, *Poison, Play, and Duel: A Study in* Hamlet (Lincoln: Univ. of Nebraska Press, 1971), pp. 32-34. Alexander's book did not come to my attention until the present study was virtually on its way to the publisher. His thinking on some of the crucial issues, such as the Ghost and Hamlet's divided mind, is somewhat similar to mine.

been doing at Wittenberg, Luther's university and a stronghold of Protestantism?

For purposes of this study, the most important fact about institutional religion *circa* 1600 is that religious controversy on the most basic issues was raging everywhere in Europe. Shakespeare has woven the texture of this confusion, and the anxiety confusion bred, into the fabric of his play;[5] or, more exactly, he has dramatized the situation of men who, though deeply religious, are left to their own devices in deciding what to believe, in placing themselves in the theological cosmos when faced by rival systems, all of which claim to be the truth. Such was the dilemma of many Renaissance Christians, and such is the dilemma of Hamlet. While it may be a mistake to pounce upon Hamlet's attendance at Wittenberg quite so eagerly as J. Dover Wilson has done, it would also be a mistake to ignore it entirely, since Shakespeare has troubled himself to name this particular university rather than any other.[6] Wittenberg's significance in the play lies not so much in its association with Lutheranism (Hamlet makes a very strange Lutheran indeed), as in its reputation as a center of dispute; for dispute necessarily implies contradiction, search, and confusion, the very stuff the metaphysics of *Hamlet* is made of. Much the same can be said of the purgatorial Ghost; its dubiety throws Hamlet back on his own resources. In the world of this play, heaven acts as it sees fit and leaves men to figure out as best they can the why's and wherefore's and even the what's. Religious dispute itself plays a notable part in the drama: the gravediggers provide a broad burlesque of formal theological disputation, while the sole representative of organized religion, the churlish Priest, makes his brief appearance for the purpose of starting a theological argument.

Thus the critic can no more arrive at a plausible explication of *Hamlet* by relating it to theological systems of Shakespeare's time than the Prince himself could have solved his

[5] See Michael Taylor, "The Conflict in *Hamlet*," *Shakespeare Quarterly*, 22 (1971), pp. 149-150.
[6] *What Happens in* Hamlet, pp. 68-72.

problems by consulting a sympathetic confessor. The bitterly disputed tenets of religion, as well as the skepticism that followed the breakdown of papal hegemony, form a signal part of the highly problematic *Hamlet*-world. As I maintained in Chapter One, the tension between issues in Shakespearean tragedy is more important than the issues themselves, and the prime matter of his dramaturgy is not the truth sought but the search itself.

In their persistent, occasionally frantic search for openness and truth, all the characters of the play share a predilection for the same basic tactics, secrecy and deception. Early in the action, Polonius sets the pattern in his directions to Reynaldo. To discover the truth about Laertes' life style, Reynaldo, keeping his own purposes secret, is to tell lies about him: "Your bait of falsehood takes this carp of truth" (II.i.63). Throughout the play, every one of the major characters with the exception of Horatio (and even he as accomplice) employs this tactic; they all resort to deceptions and subterfuges to catch the carp of truth. The problem is that in the *Hamlet*-world the truth has a way of coming up a barracuda, and, in the course of this perilous angling, each of the characters in turn procures his or her destruction, Polonius being the first to go. In effect, they are all faced with the same problem: in an uncertain world where mistakes can be fatal, they feel that the situation may require some action of them. It must be the "right" action, that is, the action that is congruent with truth. But the truth they find endlessly elusive. The inscrutability of the metaphysical universe, their own false assumptions, the false assumptions of others, their areas of ignorance, and the tangle of secrets and subterfuges—all these combine to confound everyone's attempts at accurate assessment and hence at right action.

Modern criticism, especially by its study of the imagery of *Hamlet*, has made us acutely aware of the relentless emphasis upon moral, political, and physical decay in all parts of the drama. What has not received enough attention, however, is the degree to which all the major characters, especially the

34

Prince, are aware of life's having fallen off from a previous standard of excellence, of moving through a decadent present toward an uncertain and unattractive future. To a remarkable extent, they are all fond of talking about the past and comparing the present to it unfavorably. Hamlet sees his mother's marriage as a falling off from a paragon to a beast, while he is also conscious of his own relationships with Rosencrantz, Guildenstern, and Ophelia deteriorating from affection and trust, even love, to suspicion and revulsion. Moreover, he is painfully aware of a decline in his whole evaluation of reality. In his speech beginning "I have of late—but wherefore I know not—lost all my mirth" (ii.ii.292-306), he recalls what must surely have been his former appreciation of nature and man, contrasting it with the "sterile promontory" and "quintessence of dust" that are now central to his world-picture. But on the other hand, those around him regard Hamlet himself as having undergone a spectacular change for the worse. In Ophelia's view, he has declined from the Renaissance ideal to a raving lunatic. Her cry, "O, woe is me / T'have seen what I have seen, see what I see!" (iii.i.160-161), rings through many passages of the play; the worst part of having to endure the corrupt present is the memory of a splendid past.

Polonius, too, is fond of talking about the good old days when his advice to the king was never wrong, when he played Caesar at the university and suffered much extremity from love. But he himself is the principal embodiment of yet another kind of decay, the senility of old age, a theme that is further reinforced by the impotent and bedrid Norway, who fails to keep his nephew from threatening the political order, and the aged and ailing Player King, who presents life as a process of increasing physical and moral debilitation ending in the grave.

The grave itself is very much in evidence, and provides the most graphic depiction of decay as the hero offers for our contemplation a whole collection of bones and dust. The Gravedigger, like so many characters in the play, is fond of reminiscing about the past, and speaks of the great day thirty years before when King Hamlet defeated Fortinbras. It was, by no coincidence, the day that Prince Hamlet was born, and was also, by no coincidence whatsoever, the day that he, the Gravedigger, took up "Adam's work."[7] The implication would seem to be that the beginning of life is also the beginning of death, and the moment of glory holds the seeds of its own dissolution. It is particularly significant that the *momento mori* which Hamlet contemplates is the skull of a jester. One is forcibly reminded of the image of death as jester in *Richard II*: "And there the antic sits, / Scoffing his state and grinning at his pomp" (III.ii.162-163). In *Hamlet*, as in the earlier play, death provides the final *reductio ad absurdum* to all life's pretensions, reducing Alexander to a bung and Caesar to a chink in a wall. It will be well to remember the image of "antic death" when we come to consider Hamlet's own "antic disposition."

Perilousness, elusiveness, and decay: such are the problems of life in the *Hamlet*-world, complex problems to which all characters except the Prince attempt to apply simplistic solutions. The actions of Claudius and Gertrude, Polonius and Laertes are less perplexing, more consistent than those of the hero, for each of them brings to the *Hamlet*-world a simplistic view and coherent technique which he or she (mistakenly) feels is capable of coping with its problems. For Polonius the panacea is policy; life is largely a process of circumvention, and all one need do is be sufficiently clever:

> If circumstances lead me, I will find
> Where truth is hid, though it were hid indeed
> Within the center.
>
> (II.ii.157-159)

These three lines are a compact summary of his way of life. He clings tenaciously to his belief that love caused Hamlet's madness long after everyone else has abandoned the theory.

[7] Noted by Levin, *The Question of* Hamlet, p. 55.

A point of honor is involved, and he is determined to prove himself right at whatever cost. And his willingness to die if he should be wrong is no idle reference; he does.

Claudius, on the other hand, is a politician in the modern rather than the Elizabethan sense of the term: all his actions are directed toward the acquisition and maintenance of power. When we first see him he is measuring out power as if it were a precious substance (which, for him, it is):

> Giving to you no further personal power
> To business with the king, more than the scope
> Of these delated articles allow.
>
> (I.ii.36-38)

And at the moment of his death, he instinctively places faith in his retainers, even though Laertes has told him that the poison knows no remedy. In his eyes, the catastrophes that befall his court, including the deaths of Polonius and Ophelia, consistently appear as political rather than personal disasters. He cannot repent and save his soul because he cannot give up his crown, his ambition, and his queen; yet, when it comes to a choice between the crown and the queen, he unhesitatingly opts for the former. He could easily prevent Gertrude's drinking from the poisoned cup by telling her what is in it. But to do so would gravely threaten his position, so he watches her drink and then cooly tries to cover up when she collapses.

Polonius wants to discover the cause of Hamlet's madness to prove himself right. Claudius wants to discover the cause of Hamlet's madness because he senses danger. Gertrude really does not care about the cause of Hamlet's madness; she simply wishes it would go away. Her method of dealing with the problems of the *Hamlet*-world is even simpler than her husband's; she does her best to ignore what she does not wish to see. To avoid facing unpleasant facts, she is capable of averting her eyes from a great deal, including her own ambiguous situation. It is exactly this obtuseness that most infuriates her son. At the play, she wishes to be merry and make a fuss over him, while he is interested in administering

37

doses of wormwood. Above all, his need is to make her see her actions through his eyes. "Have you eyes," he rants at her, "Ha! Have you eyes?" (III.iv.66-68).

Laertes' approach to life in the *Hamlet*-world is unquestioning adherence to the concept of family honor. The obscure funeral of Polonius, "No trophy, sword, nor hatchment o'er his bones, / No noble rite nor formal ostentation" (IV.v.212-213), seems to infuriate the son almost as much as the murder, and his reaction to Ophelia's maimed rites is the same. His allegiance seems to be not so much to his father as to the idea that wrongs must be revenged. Thus the contrast between Laertes and Hamlet is not simply that one can act while the other cannot, but rather that one accepts conventional norms at face value while the other does not.

Generally speaking, we may note two similarities among all of the important secondary characters in this play: in dealing with the problems of the *Hamlet*-world, they all tend to put their eggs in one basket, and they are all disastrously ineffective. One by one the protagonist overturns the baskets. In the end, the power of Claudius, the policy of Polonius, the obliviousness of Gertrude, the vengeance-mindedness of Laertes, the obedience of Ophelia, the time-serving of Rosencrantz and Guildenstern all come to the same thing: Yorick grins at them all.

In contrast to the secondary characters, Hamlet's approach to the *Hamlet*-world is complex, multifaceted, and complementary; he is quite capable of believing simultaneously two or more things which logically should cancel each other out, and nowhere is this more true than in his view of himself. On one hand, he is acutely aware of himself as part of the corrupt and revolting world he sees around him. The first private words we hear from him concern his "too, too sullied flesh," and throughout the play he shows a marked tendency toward self-deprecation. This tendency can vary from engaging modesty with his friends to virtual orgies of self-excoriation such as the rogue and peasant slave speech. To Ophelia he gives a telling glimpse of that side of his self-awareness which is conscious of being trapped in a corrupt and incongruous reality: "What should such fellows as I do crawling between earth and heaven? We are arrant knaves all; believe none of us" (iii.i.127-129). Moreover, he does not exclude himself from the corruption of the flesh, the *reductio ad absurdum* which death applies to the struggles of life: "We fat all creatures else to fat us, and we fat ourselves for maggots" (iv.iii.21-23).

But Hamlet's problem is not an inferiority complex; quite the contrary. If he has a painful awareness of himself as sharing in humanity's corruption, he has an equally strong sense of himself as separate from and superior to it. It is from this sense of superiority that his moral feeling derives. Now by Hamlet's moral feeling I do not mean those qualities about which nineteenth century critics were so rhapsodic: rather I mean his urgently felt compulsion to make moral judgments about everything and everyone around him. Hamlet is a born critic and judge of life, and a tireless experimenter with life-views. His moral sense is the principal point of contact between his extraordinary mind and his enormous capacity for passion. Hamlet's moral judgments are not intellectual only, but inform his nature and determine his emotional relationships to all those around him.[8] He arrives at judgments intuitively, usually instantaneously, by a series of lightning leaps from the particular to the general and then back to the particular, and pursues his judgments with all of the considerable ardor of his temperament. In every encounter he has with the faction of the court, his often brutal treatment of them stems from the passionate conviction he has in the moral assessment he has made of them. Under the influence of such conviction (rather than simply under the influence of "passion," nebulous and undefined), Hamlet is capable of quite shocking conduct. He has an almost megalo-

[8] Edward Dowden, *Shakespere: A Critical Study of His Mind and Art*, 3rd. ed. (1875; rpt. New York: Harper, n.d.), p. 117, has observed: "If all his feelings translate themselves into thoughts, it is no less true that all his thoughts are impregnated with feeling."

maniacal insistence that those around him live up to his values, and his values only; to fail in the least is to fail absolutely, as Ophelia discovers to her sorrow. Of all the characters in the play, Horatio alone passes the test with flying colors.

But at the same time, there is an ambiguity in Hamlet's mind about what his real values are, an ambiguity caused by the elusiveness of the *Hamlet*-world, by the hero's peculiar, dialectical way of apprehending it, and by the collapse of his subjective world following the revelations of the Ghost. In the course of the play, Hamlet exhibits an incredible variety of moods which flash in rapid succession across his personality, and, indeed, the variety of these moods has been largely responsible for the widely divergent views of his character—languishing melancholic, trapped avenger, ruthless egotist, ruined idealist, walking death-wish. At one time or another he is each of these things, and each represents a different way of viewing the facts of his situation, another attempt to gain a firm grasp upon the maddeningly elusive realities and to bring his actions into consonance with truth. No one mode of reaction is sufficient, and yet all have irresistible claims to be made; hence he experiments with ruthless action, suicidal contemplation, stoical resignation, and violent misanthropy. Each contradicts the others without excluding them. This is the complementary dialectic of *Hamlet*, and the numerous avenues he explores convey the impression of having virtually exhausted the range of human possibilities.

Hamlet instinctively sees universal ramifications in almost any situation; this quality of the Shakespearean tragic hero is even more pronounced in him than in the other three. His first soliloquy shows him drawing the most sweeping conclusions about the world from the specific situation at Elsinore. But this same speech also tells us something about the peculiar way in which Hamlet generalizes his experience: he tends to universalize evil while seeing good as particular, if not unique. The honest man is one plucked from ten thou-

sand, Horatio's even-mindedness and loyalty tell Hamlet a
great deal about Horatio, but little or nothing about men in
general, while Claudius' smiling villainy suggests a whole
world of evil, implicating such nonentities as Rosencrantz
and such innocents as Ophelia. The famous "dram of evil"
speech (I.iv.23-38) provides a particularly good example of
how the process of selective universalizing works. Many
critics have interpreted the passage as explicating the theory
of the tragic flaw, a thoughtful insertion by Shakespeare to
help us understand his plays.[9] I, for one, do not believe
Shakespeare constructed his tragedies around any such
theory, even assuming he was familiar with it. Anyhow,
Hamlet is not talking here so much about flaws in individuals
as about the way the world apprehends the coexistence of
good and evil. Evil exerts such a powerful hold upon the
imagination that the presence of even a dram of it obscures,
in the general view, all coexistent good. Because some Danes
are fond of reveling, the world thinks all Danes a nation of
contemptible sots. Clearly Hamlet is projecting onto the
world his own mental habits; this is the way *he* views the coexistence of good and evil, as his actions throughout the play
attest.[10] However, when he returns to Denmark after his
perplexing "sea change," he has abandoned this one-sided
manner of drawing conclusions. He is capable then of universalizing good while leaving the evil particular, and hence
is able to formulate a world-view which, if pessimistic, is at
least endurable.

Hamlet's mental habits are further characterized by deft
leaps from the particular to the general and then back to the
particular again. We frequently find him, as in the first

[9] See, for instance, the elaborate case built out of this speech by
Henry Paul, *The Royal Play of* Macbeth (New York: Macmillan,
1950), pp. 10-11.

[10] Cf. Hilton Landry, "The Leaven of Wickedness: *Hamlet*, I.iv.1-
38," in *Pacific Coast Studies in Shakespeare*, eds. Waldo McNeir and
Thelma Greenfield (Eugene: Univ. of Oregon Press, 1966), pp.
122-133.

soliloquy, contemplating a specific situation and drawing from it broad conclusions about the nature of reality in general. He then takes the general conclusion and reapplies it to his particular situation. Hence his specific observation and his theorizing mutually support one another; if his generalizations are based on observation of particular events, his interpretation of particular events is influenced by his general over-view. Frequently, Hamlet's judgment of an individual is not based primarily upon the person's actions but upon how those actions fit into his own world-view. Thus he often distorts persons or events to make them conform with his vision of universal treachery, hypocrisy, and betrayal. "No matter how definite the thing he uses to clothe and animate his insight, he so manipulates the original that he in effect transforms it. What he does mainly is fix a penetrating glance at what comes into view, isolate only what he conceives to be the core, identify that core with some tangible object or experience, extract it from the moral context, and, interested in little else, assigns it a place in his own world picture."[11]

If Hamlet shares several essential qualities in common with the other mature Shakespearean tragic heroes, there is one important property that is completely unique to his characterization, his extraordinary sense of humor. An active, ever-present sense of humor is not generally regarded as standard equipment for a tragic hero, Shakespearean or otherwise. Othello, Lear, and Macbeth lack it almost entirely; in good fortune or in bad they never fail to take themselves with dead-level seriousness. But Hamlet's sense of humor is ubiquitous. It never deserts him even at the nadir of his fortunes, and he can apply it to situations which, seen from another point of vantage, do not in the least amuse him. It, too, is a result of his penchant for seeing a situation from more than one perspective at a time. His complementarity of

[11] Marvin Spevack, "Hamlet and Imagery: The Mind's Eye," *Die Neueren Sprachen* (May, 1966), p. 208.

mind accounts for the way his humor often flashes out un-
expectedly from a serious or even morose situation, strikes
home a brilliant point, and then vanishes again as suddenly
as it had appeared.

> Thrift, thrift, Horatio. The funeral baked meats
> Did coldly furnish forth the marriage tables.
> Would I had met my dearest foe in heaven
> Or ever I had seen that day, Horatio!
>
> (I.ii.180-183)

Irony is far and away Hamlet's favorite form of humor, but
he employs it in a variety of ways, ways that reflect his own
divided view of himself. Some of his wit, such as the above
quip, is derisive mockery of the situation in which he finds
himself, and carries with it an overtone of self-mockery. We
sense something similar in his first line, "A little more than
kin, and less than kind!" (I.ii.65), and in the ironic pun in his
second: "No so, my lord. I am too much in the sun" (67).
Hamlet's double relationship to Claudius, a result of the de-
tested marriage, is utterly loathsome to him, and, in making
it the subject of his humor, he is chafing exactly those areas
of his sensibility that have already been rubbed raw. He does
the same thing again in his sardonic farewell to the King,
making the physical intimacy between Claudius and Gertrude
(intimacy about which he had been hysterical a short while
before) the subject of ribald impudence:

> HAMLET: Farewell, dear mother.
> KING: Thy loving father, Hamlet.
> HAMLET: My mother—father and mother is man and
> wife, man and wife is one flesh, and so, my mother.
>
> (IV.iii.48-51)

Hamlet is a constant gall to himself in much the way the Fool
is to Lear.

But not all his wit is turned upon himself; the lion's share
is directed at others, especially Polonius, Rosencrantz, and

Guildenstern; and in his scenes with them Hamlet uses humor to demonstrate and relish his superiority. He finds it vastly amusing that, though they are trying to find out all about him, he knows more about them than they know about themselves. He takes tireless glee in making them employ their pathetic stratagems at his bidding, amusing himself with their supposition of their own cleverness. He loves to use their misconceptions about him to turn the tables on them.

> HAMLET: Sir, I cannot.
> ROSENCRANTZ: What, my lord?
> HAMLET: Make you a wholesome answer; my wit's diseased.
>
> (III.ii.306-309)

He confirms them in their false assumptions to stymie their quest for his secrets. "Sir, I lack advancement" (III.ii.326), he tells Rosencrantz, and never fails to bring up the subject of daughters when Polonius is around, enjoying the "Oho! do you mark that?" which is sure to follow. His most brilliant use of such a ploy is when he forces the old counselor, who thinks he is humoring a lunatic, to attest to the existence of a wholly nonexistent cloud shaped like a camel, a weasel, and a whale. But here again, the humor vanishes in an instant, replaced by his outraged remark to Horatio: "They fool me to the top of my bent" (III.ii.369). This is not simply a change in mood, but rather reflects a dual viewpoint. Seen in one way, he is fooling them and enjoying it immensely; seen in another way, they are trying to play upon him like a pipe, and he finds that intolerable. The same abrupt switch from virtuoso enjoyment of his ability to lead them where he wants, to outrage at the unworthy thing they are trying to make of him, occurs in exactly the same way in the recorder sequence.

The pattern of development of Hamlet's humor corresponds to the rest of his mental development, and roughly parallels the main plot-line of the play itself. In the first two acts, his wit is light and has a marked air of prankishness about it. In the central scenes, however, his wit becomes progressively more savage in his obscene remarks to Ophelia, his cruel mockery of the dead Polonius, and his calculated impudence before the King.[12] However, after his return to Denmark, this bitterness has been expunged. As he contemplates the skulls of courtiers, lawyers, landlords, and jesters, his humor has an almost quizzical tone. In the final scene, his satirizing of Osric has a casual quality, largely devoid of rancor. He invites Horatio to share the joke, something he had not done before, having previously been his own prompter, critic, and most appreciative audience.

Hamlet himself provides the most illuminating insight into what is behind his humor. Toward the end of the closet scene he remarks, more to himself, I think, than to Gertrude:

> For 'tis the sport to have the enginer
> Hoist with his own petar, and't shall go hard
> But I will delve one yard below their mines
> And blow them at the moon. O, 'tis most sweet
> When in one line two crafts directly meet.
>
> (III.iv.207-211)

Up until this point, there has been very little in the *Hamlet*-world which the hero has found "most sweet." Usually he has been depicted as a desperate, anguished, furious man, and, in this scene, that anguish and fury have reached their apex. But, having vented his anger, he can consciously recognize something that has been evident from his actions all along: there is a certain point of vantage from which Hamlet can actually *enjoy* his predicament and relish the game of finger-in-the-candle in which all the major characters are engaged.[13] This is not to say that his appreciation of what is at stake is trivial or that he regards life cynically as

[12] Levin makes a similar point in *The Question of* Hamlet, p. 119.
[13] B. L. Reid, "The Last Act and the Action of *Hamlet*," *Yale Review*, 54 (1964), 69, notes: "One side of his nature takes both physical and intellectual pleasure in the dangerous ingenuity of his strategy." See also Taylor, "The Conflict in *Hamlet*," pp. 153-154.

merely an elaborate game; rather this is *one* of the ways he regards it, and the anguished seriousness with which he also regards it can exist side by side with this enjoyment in his mind. It is this capacity that makes his mind the most fascinating and perplexing in literature.

All of Hamlet's humor, both the self-mocking and the self-aggrandizing, has as its vantage point a third eye, detached from the situation, amused by life's incongruity and by the knavishness and foolishness by which the world turns. Thus all of Hamlet's wit is reductive; it applies the *reductio ad absurdum* to the entire situation and everybody in it, himself included. "The king is a thing . . . of nothing" (iv.ii.27-29). In the graveyard scene, Hamlet connects his own reductive wit with the *reductio ad absurdum* suggested by antic death, the skull of the jester. Like the king who finds his way through the guts of a beggar, Caesar and Alexander find themselves plugging a wall and a beer barrel. But in the process of commenting upon the extremity to which all men must come, Hamlet places himself in a most peculiar situation, playing straight-man for the Gravedigger. "How absolute the knave is! We must speak by the card, or equivocation will undo us" (v.i.128-129). Hamlet speaks truer than he knows. Trading quips unwittingly at the grave of the woman he once loved, he is in exactly the kind of ironic position into which he has so enjoyed putting others. But whether Hamlet is using his humor as a gall to himself, for amusement in the game, as a weapon, as a release, or as a *reductio ad absurdum*, humor is for him, as for Lear's Fool, not merely a way of commenting but a way of seeing.

It should be evident from the foregoing that I disagree with that long critical tradition that makes Hamlet a disillusioned idealist suffering from a severe case of moral debilitation. To see him as a confused undergraduate, a kind of Renaissance Holden Caulfield, stunned to ineffectuality by the discovery that his elders are not necessarily his betters, is to sentimentalize him and oversimplify his tragedy. Nor do I find any more satisfying the later tradition that would make

46

of him a moral invalid, if not a moral leper. Hamlet's reaction
to the problems of the *Hamlet*-world are complex and multifaceted, but the most conspicuous and consistent element in
that reaction is rage—rage that he is able to control only by a
supreme effort of his will, rage which is never far below the
surface, which is constantly breaking through despite his
best efforts to restrain it, and which, in moments of great
stress, runs entirely out of control and takes possession of him
completely. Hamlet, faced with evil, does not give up on the
world; rather he launches a furious assault upon it with all
the very considerable resources at his disposal to make it
conform to his values.

Until this point, I have been dividing Hamlet inventorially,
a process which can dozy the arithmetic of memory, and yet but
yaw neither in respect of his quick sail. The time has come to
turn to his career as depicted in the action, and the place to
start is with the first soliloquy. This speech is set apart from
most Shakespearean soliloquies in that the syntax is particularly choppy, almost strangulated, the thought being continually interrupted by uncontrollable outbursts. Moreover,
it is marked by a peculiar intellectual stasis. There is no
development of thought as in the "To be or not to be"
soliloquy; Hamlet's mind remains stationary before a specific
situation and the entire speech is given over to delineating
that situation, and his attitude toward it. The speech does not
suggest the melancholy brooding of a demoralized man
lyrically rehearsing his troubles. Rather it suggests a man
whose mind has been pushed to the very limits of endurance,
one who is literally choking on his indignation. The syntax is
broken because Hamlet repeatedly recoils from naming the
deed that now occupies the center of his consciousness;
twenty-three strangulated lines pass before he can get it out:

> . . . why she, even she—
> O God, a beast that wants discourse of reason
> Would have mourned longer—married with my uncle.
>   (I.ii.149-151)

But despite the interruptions, the speech shows an involuntary forward plunge which has something of the compulsive, one might even say something of the obsessive about it. Hamlet's mind is here feeding upon itself as if increase of appetite had grown by what it fed on: the more he considers the situation, the more he is revolted; the more he is revolted, the more he is forced to dwell on exactly what revolts him most.[14]

Although there are several aspects of the marriage that repel Hamlet, the one he stresses repeatedly is the discrepancy between what Gertrude had appeared to feel for King Hamlet and the ease and swiftness with which she put his memory aside to marry his brother. The interval between the funeral and the nuptial (a kind of emblem in his mind for the flimsiness of what had seemed so certain) keeps getting shorter and shorter: "But two months . . . nay, not so much, not two . . . within a month . . . a little month, or ere those shoes were old . . . Ere yet the salt of most unrighteous tears / Had left the flushing in her gallèd eyes. . . ."[15] Far more is at stake here than filial devotion to a father's memory or an Oedipal mother-fixation. The marriage undermines his confidence in his apprehension of reality. His mother's love for his father was something so self-evident that it would never enter his mind to question it; it was simply assumed, one of the givens of his world-picture. But now it has turned out to be something quite different from what it had appeared, and the shock of discovery casts doubt upon the reliability of all "seeming" and appearance. Time and again he returns to that point, as will the Ghost in making his terrible revelation.

Hamlet has already universalized the worst aspects of the situation at court into a broad vision of the world shot through with evil. It is significant, however, that at this point

---

[14] In *Nature in Shakespearean Tragedy*, Speaight observes that many of Hamlet's speeches depict energy feeding on emotion and emotion feeding on itself (p. 30).

[15] H. B. Charlton, *Shakespearean Tragedy* (1948; rpt. Cambridge, Eng.: Cambridge Univ. Press, 1952), p. 96.

we hear nothing of Gertrude's sensuality. There is no hint of the gross, physical revulsion with which Hamlet will later vilify her. Woman's name is still frailty, not lust. The sexual malaise, which has been so widely regarded as crucial to the characterization, does not appear until the "fishmonger" sequence, well after the Ghost has made his revelations.

For all its dynamic spontaneity, however, the speech has a carefully worked out, almost circular pattern. It begins in the particular, moves to a general statement about nature and the world, and then closes as it began, in the particular: "But break my heart, for I must hold my tongue" (159). This final, remarkable line has not received the attention it deserves. Hamlet is saying that what is breaking his heart is not simply that the situation exists, but that he must contain his feelings about it because of his position as son and subject. Furthermore, if we look back over this scene, we will find that all of Hamlet's taut, cryptic remarks have been part of a struggle to hold his tongue, or, more exactly, to speak the unspeakable under a thin veil of word-play. This is surely true of his first line, perhaps intended for the hearing of Claudius and Gertrude (there is no "aside" in either Q2 or F1), and the ironic pun in his second line. Moreover, in his first long speech, he caustically lectures Gertrude on the difference between seeming and being. The whole passage is a thinly veiled reproach for the difference between what she seemed to feel and the way she subsequently acted. His grief for his father is not mere seeming (as were her Niobe-like tears); the outward shows of grief are actions that a man might play (as she apparently did); he has within (as she so manifestly does not) that which passes show. His very appearance in black in spite of, or rather *because* of the court's desire to forget the old king and be merry with the new, makes him a kind of walking reproach of their shallowness and perfidiousness. This wilfulness, this determination to force his feelings upon the court as far as his position will let him, has far more to do with Hamlet's garb than his "classic melancholia" or his unhealthy preoccupation with the grave. Hamlet's struggle

49

to hold his tongue, to contain his outrage while still expressing it as much as he dares, further accounts for the choppy syntax of the first soliloquy. Outbursts such as "O God, a beast that wants discourse of reason / Would have mourned longer" (150-151), are exactly the kind of thing which Hamlet wants to say, must say, and finally does say to Gertrude. At this juncture, he can only spit it our in her absence.

His mother's conduct makes him suspicious of all apparent reality; the Ghost's revelations shatter his faith in the very processes by which reality can be apprehended. Only comparatively recently have such critics as J. Dover Wilson and Peter Alexander demonstrated that the Ghost, far from being a mere Senecan convention or a leftover spook from the ur-*Hamlet*, is actually a subtly drawn characterization whose importance quite transcends his few appearances.[16] What seems to have escaped comment, however, is that the preoccupations of the elder Hamlet are markedly similar to several of those which will haunt the younger. First of all, the marriage of Claudius and Gertrude seems to incense him even more than the murder. He returns to it several times, stressing the discrepancy between Gertrude's professed love and actual slightness, and emphasizing the paucity of Claudius' merits in comparison to his own. Moreover, both Hamlets share a physical loathing of Claudius not simply as a criminal usurper, but as something rank and gross in nature. Indeed, the Ghost shows an interest in the corruption of the flesh and the horrors of the afterlife which verges on morbid fascination, as, of course, does the son: witness the almost clinical description of the effect of the poison. In addition, he points conspicuously to a preoccupation already well established in the mind of the Prince, the presence of dark realities below apparently innocent surfaces and the unreliability of appearance in general, and of "seeming virtue" in particular. This emphasis in the father's speeches upon the characteristic problems of the *Hamlet*-world establishes early

[16] *What Happens in* Hamlet, pp. 55-60; *Hamlet, Father and Son*, pp. 27-36.

in the play themes that will shortly be elaborated with baroque lavishness by the son.

It is of the utmost significance that the Ghost accomplishes essentially what he came to do in just the first forty lines of the scene; he reveals the murder, accuses Claudius, and exhorts Hamlet to revenge. His long speech which follows, the only major one he has in the play, contains no further startling revelations, but merely elaborates the details. It is addressed not to the mind but to the imagination, and young Hamlet's imagination at this point is most fertile ground for what the Ghost has to say about the world and humanity. Already convinced of the ubiquitousness of corruption, already shaken by the discrepancy between the way he had thought things were and the way they are, already inclined to see "foul deeds" below every smiling surface, the Prince now discovers that even his worst premonitions came short of the mark. Convinced in his first soliloquy that he had viewed the depths, he now discovers he had not even conceived of what the depths could be.[17] The Ghost's revelations complete the undermining of his world-picture by broadening and deepening the vision of ubiquitous evil, and demolishing his faith in the reliability of apprehended appearance. Hamlet's mind is not unhinged so much as it is completely estranged. All his previous assumptions about the world have proven to be invalid, and his subjective world collapses. Shakespeare uses the image of the mind as a table or commonplace book (an image he had introduced in the previous scene in Polonius' speech to Laertes) to express the destruction of Hamlet's world-view, his renunciation of all reality he had apprehended up to the moment, of his *way* of apprehending reality:

> Yea, from the table of my memory
> I'll wipe away all trivial fond records,
> All saws of books, all forms, all pressures past
> That youth and observation copied there.
>
> (I.v.98-101)

[17] See Spencer, *Shakespeare and the Nature of Man*, p. 95.

51

There is a terrible absoluteness and finality to those repeated "all's," a renunciation of the sum total of past experience, the very substance of his world-view.[18] His apprehension now being more or less a clean slate, however, what Hamlet writes down is not the Ghost's command, but something a lot closer to his own interests and compulsions:

> O most pernicious woman!
> O villain, villain, smiling, damnèd villain!
> My tables—meet it is I set it down
> That one may smile, and smile, and be a villain.
>
> (105-108)

Just as the worst thing about Gertrude's perfidiousness was her apparent love, so, too, the worst thing about Claudius' blood-guilt is his jovial complacence. The smile seems to offend Hamlet even more than the villainy.[19]

But the same passage raises a critical problem of central importance to the action of the play: why does Hamlet think first of his mother's guilt rather than of his uncle's?[20] This can hardly be pouncing too eagerly upon the sequence of lines; at one of the most crucial junctures of the play, Shakespeare would scarcely have introduced an irrelevance, especially since he has made the specific point in the Ghost's speech that Hamlet is not to concern himself with the state of Gertrude's soul. Moreover, throughout the first two-thirds of the play, Hamlet consistently places more emphasis upon Gertrude's guilt than upon his obligation to dispose of Claudius. One possible explanation for Hamlet's reaction is that the Ghost's reference to Claudius as an "adulterate beast" who "seduced" Gertrude means that their liaison began

[18] L. C. Knights, *An Approach to* Hamlet (Stanford: Stanford Univ. Press, 1961), p. 48.

[19] A similar point is made by Levin L. Schücking in *The Meaning of* Hamlet, trans. Graham Rawson (London: Oxford Univ. Press, 1937), p. 88.

[20] Noted by Harley Granville-Barker, *Prefaces to Shakespeare* (1946: rpt. Princeton: Princeton Univ. Press, 1963) I, 63.

52

during King Hamlet's lifetime. But those words had a less specific meaning for Elizabethans than for moderns, and I find plausible John Draper's arguments that infidelity during the King's lifetime is not an issue of the play.[21] The matter of adultery is never brought up again by Hamlet or by anyone else. The Prince is not a man of over-nice sensibility when it comes to naming people's vices; in a moment of passion he can even accuse Gertrude of complicity in the murder, something he obviously does not believe. But he never accuses her of extra-marital affairs. *The Murder of Gonzago*, which parallels the events at Elsinore exactly (even to the point of taxing dramatic probability, unless we are to assume that Hamlet, far from merely inserting a dozen lines, wrote the entire thing himself), depicts the seduction as taking place after the death of the Duke, not before.

If, however, we reject the idea that adultery is added to the list of Gertrude's sins, we must otherwise explain why the Ghost's revelations intensify Hamlet's reaction toward her marriage, as they so obviously do. The answer lies not in additional crimes, but in the new relationship she assumes to Hamlet's fragmented and radically darkened attitude toward the *Hamlet*-world. We must bear in mind the absoluteness of his moral judgments. He seldom takes culpability or ignorance into account as mitigating factors. Rather, as I have said, he bases his judgments largely upon how a person or an action fits into the overall pattern of his world-view. His moral outrage is aroused by her refusal to see the reality in which she is living. As that reality becomes ever more loathsome in his eyes, her association with it and refusal or inability to see it become more and more infuriating. Of course, this does not abide by the traditional Western, Christian notion of guilt by cognizant culpability—but then again, neither does Hamlet. Gertrude is not the only character to suffer damnation by association in his mind's eye.

[21] *The* Hamlet *of Shakespeare's Audience* (Durham, N.C.: Duke Univ. Press, 1938), pp. 112-117.

When the world-picture of the tragic hero collapses, he is faced with the characteristic problem of Shakespearean tragedy, how to endure what is, for him, unendurable. Hamlet now faces that problem. It has been most usual for actors and critics to depict Hamlet as verging on the brink of actual lunacy after the Ghost's departure. Rather, I think his state can better be described as a kind of intellectual chaos in which the fragments of his shattered world-view are in violent motion and disarray. If one wishes to construe this as a definition of temporary insanity, very well, but it is important to remember that each of the Shakespearean tragic heroes undergoes, in one form or another, a similar chaotic dissolution when his world-picture collapses. Othello utters a completely incoherent speech and falls down in a fit. Lear rages on the heath, drifting in and out of madness until his final plunge. Macbeth completely loses his nerve and gives way to his hallucinations after the murder of Duncan. Hamlet, then, is not alone in uttering wild and whirling words, and he most certainly is not mad, in this scene or in any other. Various elements of his personality are in chaotic flux, and the most prominent of these can only be called exultation. When Hamlet comes into open confrontation with the truth, his reaction is always wild excitement, even enthusiasm, even if the truth encountered is appalling. We had a foreshadowing of this exaltation in his cry, "O my prophetic soul!" (I.v.40), and we will see an even more remarkable instance of it after the success of *The Mousetrap*.[22] It is never long before Hamlet is weighed down by the truth and by the obligations it imposes upon him, but his initial reaction upon first grasping it is always triumphant.

From the moment of the Ghost's departure, Hamlet is sole proprietor of the whole truth: no one else knows about the murder except Claudius, and Claudius does not know that Hamlet knows. The Prince's knowledge sets him apart from the court and frees him from the obligation to hold his

[22] See Dowden, p. 138.

tongue. He can now approach the intriguers knowing more about them than they know about him or, in many cases, about themselves. He is not above relishing this edge in the extreme, and his instinctive reaction is to guard it even from Horatio; hence his fanatical insistence upon the thrice-repeated oath. A similar spirit underlies his weird jesting with the Ghost: "Ha, ha, boy, say'st thou so? Art thou there, truepenny? . . . Well said, old mole! Canst work i'th' earth so fast? / O worthy pioner!" (150-163). This is not lunacy nor even mere hysterical gaiety. Rather, it is the jesting of conspirators, the cryptic remarks between those in the know when everyone else is ignorant. It is, in fact, the very kind of conspiratorial humor which Hamlet repeatedly forbids to his companions. His jesting here, his relish of the freedom and the power of the secret, his conspiratorial jokes with Horatio after the play, all are closely allied to that part of Hamlet's multiple viewpoint from which the conflict of mighty opposites is exciting and perversely enjoyable. His demeanor has something of the delirious freedom of the man for whom limits no longer exist, to whom the rules no longer apply, who has smashed all the forms and renounced literally everything of his past.

In the course of this crucial scene, Hamlet announces his intention to put on "an antic disposition," providing one of the most perplexing cruxes of the play. As it is integrally linked with the even larger crux of Hamlet's supposed "delay," it must occupy our attention for some considerable space. Underlying most *Hamlet* criticism is the tacit assumption that "antic disposition" and "feigned madness" are synonymous, interchangeable terms, an assumption in no way justified. Hamlet speaks only of "How strange or odd some'er I bear myself" (I.v.170). Certainly, throughout the central portion of the play all the principals think he is mad, and he actively encourages them in this belief. But is that all there is to it? So far as I have been able to determine, the only critics who have subjected the word "antic" to any close scrutiny have been Bernard Grebanier and Sidney

Thomas.[23] Grebanier, citing the *OED* as his source, concludes that the word was never used to signify madness (pp. 146-147). As a matter of fact, he is wrong, and the *OED* has apparently missed a number of important usages, including at least one in Shakespeare. Thomas, more painstaking in his researches, concludes that it was "rarely" used in Elizabethan idiom to indicate insanity: "I have found only one doubtful example of such usage: the term 'wild unshapen antic' applied by Antonio to the supposed madwoman Isabella in Thomas Middleton's play, *The Changeling* (v.iii.141)" (p. 4n). Inexplicably, both critics fail to draw attention to the occurrence of the word in *Troilus and Cressida*, a play near, perhaps adjacent, to *Hamlet* in the usually accepted chronology:

> Behold, distraction, frenzy, and amazement,
> Like witless antics, one another meet,
> And all cry Hector! Hector's dead! O Hector!
>
> (v.iii.85-87)

Surely the noun in the simile refers to deranged persons.[24] But both critics are right in the essential point: of the several

[23] Bernard Grebanier, *The Heart of* Hamlet (New York: Crowell, 1960), pp. 141-149; Sidney Thomas, *The Antic Hamlet and Richard III* (New York: King's Crown Press, 1943), pp. 5-7.

[24] Dekker also used the word in connection with madness in part one of *The Honest Whore*, although in this context, the word could well mean "grotesque" or "clownish":

> There are of mad men, as there are of tame,
> All humourd not alike: we haue here some,
> So apish and phantastike, play with a fether,
> And tho twould greeue a soule, to see Gods image,
> So blemisht and defac'd, yet do they act
> Such anticke and such pretty lunacies
> That spite of sorrow they will make you smile.
>
> (v.ii.155-161)

Quoted from *The Dramatic Works of Thomas Dekker*, ed. Fredson Bowers (Cambridge, Eng.: Cambridge Univ. Press, 1955). Considering the Elizabethan propensity to find lunatics entertaining, it is not surprising that "antic" should share in both meanings.

meanings the word "antic" had as a noun, adjective, and
occasionally as a verb, "lunatic" was certainly not the most
usual. We have already referred to a more characteristic
usage, Richard II's depiction of the "antic," death, scoffing
at his state and grinning at his pomp. There is a strikingly
similar occurrence of the word in *1 Henry VI*, as Talbot sees
his dead son: "Thou antic Death, which laugh'st us here to
scorn" (IV.vii.18). There is an attribution problem in this
play which need not concern us here; whether or not this
line is by Shakespeare, it shows that there was a common
association between "antic" and scoffer, applier of the *reductio
ad absurdum*. A similar usage occurs at the opening of the
"Gulling Sonnets" of Shakespeare's contemporary, Sir John
Davies:

> Here my Camelion Muse her selfe doth chaunge
> to divers shapes of gross absurdities
> and like an Antic mocks with fashion straunge
> the fond admirers of lewde gulleries.[25]

This "fashion straunge" could well serve as a description of
Hamlet's "strange" behavior. Lear's Fool is this type of antic,
and so, in certain moods, is Hamlet.[26]

Shakespeare's other uses of the word stress the pejorative
sense of "clown," for the most part, as in the Boy's comment upon Nym, Bardolph, and Pistol in *Henry V*: "three
such antics do not amount to a man" (III.ii.28).[27] Accord-

[25] *The Poems of Sir John Davies*, ed. Clare Howard (New York:
Columbia Univ. Press, 1941), p. 223.
[26] Thomas links Hamlet with the Vice tradition. See pp. 53-65.
[27] Spevack lists the following additional uses:

> If black, why nature, drawing of an antic,
>
> (ADO 3.01.63)
>
> Or show, or pageant, or antic, or firework,
>
> (LLL 5.01.112p)
>
> We will have, if this fadge not, an antic.
>
> (LLL 5.01.147p)
>
> I never may believe / These antic fables, nor
>
> (MND 5.01.3)

57

ingly, a survey of these usages reveals that while "antic" could mean "insane" or "madman," it more usually meant "clown," including the kind of jester or scoffer who reduces those around him to absurdity by pointing out their follies and misconceptions. There is no airtight way of proving that this is what Hamlet has in mind when he warns his friends that some strange behavior is in store; all we can do is point out that this is exactly what he does.

Those scenes in which Hamlet is using his antic disposition are characterized not merely by odd behavior of any kind, but rather by the "putting on" of a "disposition"; that is, Hamlet is consciously encouraging those around him to believe him mad. This occurs first with Polonius in the "fishmonger" sequence, and then again when the minister announces the arrival of the players; it occurs again in the presence of the assembled court before and during the presentation of *The Mousetrap*, then with Rosencrantz, Guild-

---

Were he the veriest antic in the world
(SHR IN.1.101)

With the rusty curb of old father antic the law?
(1H4 1.02.61p)

Slave / Come hither, cover'd with an antic face,
(ROM 1.05.56)

The pox of such antic, lisping, affecting
(ROM 2.04.28p)

A sound, / While you perform your antic round;
(MAC 4.01.130)

And all we'll dance an antic 'fore the duke,
(TNK 4.01.75)

The wild disguise hath almost / Antick'd us all
(ANT 2.07.125)

Go anticly, and show outward hideousness,
(ADO 5.01.96)

There appears / Quick-shifting antics, ugly in
(LUC 459)

Marvin Spevack, *A Complete and Systematic Concordance to the Works of Shakespeare*, 6 vols. (Hildesheim: Olms, 1968-70).

enstern, and Polonius after the King has retired in disorder;
then with the two schoolfellows after the murder of Polonius;
then with Claudius before the Prince's departure; and finally,
though perhaps only peripherally, with Osric.

In addition there are other scenes in which those around
Hamlet believe him to be mad, but in which he is not attempting to encourage them in this belief. Rather, something has
happened which arouses his rage to the bursting point or
otherwise excites him, and, though he is not literally mad in
the sense that Ophelia and Lear are mad, neither is he putting
on a disposition of any kind. Such scenes are the episode after
the departure of the Ghost, the nunnery scene with Ophelia,[28]
the closet scene, and the wrestling in the grave. What interests
us at the moment are the scenes in the first group, where
Hamlet is deliberately stringing everyone along, indulging in
the kind of behavior he had in mind when he warned his
friends not to give him away.

We may immediately note several things he is *not* doing in
these scenes. He is not protecting himself; rather he is toying
with Claudius and his spies, arousing the King's suspicion
until, even before the presentation of the play, Claudius has
resolved on the expedition to England. Hamlet is not gathering evidence in these scenes; he at no time solicits information
from those he is gulling, but rather tells them a good deal
about himself and themselves, as noted by Rosencrantz and
Guildenstern when they report back to their royal employer:
"Niggard of question, but of our demands / Most free in his
reply" (iii.i.13-14). The antic disposition has no essential
connection with his principal evidence-gathering stratagem,
the presentation of the play. He is not using feigned madness
to cover up real madness or near-madness. In the scenes
where he is putting on a disposition, the Prince is in perfect
control of himself and of the situation. Indeed, his gulling of
the others depends upon a particular lucidity and sharpness

---

[28] It will be my contention that Hamlet is not feigning madness
for the benefit of the King in this scene. See below, pp. 72-74.

of mind. When Hamlet feels he is about to lose his grip on himself, he either gets everyone out of the way so that he can give vent to his feelings in private (as in the rogue and peasant slave speech), or else lets fly regardless of the consequences (as in the fight in the grave). At such moments of stress he does not use the antic disposition; rather, it is at precisely such times that he abandons it.

Those critics who hold that Hamlet uses the antic disposition to unburden himself come closer to the mark;[29] he does use it in order to speak, and what he feels impelled to tell is *the truth*. His stratagem not only gives him license to speak otherwise unspeakable truths (no small consideration to a man whose heart is breaking because he must hold his tongue), but also allows him to tell the truth in a way that reduces his hypocritical auditors to absurdity.[30] The antic disposition is one of several methods he has of forcing truth upon a world that operates largely by fraud and hypocrisy. Polonius' position is that of a shrewd and wise counselor; Hamlet knows him to be a fool, and, under the guise of madness, tells him so. Rosencrantz and Guildenstern are trying to pass themselves off as friends and believe themselves to be loyal and favored subjects; Hamlet knows them to be shallow time-servers who have made themselves puppets in a treacherous conspiracy, and, under the guise of madness, he tells them so. Ophelia is a paragon of apparent virtue, while Gertrude seemed the epitome of wifely devotion. Disgusted with what he believes to be the charade of love, he uses the guise of madness to berate them before the assembled court for their faithlessness. His devotion to truth is so absolute that

[29] The idea was apparently suggested first by Karl Werder in *The Heart of Hamlet's Mystery*, trans. Elizabeth Wilder (New York: Putnam, 1907), p. 92, who held that Hamlet's task was objectively impossible, and therefore the hero had to unburden himself. More recently, Levin has connected Hamlet with a line of all-licensed fools in Elizabethan-Jacobean drama (*The Question of* Hamlet, pp. 111-128).

[30] "Hamlet speaks the truth to them and makes them tell their lies" (Werder, p. 99).

he cannot even resist telling Claudius' spies that he is not really mad: "I am but mad north-north-west. When the wind is southerly I know a hawk from a handsaw" (II.ii.369-370). The reference is cryptic and the revelation itself is phrased cleverly to fit their conviction that he is mad. But it is the truth, and he tells it, and their inclination to disbelieve it and cling to a misconception is exactly the kind of irony Hamlet relishes.

In every instance, then, Hamlet uses his antic disposition to strip away what he conceives to be a deceptive appearance and to point a derisive and reductive finger at the truth that lies beneath. Feigned madness is not a conscious or unconscious means of putting off what he is incapable of doing; rather it is a declaration of total war against the court and its values. All along the court has been feigning reasonableness; nothing could be more level-headed than Claudius' opening speeches.[31] But this is utter sham; beneath the surface of smiles, this court is based upon the same jungle law as Macbeth's or Goneril's. By means of his antic disposition, Hamlet separates himself from this tissue of lies, places himself above it, and frees himself to deal with it in terms commensurate with its nature. Hence the antic disposition is closely linked with Hamlet's reductive wit; is, in fact, almost identical with it.

One final, if somewhat parenthetical, word on this complicated problem: it is difficult to argue anything from the sources of *Hamlet*, since Shakespeare may have been working from the ur-*Hamlet*, a shade as elusive as anything to be encountered at Elsinore. Yet there is some evidence that Shakespeare may have read either Saxo's account or Belleforest's, or both, and, for what it's worth, both contain references to Hamlet's using his disguise in the service of truth. Saxo reads: "for he was loath to be thought prone to lying about any matter, and wished to be held a stranger to falsehood; and accordingly he mingled craft and candour

[31] See Terence Hawkes's analysis in *Shakespeare and the Reason* (New York: Humanities Press, 1965), pp. 46-59.

in such wise that, though his words did not lack truth, yet there was nothing to betoken the truth and betray how far his keenness went."[32] Bellforest reads: "the answers that ever he made (during his counterfeit madness) never strayed from the trueth (as a generous minde is a mortal enemie to untruth)" (p. 229).

C. S. Lewis has described Hamlet as a man given a task by a ghost.[33] Exactly so. His tragedy does not lie in that he is constitutionally incapable of carrying out that task, or that the task itself is impossible, in practical terms, of execution. The problem is that what he is told to do and what he wants to do—what he is inwardly impelled to do—are two decidedly different things. The Ghost's primary interest in revenge is to set things to rights: the fratricide-regicide must not be allowed to enjoy his usurped throne and incestuous marriage. But Hamlet's own inner needs are less clear-cut. With his former vision of reality in shambles, he must impose some form of new coherence upon his personal world. Hamlet does not have the emotional constitution of a nihilist; that life should have meaning is desperately important to him. Yet he is forced to contemplate a world where all values are sham, where death is a consummation devoutly to be wished, where love makes monsters out of men and all women are false, where procreation itself merely perpetuates corruption, where all human endeavors serve merely to provide the worm's banquet. Hamlet does not so much vacillate between militant idealism and misanthropic pessimism as he is caught in the tension between them, torn by the irresistible demands they make upon his emotions and mind.[34] Throughout the play, his struggle is not simply with his royal antagonist, but with the larger problem of what is real and how reality is to be

[32] In *The Sources of Hamlet,* ed. Israel Gollanz (London: Oxford Univ. Press, 1926), p. 107.
[33] "Hamlet: The Prince or the Poem," p. 147.
[34] Schücking noted that Hamlet is ready to believe in times of great stress, but never entirely loses his skepticism (*The Meaning of Hamlet,* p. 85).

apprehended. He launches a multifronted attack upon the
Hamlet-world itself, attempting to gain a new grasp on reality
through trial and error, to assess the worth of human life as
seen from several possible perspectives, and, paradoxically,
to enforce upon the court values in which he instinctively
believes, even though the intellectual underpinning of such
belief has been demolished. Underlying all his struggles is a
desperately felt need for congruence between appearance
and reality, a need to unmask hidden evil and show things
as they truly are, and a relentless search for factual and
philosophical truth, the only basis upon which right action
can be founded. Thus his much discussed delay is a delay
only when viewed from the standpoint of the Ghost and his
purposes: in pursuing the course dictated by his own inner
needs, Hamlet is scarcely less resourceful or energetic than
Iago.

In his struggle to establish congruence between appearance
and reality, Hamlet employs three principal means. The first,
as we have seen, is the antic disposition. The second is the
tirade of denunciation, veiled at first or delivered in private,
but becoming progressively bolder until we reach the merciless excoriation of the closet scene. The third method is the
play within a play, a shrewd device for bringing reality out
from behind its elaborate disguises, as well as for depicting
mimetically what really happened.[35] Now all three of Hamlet's
methods of attacking sham have one very basic thing in
common—they all depend upon the effective use of words.
Taken together they form the elaborate intrigue which may
properly be called Hamlet's revenge of words.[36] In mounting

[35] Reid, in "The Last Act and the Action of *Hamlet*," notes the
connection between the function of *The Mousetrap* and Hamlet's observations on the purpose of playing (p. 69). See also Hawkes,
Shakespeare and the Reason, p. 63.

[36] For incisive commentary on the role of words *qua* words in
Hamlet see: Richard Foster, "Hamlet and the Word," *Univ. of To-
ronto Quarterly*, 30 (1961), 229-245; John Paterson, "The Word in
Hamlet," *Shakespeare Quarterly*, 2 (1951), 47-55.

a revenge of words, the Prince is using the most effective weapons for his purposes. Since words have been used to build the elaborate screen of deceptions and to subvert the reliability of appearance, words alone can suffice to uncover truth and restore congruence. Words as wielded by Hamlet become devastating weapons indeed, and the link between words and weapons is made repeatedly in the imagery at exactly that point where the revenge of words is reaching its terrible culmination. "I will speak daggers to her, but use none" (III.ii.381), Hamlet says, and, when she has a sample of what he means, Gertrude concurs in the aptness of the metaphor: "These words like daggers enter in mine ears" (III.iv.96). Without solid foundation in truth, the use of actual daggers would at best be ineffective, and at worst might be pernicious.

But in pursuing his own purposes, the revenge of words, Hamlet brings his actions into diametrical opposition with the purpose of the Ghost, a revenge of blood, thus involving himself in an impossible dichotomy. The Ghost's command has behind it multiple authority: the will of heaven, the demands of honor, and the obligation of filial duty. Hamlet is far from insensitive to the weight of these authorities, and at several points he upbraids himself bitterly for failing to sweep to his revenge as he had promised. The rogue and peasant slave soliloquy is a vivid depiction of a man to double business bound, caught up in not one but several dilemmas, his mind torn between conflicting, mutually exclusive beliefs. Prior to the beginning of the speech, Hamlet has hit upon the stratagem of the play and has made arrangements for its presentation. Logically, then, he must have doubts about the Ghost and feel the need for corroboration. Yet, when the speech begins, it becomes instantly apparent that he is firmly convinced that Claudius killed King Hamlet, and that he accepts without reservation the need for revenge. But what kind of revenge? The soliloquy is conspicuously concerned with words; what sets Hamlet off on his tirade of self-reproach

Is not that the player can *do* anything but that he can use words so effectively in the service of a mere fiction.[37] Hamlet speculates what a man of the player's prowess would do in his own situation:

> He would drown the stage with tears
> And cleave the general ear with horrid speech,
> Make mad the guilty and appal the free,
> Confound the ignorant, and amaze indeed
> The very faculties of eyes and ears.
>
> (II.ii.546-550)

These are, of course, the kinds of effects that Hamlet wants to produce and finally does produce through *The Mousetrap*. What he rebukes himself for is not that he cannot do anything, but that he cannot *say* anything:

> Yet I,
> A dull and muddy-mettled rascal, peak
> Like John-a-dreams, unpregnant of my cause,
> And can say nothing.
>
> (551-554)

Once again we are reminded of the closing line of the first soliloquy. But the tension between Hamlet's purposes and the violent revenge to which he has been bidden is unbearable. Reviewing his own conduct, he comes to a most characteristic conclusion: he certainly is not a coward, and he certainly is a coward. As the climax of the speech approaches, his disgust and rage begin to feed upon themselves as in the first soliloquy, and he launches into an orgy of vituperation, bellowing exactly the things he wants to say to Claudius' face, but cannot. However, having indulged his fury, he characteristically turns completely around, regards the situation from a radically different perspective, and renounces the revenge of words:

[37] Foster, p. 236.

Why, what an ass am I! This is most brave,
That I, the son of a dear father murdered,
Prompted to my revenge by heaven and hell,
Must like a whore unpack my heart with words
And fall a-cursing like a very drab,
A stallion! Fie upon't, foh!

(568-573)

His passion, having found a momentary outlet, subsides, and
he calls his intellect back into play: "About, my brains"
(573). This is the turning point of the speech, incorporating
yet another of the startlingly abrupt changes of viewpoint
which are so characteristic of the Prince. We are back in the
presence of Hamlet the intellectual skeptic, doubtful of all
surfaces and determined to bring things out into the open.
Immediately the revenge of words moves back into the forefront; guilty creatures at a play "proclaim" their malefaction,
for murder "will speak" with most miraculous organ. Clearly,
the purpose of the play is not to establish guilt but to unmask it; even in his most skeptical moment, Hamlet inad-
vertently reveals that he accepts the Ghost's account and
hence should be in no need of proof:

I'll have these players
Play something like the murder of my father
Before mine uncle.

(580-582)

If Hamlet, then, does not need to be convinced, the point
of making Claudius blench is not to convict him but to make
him drop his disguise, to appear, if only for an instant, as he
really is, to create a situation in which he can no longer
smile and be a villain. Hamlet the enthusiast is once more
caught up in the game, sanguinely anticipating the outcome:
"The play's the thing / Wherein I'll catch the conscience of
the king" (590-591).

Hamlet's invention, preparation, and execution of his stratagem and the extraordinary consequences that ensue form the

main line of the action in Acts II, III, and IV, counterpointed
by Claudius' attempts to spy out what his nephew is up to and
his growing conviction that Hamlet is not in essential madness
but mad in craft, and very, very dangerous. But the presentation is far from direct, being embellished by digressions and
digressions from digressions which present a whole host of
ancillary issues. The middle section of the play consists largely
of a series of confrontations between Hamlet and the other
inhabitants of the *Hamlet*-world, confrontations in which
every facet of the hero's relationship to that world is minutely
examined from several different vantage points, confrontations involving Hamlet and Polonius, Hamlet and his two
false friends, Hamlet and Ophelia, Hamlet and Horatio,
Hamlet and the players, Hamlet and the court, Hamlet and
Claudius, Hamlet and Gertrude, not to mention Hamlet and
Hamlet, and Hamlet and the Cosmos. Perhaps the most important of the subsidiary plot lines is the demise of the short,
unhappy love affair between Hamlet and Ophelia.

Ophelia is, of course, the principal if not the only embodiment of romantic love in the play, and her fragility and pathos
are linked to the problematic nature of love in the *Hamlet*-
world. The value of love as an ameliorating agent is given
far less emphasis in this play than in *Othello* or *King Lear*.
Like so many affirmative values in *Hamlet*, love has fallen
off from past excellence and has been poisoned by the corruption of the times. Once praiseworthy, even trustworthy,
it has declined and decayed, leaving a painful memory and an
anguished sense of loss. Love is poisoned by the uncertainties
and rancor of the *Hamlet*-world, undone by association with
its complex and endless stratagems, and crushed before it
has a chance to exert itself as a saving grace. This is what the
pathetic life and lyric death of Ophelia dramatize.

The first mention of love between Hamlet and Ophelia
is introduced in an atmosphere of uncertainty and suspicion.
Laertes and Polonius both caution Ophelia that Hamlet's
overtures are not what they seem, and in responding to them,
she is endangering her virginity. "Fear it, Ophelia, fear it, my

dear sister. . . . Be wary then; best safety lies in fear" (I.iii.33-43), carps her brother, and it is therefore no surprise that when we next see her she is saying, "O my lord, my lord, I have been so affrighted!" (II.i.75). She remains frightened for the rest of her unhappy life. The immediate cause of her distress in this case is Hamlet's astonishing entrance into her chamber. Scrutinizing her closely, he sees something, or more likely, *fails* to see something he wants to, and heaves a piteous sigh of disillusion.[38] In Hamlet's love poem, we get a glimpse of the problems he is having with love, especially in the paradoxical line "Doubt truth to be a liar" (II.ii.118). The meaning of "doubt" has shifted from "call into question," its denotation in the first two lines, to "fear" or "suspect," as in "I doubt some foul play" (I.ii.256). That all apparent truth may really be false is, of course, Hamlet's central preoccupation.

But the problem is not simply that Hamlet doubts the sincerity of love; the misanthropic side of his nature sees sex and procreation as a disgusting and pointless charade: "For if the sun breed maggots in a dead dog, being a good kissing carrion—Have you a daughter? . . . Let her not walk i' th' sun. Conception is a blessing, but as your daughter may conceive, friend, look to't" (II.ii.181-186). An old and widely held theory proposed that the sun could engender vermin or reptiles in carrion or in scum. Hamlet expands this into an antic conceit: if Ophelia walks in the sun, she too may conceive by it. Thus human generation is equated with the breeding of maggots. Of course, in a less cryptic sense, Hamlet is also saying to Polonius, "You do well to keep your daughter locked up, for if you let her out, being a woman, she will be seduced."

The same theme of generation as the mere breeding of sinners carries over into the famous and controversial nunnery scene, the first time we actually see Hamlet and Ophelia together. It is not a matter of mere organizational conveni-

[38] Dowden, p. 131. Cf. Wilson, *What Happens in* Hamlet, pp. 111-112.

ence, far less organizational caprice, that this encounter follows immediately upon the "To be or not to be" soliloquy. D. G. James has suggested that *Hamlet* is not a tragedy of excessive thought but of defeated thought. "Hamlet does not know and he knows no way of knowing."[39] If this is true, and I believe it is, then this speech dramatizes the most signal and complete defeat of thought. In his search for the true nature of reality, Hamlet is here confronting in the most absolute terms the problem of right action based upon certain knowledge that reality is one thing definitely and not another.

The voluminous commentary upon this speech has centered on two main problems. Are we to understand that Hamlet is contemplating suicide? Is it likely that Burbage delivered the soliloquy with the bare bodkin actually in his hand? The second problem has to do with the sequence of thought in the opening five lines. Is Hamlet first posing one problem, then shifting abruptly to another, then coming back to the first? Dr. Johnson suggested that the train of thought "is connected rather in the speaker's mind, than on his tongue," thus implying the kind of free association which modern psychiatry has found so intriguing.[40] Or are we to understand that "to be" in its fullest sense is "to act," and thus Hamlet is not really changing the subject in the second line, but merely recasting the problem in different terms? I propose that the organization of the speech is dialectical, its viewpoint is complementary, and its topic is the limitation and ultimate impotence of the mind in the search for truth.[41]

"To be, or not to be—"(III.i.56): these words mean exactly what they say, to exist or not to exist. The line sets up the terms of the primary dialectic. Hamlet first considers the

[39] *The Dream of Learning*, p. 42.

[40] *Johnson on Shakespeare*, ed. Arthur Sherbo, The Yale Edition of the Works of Samuel Johnson (New Haven: Yale University Press, 1968), p. 981.

[41] Levin's reading of the opening lines is similar to mine, though he comes to a different conclusion about the significance of the speech (*The Question of* Hamlet, p. 69).

thesis, being, which at once suggests a further question: *how* is one to be. The result is a secondary dialectic:

> Whether 'tis nobler in the mind to suffer
> The slings and arrows of outrageous fortune
> Or to take up arms against a sea of troubles
> And by opposing end them.
>
> (57-60)

From different viewpoints, Hamlet can appreciate both the noble stoicism of Horatio and the ruthless if somewhat mindless action of a Fortinbras. In his complementary apprehension of reality, both possibilities have irresistible claims to adherence, yet they contradict each other. This conflict is one of the dichotomies he faces throughout the play, and he never succeeds in fully resolving it. Stymied, he turns to the antithesis of the primary dialectic, non-being:

> To die, to sleep—
> No more—and by a sleep to say we end
> The heartache, and the thousand natural shocks
> That flesh in heir to. 'Tis a consummation
> Devoutly to be wished. To die, to sleep—
>
> (60-64)

Death may be non-being, nothing more than a sleep, the obliteration of consciousness, and an end to the thousand natural shocks that are part of the human condition. If so, such a consummation is not to be dreaded but longed for. But this idea immediately suggests its opposite, and the result is another secondary dialectic:

> To sleep—perchance to dream: ay, there's the rub,
> For in that sleep of death what dreams may come
> When we have shuffled off this mortal coil,
> Must give us pause.
>
> (65-68)

Hamlet, then, is not moving randomly from problem to problem; the speech is entirely cohesive within its dialectical framework, and quite consistent with Hamlet's dialectical mind.

By the time he reaches line 65, Hamlet has begun to realize that the initial problem, being versus non-being, may not lie within the purview of human choice at all, that man, whatever his desires, can exercise no choice as to whether he exists or not. Even self-annihilation may not secure the peace of non-being, but only a different—and worse—mode of being. For the next thirteen lines he expands this perception, always keeping in focus the pain and injustice he sees as lying at the center of human experience; even the patient merit which he had contemplated at the beginning of the speech and which he so admires in Horatio yields only spurns from the unworthy—Horatio's poverty against the wealth and snobbishness of an Osric.

But the bare bodkin, the alternative, is stymied by the utter inscrutability of the metaphysical universe that may or may not lie beyond life. Man does not know and has no way of knowing what lies beyond. Any attempt to solve life's problems with finality is an irrevocable act committed in invincible ignorance. Hamlet is here contemplating not only the mystery of death but the *finality* of death in conjunction with its mystery. Were one to opt for the bare bodkin and be wrong, the loss could never be recouped. The choice between being and non-being may not lie within man's power, and he has no way of knowing even whether it does or not. Thought, then, is inadequate to the original problem; it is strong enough to defeat the impulse to heedless action, but too weak to provide a clear course of action based upon certain knowledge that ultimately reality is one thing definitely and not another. Thus man is betrayed by his own highest faculty. This multiple defeat of thought and action by inscrutability accounts for the contempt—contempt of man's powers and of his own power as a man—which pervades the close of the speech.

It is of the utmost significance that Ophelia is "loosed" upon Hamlet when he is in exactly that mood depicted at the closing of the soliloquy. She never fails to intensify the self-

deprecating side of Hamlet, that perspective in his complementary viewpoint from which he appears to himself as fully
a part of a human order for which he has only loathing and
contempt. We could sense something of this in the piteous
sigh that seemed to shatter all his being, and in the heart-
sickness and ineptitude of the poem and letter. In the present
scene, his first words to her, immediately after the stalemate
of the soliloquy, express once again his self-identification
with a sinful humanity: "Nymph, in thy orisons / Be all my
sins remembered" (89-90).

There could be no worse moment to offer Hamlet a rebuff,
more evidence of the unreliability and hostility of everyone
and everything around him. His initial reaction is annoyance
and defensiveness: "No, not I, / I never gave you aught"
(95-96). We may regard this as Hamlet's bringing his antic
disposition into play, or it may be interpreted as one of his
cryptic double entendres: "No, not I. The man who gave them
was not the same as the man I am now." In any case, if antic
it be, it is the only use which Hamlet makes of his disposition
in this scene, for he cannot maintain the emotional aplomb
upon which his satirical "madness" depends. As his passion
mounts, he speaks in deadly earnest to her about subjects already well established in the play:

HAMLET: Ha, ha! Are you honest?
OPHELIA: My lord?
HAMLET: Are you fair?
OPHELIA: What means your lordship?
HAMLET: That if you be honest and fair, your honesty
should admit no discourse to your beauty.
OPHELIA: Could beauty, my lord, have better commerce
than with honesty?
HAMLET: Ay, truly; for the power of beauty will sooner
transform honesty from what it is to a bawd than the
force of honesty can translate beauty into his like-
ness. This was sometime a paradox, but now the time
gives it proof.

(103-115)

Hamlet's initial question means both "are you what you seem" and "are you chaste," but it comes to the same thing, because what Ophelia appears to be is a virtuous maiden. The "paradox" to which he refers concerns, I believe, the Neoplatonic concept that beauty and goodness are invariably allied, and that beauty of the face is a reflection of the beauty of the soul. The idea was a commonplace of the Elizabethan courtly tradition, though it met with considerable skepticism, and even Castiglione's Peter Bembo encountered incredulity among his auditors as he stoutly defended the tenet.[42] Shakespeare did not believe it for an instant, in all probability but the discrepancy is one of the central preoccupations of his work. Beauty in the service of evil seemed to suggest to him the ugliest fly in the cosmic ointment, the shocking inconsistency that cast doubt upon the entire ordered, benevolent system which was part of the spiritual heritage of the Renaissance. Surely only some such sweeping association can account for the presence everywhere in his works, from the earliest to the latest, of lovely exteriors masking monstrous evil that itself suggested some fundamental taint in the universe. Such discrepancy implied not only a prince of lies such as "honest" Iago, but also the carnivorous anarchy of the *Lear*-world.

In rising agitation, Hamlet begins the first of his "nunnery" speeches: "Why wouldst thou be a breeder of sinners?" (121-122). He is better than average, but even better than average is so bad that human procreation merely perpetuates vice. Better to retire and live in celibacy. "Nunnery" still means "convent," though its other meaning is only a few lines away.

For no apparent reason, Hamlet now asks, "Where's your father?" (130). A long theatrical tradition has it that Polonius coughs or moves the curtain, or does something to make Hamlet aware of the eavesdroppers. This may or may not have been Shakespeare's intention.[43] In any case, I think it

---

[42] *The Book of the Courtier*, trans. George Bull (Harmondsworth, Eng.: Penguin, 1967), p. 329.

[43] Schücking, with his usual close reasoning, argues effectively that it was not (*The Meaning of* Hamlet, pp. 121-122).

is a mistake to explain away the rest of the scene by assuming that Hamlet feigns madness for the benefit of the King's hearing. He has been speaking in a steadily mounting crescendo of passion which continues to increase until the near hysteria of the scene's end. His tone has nothing of the cool irony we associate with the other "antic" scenes; rather it has more the ring of the first soliloquy or the closet scene. Hamlet's revulsion is feeding upon itself: the more he contemplates the world, the more revolted he becomes; the more revolted he becomes, the more he is impelled to contemplate the source of his revulsion. The repeated "farewell" conveys the impression that Hamlet wants to be done with the matter, perhaps even begins to make his exit, but is drawn irresistibly back to unleash another tirade, a pattern which will recur in the closet scene. The subject of his tirades is the same preoccupation that has bedeviled him throughout the play: women are not what they make themselves out to be; they assume innocence, playfulness, and naïveté to cover up their wantonness; love makes monsters out of men and drives them mad. The sense of "nunnery" changes to "brothel," since carnal lust is beneath all the appearances of charm and virtue. Finally, since marriage and procreation simply perpetuate corruption, "we will have no more marriage" (147).

It is a dismal view of romantic love, a conscious parody of the courtly tradition, and, surprisingly, there is little in the play to counterbalance it—perhaps nothing except the asexual love between Hamlet and Horatio. In her bawdy St. Valentine's song, Ophelia has come to a view of love similar to Hamlet's, but with the roles reversed. Now it is men who dissemble in order to prey upon the sincere affections of women. "We are arrant knaves all; believe none of us," Hamlet had told her, and she seems to have taken the lesson to heart: "It is the false steward, that stole his master's daughter" (IV.v.171-172). In *Othello*, we shall see a dialectical treatment of love as the most affirmative but most dangerous of human passions. In *King Lear*, it will be both the only value that makes life endurable and the one that renders

human beings most vulnerable to suffering. No such dialectic
is established in *Hamlet*. Ophelia's significance in the drama
lies not in what she does, nor even in what is done to her,
but rather in what fails, what is defeated without even a real
struggle. The pastoral description of her death reinforces the
impression of something pretty but ineffectual, lacking power
to save itself, let alone others.

When next we see Hamlet after the nunnery scene, calm
has returned once again, but it is, of course, a calm before
even greater storms. It is ironic that the Prince delivers his
praise of Horatio's noble stoicism on the brink of casting such
values irrevocably to the winds. He assumes the antic disposition as the court gathers, and never have we had so strong a
sense of Hamlet's enjoying immensely the game of hide-and-
seek of which he is, at this point, in such perfect control. In
this scene and those immediately following it, he brings his
revenge of words to its triumphant conclusion, though
tripping the mechanism of disaster in the process. The attack
he mounts is all-encompassing; no one is spared. The hidden
guilt of the King, the Queen's perfidiousness, the fatuous
"busyness" of Polonius, the shallow hypocrisy of Rosencrantz
and Guildenstern, the supposed wantonness of Ophelia—all
are exposed to Hamlet's scathing contempt. Unmasking evil
is only half the game; brutal mockery and merciless excoriation make up the other and by far more important half.

The complete success which Hamlet achieves in bringing
foul deeds to the surface produces in him a state of exultation
strongly reminiscent of his mood after the revelations of the
Ghost: he is full of wild and whirling words, cryptic jokes and
jingles, and brilliant sallies of wit against his antagonists,
whom he has so completely nonplussed. Yet Hamlet is pe-
culiarly uninterested in Claudius once he has unmasked him.
Upon being informed that the King has retired marvelously
distempered, he replies with a characteristic but wholly irrelevant joke: "With drink, sir?" (III.ii.290). But Gertrude's
reaction to the play, the bulk of which had been directed
against her rather than her husband, interests the Prince in-

75

tensely. When he steels himself to do deeds that day would quake to look upon, it is not Claudius of whom he thinks, but "Soft, now to my mother" (377). He is about to bring his revenge of words to its conclusion, the conclusion toward which it has been pointed from the first,[44] and not even the perfect chance to dispatch the guilty King deters him from the pursuit of his private purposes. "My mother stays" (III. iii.95), he reflects behind the praying criminal, revealing the business that is uppermost in his mind.

But this is not to dismiss the reason that Hamlet himself gives for allowing the prolongation of Claudius' sickly days. Throughout the play, Hamlet shows a propensity for wishing to see his enemies in hell; justice may be in the hands of heaven, but Hamlet is always anxious to see personally that heaven does not let anyone off too lightly. In this he over-reaches, and gets tripped up in a way characteristic of the *Hamlet*-world: he mistakes an appearance for the reality. Claudius cannot repent and does not achieve grace, and his final lines, "My words fly up, my thoughts remain below. / Words without thoughts never to heaven go" (III.iii.97-98), are the crowning irony of a play not otherwise deficient in ironies. Moreover, Hamlet makes his blunder not because of his skepticism, but because of his faith. When it comes down to the wire, Hamlet believes passionately in the universe expounded by orthodox Christian theology. If part of his previous anguish had been the inability to find absolute answers on an intellectual basis, his fatal misjudgment is grounded upon unconditional acceptance of heaven and hell, and belief that repentance and grace can win salvation for even the rankest sinner.

But there is another reason why Hamlet feels disinclined to carry out a revenge of blood at this point: praying is not a characteristic activity of the man whom he conceives Claudius to be. All along he has had a physical disgust for his uncle; if the world is a garden grown to seed, Claudius is

---

[44] Granville-Barker makes this point (I, 234); see also James, *The Dream of Learning*, p. 51.

one of the rank, gross things that possess it merely. At this crucial juncture, Hamlet, as always, demands congruence—everything must fit. He contemplates with positive relish the circumstances he will wait for:

> When he is drunk asleep, or in his rage,
> Or in th' incestuous pleasure of his bed,
> At game a-swearing, or about some act
> That has no relish of salvation in't—
>
> (89-92)

If Hamlet spares Claudius because he considers the matter too closely, he stabs Polonius because he does not consider the matter at all. This is the other side of the thought-passion dialectic. His action is emblematic of the *Hamlet*-world itself: he stabs through a curtain at something he cannot see, which he thinks to be one thing but which turns out to be quite another. This is precisely what all these characters have been doing in one way or another since the beginning of the play. But so relentless is Hamlet's determination to make his mother see her actions through his eyes that he does not let even this disastrous accident, with its ominous implications for his future, deter him for an instant:

> Leave off wringing of your hands. Peace, sit you down
> And let me wring your heart, for so I shall
> If it be made of penetrable stuff.
>
> (III.iv.35-37)

All of Hamlet's previous actions from the first soliloquy—the scathing denunciations of the court, the bitter abuse of Ophelia, the self-castigation, the elaborate mounting of the play, the sparing of Claudius—all of them have pointed toward this scene where the imposthume breaks[45] and the process of reconstructing the hero's private world begins. Hamlet is not merely delivering a severe scolding, and his subject is not Gertrude's fall from grace alone. Throughout

---

[45] See Francis Fergusson, *The Idea of a Theater* (Princeton: Princeton Univ. Press, 1949), p. 105.

the high voltage speeches of the scene are interwoven the issues and dichotomies which I have attempted to show operating throughout the play. The Prince begins by talking not about her act itself, but about what her act has done to *him*, about the undermining of his world itself:

> Such an act
> That blurs the grace and blush of modesty,
> Calls virtue hypocrite, takes off the rose
> From the fair forehead of an innocent love,
> And sets a blister there, makes marriage vows
> As false as dicers' oaths. O, such a deed
> As from the body of contraction plucks
> The very soul, and sweet religion makes
> A rhapsody of words!

(41-49)

In each of these phrases, a value that had existed in the past has been corrupted, negated, or made hollow—modesty, virtue, innocent love, marriage vows, the marriage contract, and sweet religion. All of these are traditional values, the staples of his world-view until Gertrude's actions cast a pall of suspicion on them in Hamlet's mind. One might argue, along with T. S. Eliot and G. Wilson Knight, that Hamlet's extreme reaction reflects innate morbidity on the Prince's part or shoddy artistry on Shakespeare's; and such objections cannot be satisfactorily countered by pointing out that an irregular marriage would shock an Elizabethan sensibility far more than a modern one.[46] The point is that in the *Hamlet*-world, affirmative values are delicately balanced against other possibilities, possibilities to which the mind of Hamlet is particularly open. The smallest nudge is capable of upsetting that balance and bringing the entire system crashing down. We will see something similar in the other tragedies, especially *Othello*. When the tension between value systems is so taut in the mind of the hero, the precipitating

---

[46] T. S. Eliot, "*Hamlet*," in *Elizabethan Essays* (London: Faber and Faber, 1934), pp. 60-62; Knight, pp. 25-31, 43-50.

factor may be quite unequal to the cataclysmic effects pro-
duced. Doubt of one thing implies doubt of another, and then
another and another, until the entire structure of the hero's
subjective world comes down in ruins like a building from
which one small but crucial stone has been removed.

Throughout the first half of the scene, Hamlet's tone is as
much exhortatory as accusatory; he is trying to make her
see her act with his eyes, and manages to avoid the self-
goading fury for which he has shown such a propensity.
Gertrude initially stands up to him with considerable courage,
but finally her nerve fails her, and she accepts his version of
her conduct as the true one:

> O Hamlet, speak no more.
> Thou turn'st mine eyes into my very soul,
> And there I see such black and grainèd spots
> As will not yield their tinct.
>
> (89-92)

She does not deny his accusations; she simply does not want
to hear them: "O, speak to me no more. . . . No more, sweet
Hamlet. . . . No more." For him it is the taste of blood. He
leaves his admonishing entirely and embarks upon a hysterical tirade of abuse so vindictively cruel that it literally ex-
hausts the patience of heaven.

The Ghost's second visitation is the climax to the tension
which has been building between his purposes and those of
the hero. Heaven has appointed Hamlet its minister in only a
most limited sense, and its scourge not at all; that is an office
he has taken upon himself in specific defiance of all orders.
If on the one hand the Ghost has come to whet Hamlet's
almost blunted purpose, on the other his visitation is to halt
any further excesses in the Prince's furious battle with the
Hamlet-world, to step between the weak, sensuous Queen
and her implacable son. Hamlet instinctively grasps both sides
of the spectre's mission: he is being chided for being tardy,
for having lapsed in time and passion, but he also realizes
that a damper is being placed upon his actions:

79

Do not look upon me,
Lest with this piteous action you convert
My stern effects. Then what I have to do
Will want true color—tears perchance for blood.
(128-131)

As the Ghost's first appearance marked the collapse of
Hamlet's personal world, so now after his second departure
we begin to sense a marked shift in both the tone of the play
and the character of the hero. The process, however, is
neither sudden nor straightforward; if we begin to get
glimpses of the Hamlet who is to be, the old problems and
preoccupations are still very much in evidence. Such multi-
plicity of viewpoint is, of course, thoroughly characteristic of
both the play and the hero, perhaps the most characteristic
thing about them. Hamlet's "regeneration"—if one wishes to
apply that well-worn term to the détente he finally reaches
with the *Hamlet*-world—embodies two antithetical strains.
On one hand there is the dawn of a cautious, limited optimism, especially evident in his partial reconciliation with the
Queen. Virtue may be able to inoculate our old stock after
all, and even an assumed appearance of virtue, that odium
of Hamlet's personal world, may in time induce the genuine
article:

Assume a virtue, if you have it not.
That monster custom, who all sense doth eat,
Of habits devil, is angel yet in this,
That to the use of actions fair and good
He likewise gives a frock or livery
That aptly is put on.

(161-166)

But on the other hand, there is a grim side to Hamlet's latest
reappraisal of reality, a side epitomized by a sudden shift in
his attitude toward death. Up until this point, he has been
interested in death primarily as a metaphysical problem—
what happens to the soul afterward. But now the irony of

Polonius' death as a result of being "too busy" awakens in Hamlet a strong, sardonic sense of the physicality of death, the decay of the body, and the *reductio ad absurdum* which the worm's banquet applies to life. This preoccupation starts with his jesting over the corpse, proceeds through his grim game of hide-the-body, through his morbid reflection upon the progress of a king through the guts of a beggar, and culminates in the graveyard scene, where the decay of the body has become his favorite if not his only subject. It is perhaps the heightened sense of absurdity, the perception of worms as the ultimate benefactors of all man's industry and cleverness, that increases Hamlet's appreciation of the contest with Claudius as a game. Nowhere else, not even in the *Mousetrap* scene, does Hamlet so clearly relish his ability to lead by the nose the hypocrites and intriguers around him.

"Come, sir, to draw toward an end with you," he quips, and lugs the guts into a neighboring room. Hamlet is keenly aware that the dead Polonius is a parody of the live one:

> Indeed, this counsellor
> Is now most still, most secret, and most grave,
> Who was in life a foolish prating knave.
> (214-216)

Throughout the play, Polonius has been hiding himself in order to seek out truth; so now once more he will be concealed, but this time he himself will be sought. It is exactly the kind of irony, the "fine revolution," which Hamlet finds quite irresistible in Acts IV and V. Besides, the game gives him another opportunity to bait his adversaries, to demonstrate his superiority, and to insult Claudius to his face: "In heaven. Send thither to see. If your messenger find him not there, seek him i' th' other place yourself" (IV.iii.33-36).

In the Folio version of the text, Hamlet's cryptic farewell to his "mother" is the last we see of him until the graveyard scene. There is a short scene depicting Fortinbras' army crossing the stage, but Hamlet does not meet them, does not question the Captain, or deliver his final soliloquy. There has been

much speculation as to whether F1 represents a stage cut or
Q2 contains an interpolation, perhaps with topical over-
tones.[47] To be sure, the scene as it stands in full does present
some problems, large and small. It does not seem wholly
probable that Hamlet's companions, who believe themselves
to be deporting a dangerous lunatic under royal warrant,
would obligingly comply with his request, "I'll be with you
straight. Go a little before" (IV.iv.31). This, however, is by
no means the wildest improbability in this play. Even more
perplexing are the problems of relating what Hamlet has to
say in this speech with what he has said before, or with the
direction he will eventually take. His sentiments toward the
end of the speech seem more fitting for Harry Percy, and, in
fact, Hotspur does make an almost identical pronouncement:

> I'll give thrice so much land
> To any well deserving friend;
> But in way of bargain, mark ye me,
> I'll cavil on the ninth part of a hair.
> (*1 Henry IV*, III.i.135-138)

But Hamlet has a propensity for assuming a viewpoint suggested to him by his surroundings, trying it on for size, so to
speak, without its being a definitive pronouncement. When it
comes to world-views, he is, as I have said, a tireless experimenter.

Moreover, we are here at a turning point in the play, a
turning point involving not only character and action but
theme and tone as well. The beginning of this pivotal movement is signaled not so much by the withdrawal of Hamlet
for a long period as by the introduction in adjacent scenes of
his opposite numbers, Fortinbras and Laertes. But the purpose of their simultaneous reemergence is certainly not to
contrast their "action" with Hamlet's "inaction," because
Hamlet has been far from inactive. Rather the question is,
upon what foundation should action be based? This, of

[47] See **G. B. Harrison**, *Shakespeare's Tragedies*, pp. 104-105.

course, is not a new problem in the *Hamlet*-world; an elaborate dialectic has been operative throughout the play between thought and passion as the basis of action, between dispassionate stoicism and violent, ruthless opposition. If heretofore the main concern has been the difficulty of establishing values upon which action can be based, now, as the conclusion approaches, our attention is turned to the consequences of action which has been taken without thought, and which drives ruthlessly on, directed largely by passion. It is this kind of action and its relative value which Hamlet's speech examines.

In the course of his reassessment of reality, Hamlet has reached the conclusion that thought leads only to further uncertainty and vacillation. And now he sees an army headed off on an expedition which makes no sense whatsoever. Instinctively applying the criterion of reason, he comes up with a characteristically glum conclusion:

> This is th' impostume of much wealth and peace,
> That inward breaks, and shows no cause without
> Why the man dies.
>
> (IV.iv.27-29)

For any other kind of mind, this would be the end of the matter; but Hamlet turns about, as we have seen him do so many times before, and evaluates the situation from a point diametrically opposed to his previous coign of vantage. In an earlier soliloquy, he accepted the stalemate between thought and certitude as inevitable, but here he scuttles the entire problem by complete endorsement of Fortinbras' way of doing things, exposing what is mortal and unsure to all that fortune, death, and danger dare:

> Rightly to be great
> Is not to stir without great argument,
> But greatly to find quarrel in a straw
> When honor's at the stake.
>
> (53-56)

Like all Hamlet's soliloquies, this one is a waystation in the pilgrimage of a mind in search of values in a world most tricky and ambiguous about yielding them. Moreover, it would be a serious mistake to suppose that Shakespeare is offering Laertes or Fortinbras as an alternative to Hamlet's ineffectuality, or suggesting that they, at least, know how to get a job done. Though Laertes' uncritical determination does succeed in getting him his revenge, it also makes him the ignominious instrument of a usurper-regicide, debases such nobility as he has, and brings about his just death—all because he specifically lacks the circumspection and skepticism about appearance and the passion for truth that characterize Hamlet. Once again, the play's viewpoint is complementary. Among the most curious things in the very curious critical history of *Hamlet* is that, while one school, deriving largely from Coleridge and Goethe, sees *Hamlet* as a tragedy of excess thought, another group, best exemplified by L. B. Campbell, sees the play as a tragedy of excess passion.[48] Both are right insofar as each recognizes one branch of the thought-passion dichotomy, though neither recognizes the dichotomy itself. In the "To be or not to be" soliloquy, thought is pushed to its furthest limit and falters; in the grotesque fight in Ophelia's grave, the "quarrel in a straw" ethic is pushed to its extreme, and it, too, falters. Even at the end of the play, the thought-passion dichotomy is not resolved. It is significant, I think, that the important task of restoring order to the *Hamlet*-world is split between two characters, Horatio and Fortinbras. The former must calmly and carefully explain what has happened so that further error and mayhem are avoided, while the latter must seize the initiative to restore political order with a firm hand and assume control of practical affairs. Each represents an approach to life which Hamlet had experimented with and found inadequate to the

[48] *Goethe's Literary Essays*, ed. J. E. Spingarn (1921; rpt. New York: Unger, 1964), p. 153; Campbell, *Shakespeare's Tragic Heroes*, p. 109; *Coleridge's Shakespearean Criticism*, I, 37-40.

total problem. Finally they coexist in a tenuous but necessary compromise forged in the heat of the disaster.

The final scenes of *Hamlet* are less skillfully wrought than those earlier acts where we had Shakespeare's dramaturgy at its incomparable best. The problem is not so much that the narrated adventures at sea are contrived and improbable as that a most significant change has taken place in the hero which we have not been permitted to see—at least not as clearly as we see comparable changes in Othello, Lear, and Macbeth. Hamlet's "regeneration" is revealed as an accomplished fact, and the causes which he himself gives for it do not seem altogether equal to the problems that have been raised. Moreover, Hamlet's sea change is difficult to define precisely, because in many ways he has not changed much at all; he is still the same man doing all the same things—contemplating death, musing upon the absurdity of life, flaring into passionate outbursts, performing rash and outrageous deeds, gulling the fops and toadies of the court, assuring the damnation of his enemies, enumerating the crimes of the King, asserting the urgency and justice of revenge, but not doing very much about dispatching Claudius until it is too late. There is an unmistakable change in tone and attitude, however, and it signifies nothing less than the reintegration of his subjective world. When he returns to Denmark, he is no longer struggling with the characteristic problem of the Shakespearean tragic hero, how to endure what is, for him, simply unendurable.[49]

If Hamlet in Act v is no longer torn by the dilemmas which tormented him earlier, at least part of the reason is that he has been eminently successful in accomplishing those purposes dictated by his inner needs. At a price already terrible and due to go much higher, he has unmasked the smiling villain and forced the Queen to see herself with his eyes, and in the

[49] For a particularly good account of Hamlet's sea-change see Mack's "The World of *Hamlet*," p. 55. Also cf. Richard Levine, "The Tragedy of Hamlet's World View," *College English*, 23 (1962), 543.

process has rid himself of much of the often hysterical rage he felt toward the *Hamlet*-world in general. Claudius is still a criminal of the worst kind, but the Prince can now enumerate his crimes without the pathological loathing that characterized his speech in the prayer scene. Previously Hamlet's grievances were concerned not so much with what Claudius had *done* as with what he *was*. Hamlet has also successfully swept from his sight the spies, parasites, and hypocrites whom he found so loathsome, again not so much because of what they did as because of the standing affront they offered the values of honesty and loyalty. He has vindicated himself by delving a yard below their mines and blowing them at the moon. Because so many of his own inner needs have been satisfied, Hamlet can impose a certain distance between himself and the corruption around him. He is no longer trying to extricate himself from the web of evil, nor is he looking to the world for vindication of his values. His world-view is far from cheerful; the beauty of the world and the paragon of animals are gone forever and can never be regained. In their place is a *contemptus mundi* purged of real rancor, directed toward the general pattern of ashes to ashes and dust to dust.[50] In the graveyard scene, as he catalogs the great and the mundane reduced to the same dust, he generalizes them into types—the courtier, the lawyer, the landowner—or thinks of those removed in time to an almost mythical past— Alexander and Caesar. He now applies the *reductio ad absurdum* to the general picture of human vainglory rather than specific individuals of his own acquaintance. He had contemplated with absolute glee the corruption of Polonius' body or the progress of Claudius through the guts of a beggar, as if such an ignoble end was all they deserved. But now he shows a muted compassion for those anonymous souls who have all come to the same end: "That skull had a tongue in it,

[50] D. R. Howard, "Hamlet and the Contempt of the World," *South Atlantic Quarterly*, 58 (1959), 167-175, perceptively traces the influence of the medieval *de contemptu mundi* tradition throughout the play.

and could sing once. . . . Did these bones cost no more the breeding but to play at loggets with 'em? Mine ache to think on't. . . . Alas, poor Yorick" (v.i.71-172). Most significantly, in this scene and the one following, Hamlet can relate himself to the common human condition without the feeling of intense loathing and revulsion, the need to extirpate himself that characterized his struggles in the earlier scenes.

In his long conversation with Horatio, he reveals a moral certitude that he has not displayed before, magnifying a narrow escape into a managing divinity and finding a special providence in the sparrow's fall. His attitude is not, I think, the fatalism it is so often taken to be. He shows not so much an acceptance of some external principle or force of fate as resignation to the inherent *mysteriousness* of events. That the sparrow will fall is certain, but there is no way of telling when or why. "The readiness is all. Since no man of aught he leaves knows, what is't to leave betimes?" (v.ii.211-212). The problem of "knowing," more than any other in the play, has tormented Hamlet, but here he accepts that, even at the point of death, no man has achieved knowledge about the true nature of reality. Resignation is the only course possible. "To be, or not to be," Hamlet had asked, and had concluded that man cannot even know whether or not such a choice lies within his power. "Let be," he now concludes (212), giving his earlier question the only answer he can see.

The problem, however, is with him to the end. Claudius has once again successfully tampered with the surface of reality, and even after the King is dead, Hamlet's last concern is that Horatio report his cause aright, or once again appearance will be misinterpreted by the world at large. The facts of the *Hamlet*-world remain unchanged, and it is those facts that undo him. But Hamlet has managed to reconstruct his subjective world, and hence life is no longer unendurable, and hence the peculiar tone of the end of the play. For all the carnage on stage, there is a lyrical quality to Hamlet's demise, an acquiescence closely related to the *contemptus mundi*, which separates this play from the other mature tragedies.

For Othello, Lear, and Macbeth, the problem of how to endure the unendurable reaches its apex immediately before death, while for Hamlet, the problem has ceased to exist by the beginning of Act v. For them, death is the termination of what can no longer be borne, while for him, death is "felicity" and "silence." The endings of the other plays are more powerful, if less lyrical, perhaps more fully tragic than Hamlet's quiet goodnight. At his death he commands more of our sympathy than Macbeth and more of our admiration than Othello; but we are not so overwhelmed by the magnitude of his fate.

Hamlet's problems have not been artificial nor primarily of his own making; they are thrust upon him by the nature of the *Hamlet*-world, as they are thrust in one way or another upon all the major characters. Given the circumstances of such a world, the problems cannot be solved, only evaded. Hamlet alone refuses to evade them, and that is what makes his struggle both heroic and tragic. Shakespeare was not simply making the banal statement that things are often other than they seem or that the metaphysical universe is inscrutable. His dramatic premise seems to have been that the discrepancy between appearance and reality is intolerable to a mind that places prime value upon truth, and that the inscrutability of the universe presents an unsolvable dilemma to a man who demands absolute values based upon absolute truth. Hamlet is such a man and has such a mind, yet the world he must deal with is filled with deceptiveness and unanswerable questions. Hence the play itself is, among a great many other things, an elaborate dialectic upon the need for absolute values and the impossibility of absolute values. The tension between them is the tension of tragedy.

THREE

OTHELLO: HIS VISAGE IN HIS MIND

IF much of modern *Hamlet* criticism has been a healthy corrective to the effete, languishing idealist seen by earlier generations, much of the modern commentary on *Othello* has been an exercise in critical perverseness. Beginning principally with T. S. Eliot and F. R. Leavis (though the tradition goes back sporadically to Rymer and the very beginnings of systematic Shakespearean criticism), a large and influential body of recent commentators have been unhappy with the hero of this play.[1] Othello is too easily gulled, perhaps even plain stupid. He is grandiose and obtuse. He does not really love Desdemona, nor is he capable of appreciating her love for him. He achieves no insight into himself. He indulges in self-delusion, self-dramatization, self-

---

[1] T. S. Eliot, "Shakespeare and the Stoicism of Seneca," *Elizabethan Essays*, pp. 39-40; F. R. Leavis, "Diabolic Intellect and the Noble Hero," *The Common Pursuit* (1952; rpt. New York: New York Univ. Press, 1964), pp. 136-159; Thomas Rymer, "A Short View of Tragedy," in *The Critical Works of Thomas Rymer*, ed. Curt Zymansky (New Haven: Yale Univ. Press, 1956), pp. 82-176. To the list of critics who take a similarly dim view of the Moor we may add: Robert Heilman, *Magic in the Web* (Lexington: Univ. of Kentucky Press, 1956), pp. 137-168; Matthew N. Proser, *The Heroic Image in Five Shakespearean Tragedies* (Princeton: Princeton Univ. Press, 1965), pp. 102-111; G. R. Elliot, *Flaming Minister* (Durham, N.C.: Duke Univ. Press, 1953), pp. 63-67; Leo Kirschbaum, *Character and Characterization in Shakespeare* (Detroit: Wayne State Univ. Press, 1962), pp. 145-158; Traversi, *An Approach to Shakespeare*, pp. 128-150; Albert Gerard, "Egregiously an Ass: The Dark Side of the Moor," *Shakespeare Survey*, 10 (1957), 98-106; Lawrence Lerner, "The Machiavel and the Moor," *Essays in Criticism*, 9 (1959), 339-360. Dame Helen Gardner offers a perceptive analysis of the play's recent critical history in "*Othello*: A Retrospect, 1900-67," *Shakespeare Survey*, 21 (1968), 1-11.

justification, egregious pride, and—God save the mark!—
bovarysme. Because such critics find the Moor a fit object for
condescension, they assume Shakespeare condescended to
him and intended us to as well. "Nothing dies harder than the
desire to think well of oneself," Eliot observes, and con-
gratulates Shakespeare on having dramatized the insight so
cleverly.[2] Othello is distasteful; he is not a gentleman; he is
not an intellectual. When the anti-Othello critics talk about
the Moor's failure to "comprehend" what he has done and
what he is, one gets the unmistakable impression that they
mean he fails to formulate abstract, intellectual concepts in
the way that Hamlet "comprehends" or in the way that they
themselves are accustomed to comprehending literature.[3] But
Shakespeare, I feel certain, recognized no such boundaries of
comprehension; like Lear and Gloucester, Othello ultimately
"sees feelingly," and, in that mode of perception, his comprehension of what he is and what he has done is more profound than Hamlet's.

It must be admitted, however, that the problem of balancing Othello's gullibility against his grandeur is as difficult as
any in Shakespeare. Moreover, it should not come as a complete surprise that such readings should emerge at the time
they did or from the particular critics involved. It is part of a
wide-ranging critical attempt to deromanticize the play, and
fits in with an even broader attempt to deromanticize Shakespearean criticism and, indeed, poetry in general. As in so
many cases, disagreement with Bradley provides the base
from which the attack is launched. But the problem which a
critic attempting to deromanticize *Othello* immediately faces
is that the play itself is unabashedly romantic, being Shakespeare's first attempt at romantic tragedy since *Romeo and
Juliet*, and the most romantic play in the canon save only
Antony and Cleopatra. It is other things too, but the romantic
element is there, and to refuse to consider it, or to see it
simply as the detached author unmasking weakness and error,

[2] "Shakespeare and the Stoicism of Seneca," p. 40.
[3] See, for instance, Gerard, "Egregiously an Ass," p. 105.

is to discard more of the drama than any prudent critic can afford to, rather like trying to comment upon *The Faerie Queene* while undercutting the medieval chivalric and allegorical traditions, or commenting upon *Paradise Lost* while taking violent issue with Christianity.

More than any other Shakespearean play, *Othello* has received a critical reception strangely at variance with our reaction in the theater. In the rare presence of a great interpreter, Othello is a magnificent figure, not so much for his "nobility" as for the heights and depths of human experience he explores, and his demise is one of the most devastating in world drama. The attempt to deromanticize the play in general and the hero in particular emphasizes what Othello does, whereas the crucial matter of the tragedy is what Othello suffers.[4] The essence of Othello's tragedy is the range and intensity of feeling accessible to the romantic sensibility. Shakespeare has infused into the characterization not only an expanded capacity for feelings of both a positive and negative kind but also an unprecedented power to articulate feeling. Othello far exceeds Hamlet in this, though he himself will shortly be excelled by Lear. *Othello* is only partially a play about love, and even less a play about jealousy. I construe it to be primarily a play about suffering, and, more precisely, a play about suffering in ever-deepening isolation. It is the isolation of these characters from one another, an isolation caused primarily by mutually exclusive world-pictures, that makes their errors possible, and I do not refer to Othello's errors alone.

Like the *Hamlet*-world, the *Othello*-world can be differentiated into spheres or loci which reinforce each other by parallel and contrast. In *Othello*, however, we have only two principal spheres, the world of Venice and the world of Cyprus. The metaphysical universe, which looms so large and problematic in *Hamlet* and *King Lear*, is relegated to a po-

---

[4] Coleridge seems to have been the first to make this point (*Coleridge's Shakespearean Criticism*, I, 125). See also Dowden, pp. 214-215; and Bradley, p. 194.

sition of much less importance in the world of *Othello*; insofar as it is involved at all, it is the well-defined heaven and hell of Christian orthodoxy, and its nature and existence are never specifically challenged. The contrast between the two spheres sets order against anarchy, social institutions versus rampant individualism.[5]

The world of Venice has its problems—impending war, midnight elopements, and outraged fathers—but it also has institutions capable of dealing with them. The Senate, though meeting in a crisis atmosphere, displays exactly that kind of level-headedness and perspicacity that will be so lacking on all sides at Cyprus. Moreover, Venetian society has a knack for neutralizing its dissidents and keeping its mavericks within the social fabric. Brabantio is so opposed to Desdemona's marriage that he literally goes home and dies of it, but not before assenting to the findings of the Duke and withdrawing his charges in favor of the affairs of state. Desdemona has gone about her marriage in a highly unorthodox manner by Renaissance standards, yet when she places her case before the Senate, she is able to make an orderly transition of duty from father to husband. Othello is so confident of the value of his service and the durability of his relation to the state that he retains unruffled composure under severe provocation. Most significantly, in Venice Iago is effectively neutralized. His plan to have Brabantio wreck Othello's marriage backfires completely; instead, the orderly proceedings give Othello a chance to vindicate his honor and have the legality of his marriage recognized. In Venice, all the Ancient can do is inveigh against the military system, nurse his grudges, plan, and wait.

The restraint of a mediating force is entirely removed on Cyprus, however, and the individualists are thrown completely upon their own devices. On Cyprus, Othello is master, not employee, Desdemona is alone with the life she has chosen for herself, and Iago is completely in his element. The

[5] See John Draper, *The Othello of Shakespeare's Audience* (Paris, Didier, 1952), pp. 23-34.

removal of Othello and Desdemona from the rich, orderly society in which their love flourished, through storm and danger to an isolated and besieged outpost where their love will be destroyed is but the first step in a far more profound estrangement which will eventually find them cut off from each other and from the world they had known.[6] The elaborate development of Venetian society in Act I gives us a frame of reference in which to view the starker, more primitive island setting where the tragedy actually takes place.

And *what* an island! ". . . A town of war, / Yet wild, the people's hearts brimful of fear" (II.iii.203-204). Chaotic dissolution seems never more than a step away. It is a world of quarrels, brawls, and riots, of waylayers in the streets, of drunken gallants, "That hold their honors in a wary distance, / The very elements of this warlike isle—" (II.iii.52-53), and of tempestuous campfollowers. But beyond the general uneasiness and violence, there are other patterns woven into the world of Cyprus that are even more essential to the tragedy.

First of all, there is a ubiquitous, deeply ingrained disproportion between cause and effect, between intended purposes and achieved results. On every side, events in this world seem to roll on like an avalanche, gathering size as they gather speed, to end in consequences out of all proportion to the events that initiated them. The most obvious example is Othello's jealousy itself, which is founded upon trifles light as air, but it is by no means the only example. What starts as a foolish young man's amorous exploit in Venice ends in a multiple stabbing in a back alley of Cyprus. A cup of wine which Cassio takes to please the gallants precipitates a quarrel, the quarrel develops into a brawl, the brawl into a riot, and the riot leads to his dismissal and the loss of his reputation. Emilia steals a handkerchief and fails to own up to it, thereby contributing to the death of her mistress. Desdemona sues somewhat too vehemently for a friend and winds up

[6] Harry Levin, "*Othello* and the Motive Hunters," *Centennial Review*, 8 (1964), 10.

93

being strangled. In part, events in the *Othello*-world run amok because Iago, who has talent for exploiting this kind of disproportion, is always pulling the strings; but he himself is a conspicuous victim of the action's avalanche effect. As many critics have pointed out, his original intentions are relatively modest in comparison to the spectacular effects he achieves, and as events go out of control he becomes a casualty of his own intrigues.

The capacity of trifles to produce catastrophes regularly is unique to *Othello* among the four mature tragedies. In the other three, events of momentous weight and importance initiate the action, and, once begun, the plot is sustained by developments of tragic dimension. In *Hamlet, King Lear,* and especially in *Macbeth,* once the die is cast in the first half of the play, all the rest follows with inexorable logic. But in *Othello,* the die is not irrevocably cast until well into Act v. At any point before that, the situation could be salvaged by a word, and (if we are to believe old theater stories) some impulsive members of the audience have occasionally tried to provide it. The disproportion between cause and effect, intention and result, is as important to the quality of life in the *Othello*-world as elusiveness is to the quality of life in the *Hamlet*-world.

In the matter of elusiveness itself, however, the world delineated by *Othello* is exactly opposite to the world of *Hamlet.* In the later play, the true facts are tantalizingly accessible, almost at the fingertips of the several deluded characters. Like a spider's web, Iago's plot is the most fragile of lethal constructions; the merest wave of the hand could tear it away. If any one of the characters made a single, almost self-evident connection, the whole picture would instantly become clear. They all flirt with such connections, seem to skirt the very edges of them, but never quite make them until it is too late. Emilia comes improbably close to guessing that a frustrated office-seeker has traduced Desdemona, but, until the damage is irreparable, she never connects that insight with the man who asked her to steal the handker-

94

chief. Cassio known well enough who got him drunk, but he
trusts that man's advice afterward. Lodovico guesses Othello's wits are not safe, but goes out for a stroll with him before
commending him home to his wife. Ironically enough, Roderigo, the utter fool, repeatedly comes closer than anyone to
realizing Iago's true character. The first words of the play
are his furious rebuke with the intimation that Iago has been
lying to him. In each of their subsequent encounters, the
young gull begins with a suspicion that his "friend" is not
dealing with him justly, but he is talked out of this glimmer
of sense into more outlandish folly. Each time, his conviction
is stronger than before; each time, the lie he swallows is more
improbable than the last; and each time, the action demanded
of him is more ignoble and dangerous than its predecessor.
Yet Roderigo never makes the obvious connection until the
dagger is literally in his bosom. Everyone misses the truth,
though just by a fraction of an inch; this is one of the devices
Shakespeare uses throughout the play to keep us on the edge
of our chairs with a sense of impending disaster. The truth is
withheld, though only just barely, until it can no longer save.
Then, like steep-down gulfs of liquid fire, it all comes out in
a rush.

In one way or another, each of these characters misses
making the connection that could save them all because what
he wants to see gets in the way of his judgment. All the
principal actions in this tragedy hinge to an extraordinary
degree upon what the characters believe of themselves and of
each other. Of course, such beliefs play an important part in
the three other tragedies as well, and, indeed, in any play that
purports to imitate the action of human life. But in none of
the others does so much depend upon belief and upon that
alone.[7] There is no regicide in the recent past, no ghost to

[7] Ralph Berry, in "Pattern in *Othello*," *Shakespeare Quarterly*, 23
(1972), 3-19, an article that came to my attention as the present
study was being readied for the press, says some interesting things
about trust and disbelief throughout the play. Though he does not
analyze Act III, scene iii, in detail, he seems to have been thinking
along lines similar to my own.

95

make startling revelations, no disjunction of the elements themselves to impel the action of *Othello*; it all hinges upon belief. And these characters show a marked tendency to believe what they are predisposed to believe, even when the facts, would they but look at them, indicate otherwise, even when they themselves harbor in some corner of their minds a suspicion that what they believe may not be true. All of them at some point come into proximity with an ugly truth, reject it with all their energy, and retreat into a rationalization: my daughter did not run away; she was drugged . . . I'll get my reputation back even though I have disgraced myself . . . I'll enjoy the woman who refused me even though she married another man . . . my husband is just upset by affairs of state . . . husbands are all like that . . . he looks gentler than he did. Talk about characters cheering themselves up!

In *Hamlet*, the problems posed by a perilous, elusive, and corrupt world faced all the characters, and each individual had to come to terms with them as best he could. In *Othello*, each of the major characters lives in an intensely private world; each sees the world in terms partially or wholly incomprehensible to the others. They construct their subjective worlds largely as extensions of themselves, and they are singularly vulnerable when the external world fails to conform to their idea of it. Hence, under the extreme pressure of the crisis, they become increasingly isolated from each other and fall into greater and greater misunderstanding of what the others are doing or are capable of doing. Such isolation is a salient feature of the *Othello*-world. Each character suffers intensely in a unique private hell—Iago, in his way, scarcely less than the others.[8] In *Hamlet*, there was only one world-view, the hero's, revealed in full detail, and his complemen-

---

[8] John Bayley, in *The Characters of Love* (New York: Basic Books, 1960), p. 147, notes that "Othello's tragedy is personal, ending in total loneliness of spirit." A similar point is made by Kenneth Burke in "*Othello*: An Essay to Illustrate a Method," *Hudson Review*, 4 (1951), 200.

tary mind provided the dialectical tension of the tragedy. In *Othello*, on the other hand, three world-views are fully developed, and two of them are diametrical opposites, which clash head-on in the mind of the hero. Othello, Desdemona, and Iago all speak and act in accord with the world as they perceive it, and each of them perceives it in terms incomprehensible to the others.[9]

Of course, one of the most significant facts about the *Othello*-world is that it contains Iago—and not simply contains him but supports him, for his attack upon the romantic values of Othello and Desdemona is devastatingly effective. Moreover, there is a certain unsettling credibility to much of what he has to say about human behavior, or, more precisely, his world-view concentrates to the exclusion of all else upon certain aspects of conduct which Desdemona is unwilling to see and which Othello is prone to misjudge under his Ancient's tutelage.[10] Nothing is so destructive of truth as half-truth, and half-truths are Iago's stock-in-trade. Above all, the plausibility of Iago's anti-romanticism rests not so much upon what he says as upon the course which events take under his direction. His attack is against romantic values and those who hold them, and his ability to discern the soft spots and vulnerability of those values verges upon limited genius. His most characteristic assumption is that even a constant, loving, noble nature hides a beast beneath, and it is borne out all too persuasively by the action of the play.[11]

In *Othello*, then, Shakespeare delineates a world of spaciousness, of adventure, and of love triumphant, but a world containing its own antithesis, the poisonous mineral that will gnaw its innards. If Iago looks upon Othello and Desdemona's world with contempt, they look upon his, as it unfolds, with horror and aversion, and in Othello's case,

[9] A somewhat similar point is made by Knight, pp. 115-116.

[10] William Empson in *The Structure of Complex Words* (London: Chatto and Windus, 1951), puts the case more strongly, arguing that Iago's vision is even truer than Othello's to the facts of life (p. 248).

[11] Linda Leeds, "The Two Worlds of *Othello*," Essay, Cornell Univ., 1965, p. 25.

97

paradoxically, tragically, with belief. In the first half of the play, Shakespeare depicts the inception, burgeoning, and fulfillment of love, while the antithesis ripens unseen.[12]

The first act is largely given over to the early relationship between Othello and Desdemona, and in the course of a hectic night we hear versions of their love from no fewer than four different characters: Brabantio, Iago, Othello, and Desdemona. Before the play is over, all four will turn out to be wrong. This in no way implies that love is not present or that it is not a crucial value, but rather that, at this early point, it is incompletely understood by the four parties who attempt to give an account of it.

Brabantio's view, that such a match is impossible in nature and therefore must be the result of drugs or witchcraft, is immediately discredited, but it continues to have enduring importance throughout the play, since he initially suggests what will become the most devastating argument by which Othello, with the prompting of Iago, convinces himself that Desdemona is false. It will be worthwhile to pay close attention to Brabantio, for he is one of Shakespeare's most ingeniously wrought functional characters, one of the mirroring devices which, as Mack has pointed out, Shakespeare employed with increasing frequency and skill during the Jacobean years.[13] Brabantio's reaction to the discovery of his domestic difficulties sets a pattern which will become crucially important later in the play.

When he first comes out on his balcony, Brabantio is a bastion of self-confidence, not only because of his secure and powerful position but also because nothing in his view of his daughter would lead him to believe that the lewd allegations might be true. He thinks of her as:

[12] Fritz Wölcken has observed that, in the first half of *Othello*, nothing can precipitate disaster, while in the second half, nothing can prevent it: "The First Act of *Othello*," in *Language and Society* (Copenhagen: Berlingske, 1961), p. 191.

[13] Maynard Mack, "The Jacobean Shakespeare," in *Jacobean Theatre*, eds. John Russell Brown and B. Harris, Stratford u. Avon Studies 1 (London: Arnold, 1960), pp. 27-32.

A maiden never bold;
Of spirit so still and quiet that her motion
Blushed at herself.

(I.iii.94-96)

Moreover, he has no very high opinion of Roderigo to begin
with, and believes him at the moment to be drunk. And he
quickly surmises that the youth's unidentified companion is "a
villain." Yet, in spite of all this, after Roderigo's speech of
only some twenty lines, Brabantio, far from threatening to
have him arrested, believes his story at once. He is not merely
suspicious; he does not merely want to check up on it; he
believes it instantly and completely, strongly enough to raise
his entire household before he has even looked in her room:

Strike on the tinder, ho!
Give me a taper! Call up all my people!
This accident is not unlike my dream.
Belief of it oppresses me already.

(I.i.139-142)

He believes without any good reason for believing because
something in his mind—in this case an unsettling dream,
presumably that Desdemona has run away—predisposed him
to belief, made his mind fertile ground for suggestion. Despite
all his earlier self-confidence, the premonition had been there
all along, though he had not regarded it as important. When
something touched on that premonition, giving it a correlative
in the external world, it blossomed immediately into belief.

Unlike Othello in a later situation, Brabantio can immediately secure "the occular proof." Having done so, he at
once faces all the worst ramifications of her defection:

It is too true an evil. Gone she is;
And what's to come of my despisèd time
Is naught but bitterness.

(159-161)

He at once universalizes this single instance of a child's
unruly conduct and sees parenthood itself as worthless: "Who

99

would be a father?" (163). It is not Desdemona alone but daughters in general who are deceitful: "Fathers, from hence trust not your daughters' minds / By what you see them act" (169-170). However, having faced the worst, he now recoils from the truth and seeks comfort in an illusion that salvages both his faith in parenthood and his view of Desdemona as a dutiful, obedient child. He seeks confirmation in his delusion from a man for whom he had previously had little respect:

> Is there not charms
> By which the property of youth and maidhood
> May be abused? Have you not read, Roderigo,
> Of some such thing?
>
> (170-173)

By the next scene, his speculation has ripened to a full-blown belief: "Damned as thou art, thou hast enchanted her!" (I.ii.63). Brabantio believes his charge not only because he wants to but also because his idea of "nature," an idea which seems to rest largely upon social norms, simply does not admit that a love such as Desdemona's for Othello could exist:

> —in spite of nature,
> Of years, of country, credit, everything—
> To fall in love with what she feared to look on!
> It is a judgment maimed and most imperfect
> That will confess perfection so could err
> Against all rules of nature.
>
> (I.iii.96-101)

As long as Brabantio clings to his belief that his daughter is the victim of diabolic practice, he inveighs no more against parenthood in general; but, as soon as the illusion is stripped away, his deprecation of fatherhood returns more bitter than before: "I had rather to adopt a child than get it" (191). For all his arrogance, narrow-mindedness, and self-righteousness, Brabantio is not an altogether unsympa-

100

thotic character, and the relation of his death adds pathos to the final act. In him we see in miniature the kind of complete destruction of the subjective world which is central to the experience of the tragic hero. At a later point in this study, moreover, I will refer back to several of his actions and attitudes: he believes immediately the story of a man he has no reason to believe, believes without evidence that Desdemona has done something irreconcilable with his former view of her, believes it because of a premonition in his mind that all was not well, universalizes that belief into a general picture of evil and duplicity, and then, having accepted the worst, recoils from it in a desperate attempt to reinstate his former faith. Now, all these things have analogs in the conduct of Othello, and, indeed, Brabantio's final line provides an explicit link between his situation and the Moor's: "Look to her, Moor, if thou hast eyes to see: / She has deceived her father, and may thee" (292-293).[14] Of course, there is a difference between Othello and Brabantio even more significant than the similarities: when Brabantio says of Desdemona, "O, she deceives me / Past thought!" (I.i.164-165), he is absolutely right, but when Othello exclaims, "She's gone. I am abused," (III.iii.267), he is absolutely wrong. Anti-Othello critics from Rymer onward have all asked in effect, "How can a booby who makes a mistake like Othello's possibly be a tragic hero?" I shall argue that it is precisely *because* he is so wrong that he is tragic.

The second view of Othello and Desdemona's love is expounded by Iago to Roderigo: "It is merely a lust of the blood and permission of the will" (I.iii.333). That Brabantio believed *his* version of the love is quite evident; to what extent Iago believes his is a more difficult matter. His immediate aim is to keep Roderigo spending money on false hopes. But here, as elsewhere, there is a fascinating relation between the lies Iago tells and the world-picture he believes to be the truth.

[14] Cf. Aerol Arnold, "The Function of Brabantio in *Othello*," *Shakespeare Quarterly*, 8 (1957), 55-56. He sees the main function as allowing other characters to reveal themselves.

An examination of that relation is worth a digression at this point, because it is crucial to the working of the rest of the play.

Iago is a Machiavel in the precise sense of the term; like the Florentine political philosopher, he works empirically, observing men's actions, noting the differences between the way they purport to act and the way they really do act, and pointing to the fact that events always favor the shrewd, unscrupulous operator rather than men of honor and principle. The Ancient's world-view is characterized by what we might call secular nihilism, the debunking of values in practical applied morality without specific reference to theological systems that may or may not lie behind them. Since Iago has pieced this world-view together consciously and methodically, it can best be described as his empirical construct. While the presence of such a view accounts for the dialectical tension of the play, it does not wholly account for Iago, in whom there appear to be tensions of a different sort. Bernard Spivack has analyzed in great detail the discrepancies between what Iago says he feels and what he apparently does feel, between the vindictiveness of what he does and the jovial good spirits with which he goes about it.[15] His cynical contempt for humane values can account for his detachment from his victims, but it cannot explain why he mounts such an elaborate, vigorous, and risky assault in the first place. Why imperil himself to destroy something he considers worthless to begin with? Such an action can better be explained by envy, and Heilman has perceptively analyzed that aspect of Iago's character.[16] But by logic alone, an individual should not regard a single object or set of values with both feelings of envy and an attitude of nihilism. If something is worthless, there is no point in envying those who possess it; conversely, to envy something is tacitly to acknowledge its worth and desirability. Yet envy and nihilism do obviously coexist in

[15] *Shakespeare and the Allegory of Evil* (New York: Columbia Univ. Press, 1958), pp. 16-17.
[16] *Magic in the Web*, pp. 38-41.

Iago, and, moreover, he gives startling evidence of not believing himself in the glib aloofness from values which he
affects when expounding upon the world as he sees it. For
instance, the theory of sex which he formulates as part of the
empirical construct makes every woman a whore and every
man a cuckold. He says as much glibly to Othello:

> Think every bearded fellow that's but yoked
> May draw with you. There's millions now alive
> That nightly lie in those unproper beds
> Which they dare swear peculiar: your case is better.
> O, 'tis the spite of hell, the fiend's arch-mock,
> To lip a wanton in a secure couch,
> And to suppose her chaste! No, let me know;
> And knowing what I am, I know what she shall be.
> (IV.i.66-73)

At this point, Iago can well afford to take a cavalier attitude
toward the wearing of horns; but when he actually has to
face in private the possibility that his own forehead is decked,
it is no joking matter:

> But I, for mere suspicion in that kind,
> Will do as if for surety.
> (I.iii.383-384)

> For that I do suspect the lusty Moor
> Hath leaped into my seat; the thought whereof
> Doth, like a poisonous mineral, gnaw my inwards;
> And nothing can or shall content my soul
> Till I am evened with him, wife for wife.
> (II.i.289-293)

In these passages, certainly in the second, the comic mask
of detachment falls away for an instant, as it does in the remark about the daily beauty in Cassio's life, and we get a
quick glimpse of the fires that burn within. The point is not
that Iago is jealous, but rather that his persistent fear and
outrage at the thought of being a cuckold shows that in his

heart of hearts he attaches far more importance to wifely fidelity, at least where *his* wife is concerned, than the glib philosophy of the empirical construct would lead one to believe.

If Iago consistently entertains two incompatible attitudes, envy and nihilism, it does not mean that Shakespeare has been inconsistent or has incompletely fused two dramatic traditions into a "hybrid."[17] Rather, as in *Hamlet*, he has drawn a character who views reality in more than one way. We do not have here the enormous diversity of Hamlet's powerful, searching, complementary intellect, but rather a bifurcated world-view, the result of an exceedingly warped personality. There is a deep division between the picture Iago describes of the world—the empirical construct, built from selective observation and held together largely by willpower —and the private world of envy and frustration, where his emotions are actually engaged. He debunks with his mind and envies with his heart. The relationship between these two divided halves of Iago's world-view holds the key to both his extreme vindictiveness and his apparent detachment.

Like other characters in this play, Iago believes, or tries to believe, what he wants to believe. In the world of the empirical construct, he is preeminent. If all values are either self-delusions or the fabrications of persons up to foul deeds, then clearly the man who exempts himself from all ethical restraints is at an enormous advantage. In a world of fools and whores, he, the most supersubtle Venetian of them all, is king. He perceives his own superiority in the empirical construct and relishes it immensely. But in the *Othello*-world he is not king; he is a functionary and the inner Iago knows it. There is a profound discrepancy between his role in his private world and the world of literal fact where he must fetch luggage, escort the ladies, deliver letters, endure the condescension of Cassio sober and the insults of Cassio drunk,

---

[17] Spivack argues that Iago is a hybrid of the medieval Vice and the psychological characterization of the Elizabethan stage (*Shakespeare and the Allegory of Evil*, pp. 33-37, 430-432, 447-449).

and, as he puts it himself, "must be belov'd and calmed / By debitor and creditor" (I.i.30-31). The *Othello*-world refuses to validate his grandiose convictions of his superiority. He thinks himself better qualified by merit and experience for the lieutenancy than Cassio, but Cassio has it. He thinks it possible he has been cuckolded by the man who refused him the office, and perhaps by the man who achieved it too. That Iago really does believe this and that his belief is an important factor in the play, is, I think, indisputable.[18] Not only does he mention it twice in soliloquy, but Emilia's remarks make it clear that ugly words have been spoken on this subject in the Iago household:

> Some such squire he was
> That turned your wit the seamy side without
> And made you to suspect me with the Moor.
> (IV.ii.145-147)

His coarse remark, "It is a common thing—"(III.iii.302), indicates, moreover, that the issue has not blown over between them at the time of the action. Of course, the play provides Iago no grounds whatever for his suspicions, and I think we are to understand that Emilia is speaking from experience when she tells Desdemona:

> But jealous souls will not be answered so;
> They are not ever jealous for the cause,
> But jealous for they're jealous. 'Tis a monster
> Begot upon itself, born on itself.
> (III.iv.159-162)

Surely the resemblance of this description of jealousy to that offered by Iago is no accident: "It is the green-eyed monster, which doth mock / The meat it feeds on" (III.iii.166-167). Similarly, I think we are justified in assuming that he is portrayed as speaking from first-hand knowledge when he says:

---

[18] Levin Schücking makes an effective case in *Character Problems in Shakespeare's Plays* (London: Harrap, 1922), p. 207.

Dangerous conceits are in their natures poisons,
Which at the first are scarce found to distaste,
But with a little act upon the blood
Burn like the mines of sulphur.

(III.iii.326-329)

Note the similarity to his previous image of the poisonous mineral gnawing at his inwards. More telling still is his conduct in the final scene when his wife unmasks him. He does not try to fast-talk his way out, nor does he merely accuse her of lying. In unrestrainable rage, he shouts, "Villainous whore!" (V.ii.230).

Now all this is not to say that Iago is "motivated" in the conventional sense by desire for an office or by sexual jealousy; but by the same token, surely Shakespeare did not put all this in his play just to mislead the critics. The point is that the facts of the *Othello*-world—Iago's subordinate position and his pathological suspicion that he has been cuckolded—present to Iago an image of himself which makes it necessary to insist upon the validity of the empirical construct where he can see himself as superior. He can best be understood as a man who is trying by sheer force of will to impose cohesion upon a subjective world that is in constant danger of disintegrating, to insist upon the validity of an interpretation of reality that, with at least one part of his mind, he does not quite believe in himself. He must do this because the only alternative is to recognize his envy of the beauty in other people's lives and to accept the ugliness of his own by comparison, something he is frequently on the verge of doing but always pulls back from. Like other characters in the play, Iago believes what his own psychic needs dispose him to believe. Where evidence to support his belief is lacking, he manufactures it; where facts contradict him, he attempts to alter or annihilate them. "Iago is driven by the need to make men behave as he thinks they do," John Bayley has observed, hitting the mark exactly.[19] It is neces-

[19] *Characters of Love*, p. 200.

nary that they so behave to sustain the credibility of a subjective world in which his own identity is worth his having.

The inner division of Iago's world-view informs all the
rest of the characterization. Like Hamlet, Iago is fond of
play-acting and has a marked talent for it; in fact, Richard
Flatter considers his relish for assuming roles "the most
significant trait in his character."[20] His most characteristic
method of addressing the outside world appears to be a consciously staged, highly versatile performance, which he himself enjoys from the privileged position of his self-conceived
superiority. His versatility is even greater than Hamlet's;
when the latter is play-acting, he always casts himself in the
same role, the antic prince, while Iago varies his performance
to suit both the audience and the occasion. To Cassio he is
the jolly-good fellow, a bit of a rake and the man of level-
headed morality by turns, always larding the performance
with the deference his position demands. With Roderigo he is
always the man of the world, one whose knowledge comes
from first-hand experience. He wears the mask more thinly
with his gull than with the others, enjoying his performance
more openly. The Roderigo scenes also show another side of
his character that is by no means acting—Iago the bully. To
Othello he is the cautious, concerned friend, incorruptible in
his loyalty and deferential almost to servility—until he is
sure that the Moor, like Roderigo, is safely in his power, and
then the bully comes out again. He is, of course, equally
capable of shifting ethical ground to suit the audience and
the situation; thus he can tell Cassio, "Reputation is an idle
and most false imposition; oft got without merit and lost without deserving" (II.iii.258-259), and yet a few "short time"
hours later moralize to Othello, "Good name in man and
woman, dear my lord, / Is the immediate jewel of their souls"
(III.iii.155-156). Given the context of each pronouncement,
he is right both times.

For the purposes of this particular study, the most interest-

[20] *The Moor of Venice* (London: Heinemann, 1950), p. 15. See
also Granville-Barker, IV, 221-222; and Bradley, pp. 230-231.

ing aspect of Iago's role-playing is his fondness for casting himself alternately as the man who has to suffer much at the hands of the world, and then, in the next instant, the man whose superiority and individualism put him above it all. This unconscious manifestation of the envy-nihilism tension in his character is apparent in the first glimpse we get of him. He forcefully asserts, and no doubt believes, that he really deserved the promotion. He failed to get it, so he says, because the military system based on service has fallen off from the good old days when merit counted and a fellow could get ahead even without a college education. But in his very next breath, far from presenting himself as wronged by a good system gone bad, he turns it all exactly around; the system was absurd to begin with, and he alone is shrewd enough to disregard its standards.

The wronged or injured party is a role he is fond of playing before Othello too:

> I cannot speak
> Any beginning to this peevish odds,
> And would in action glorious I had lost
> Those legs that brought me to a part of it!
> (II.iii.174-177)

When the situation goes completely out of control and his own life is threatened by the Moor's fury, the injured party is the mask he instinctively reaches for, the one that seems closest at hand in an emergency:

> O grace! O heaven forgive me!
> Are you a man? Have you a soul or sense?—
> God b' wi' you! take mine office. O wretched fool,
> That liv'st to make thine honesty a vice! . . .
> O monstrous world! Take note, take note, O world,
> To be direct and honest is not safe.
>
> . . . .
>
> I should be wise; for honesty's a fool
> And loses that it works for.
> (III.iii.373-383)

108

By one of the twists so characteristic of Shakespeare's mature tragedies, Iago literally believes these words; they are the cornerstone of the empirical construct. But, of course, in context, modified and distorted by his play-acting, they take on a completely different meaning to Othello. To negate a value while being taken for the epitome of it is exactly the kind of irony Iago relishes most.

A deep sexual malaise is another quality Iago shares with Hamlet, but, once again, there are obvious differences. Hamlet allows himself the liberty of being coarse when in a particularly ugly mood; for Iago, coarseness is a way of life, another part of his whole manner of address to the outside world from which his inner recesses are so deeply estranged. More significantly, Hamlet develops a temporary disgust for sex because he is convinced that man is essentially corrupt, and never more so than in the conduct of love affairs. Iago reverses that: he *begins* with a deeply warped sexual morbidity, manufactures from that a vision of all women as whores and all men as cuckolds, and then promulgates it to the world with obscene glee. The basis of Iago's sexual morbidity is not made explicit; if there is one simple given about the character, it is that.[21] We are shown just enough of his own marriage to conclude it is highly unsatisfactory. His pathological suspicion, in the absence of any evidence, that his wife is unfaithful, his insistent grossness, and his constant association of sex with bestiality, all suggest a man whose sexuality appears to be a source of pain and disgust to him, so he reduces all sex to a game of whores and cuckolds and makes a joke of it.

There is yet another quality that Iago shares in common with Hamlet: a sardonic, reductive sense of humor. Here

[21] William Hazlitt observed: "The habitual licentiousness of Iago's conversation is not to be traced to the pleasure he takes in gross or lascivious images, but to his desire of finding out the worst side of everything and of proving himself an over-match for appearances." From *The Complete Works of William Hazlitt*, ed. P. P. Howe (London: Dent, 1930-34), IV, 208.

again, the differences are more illuminating than the similarities. Hamlet's humor is a weapon against the vice and duplicity he sees around him in the *Hamlet*-world, while Iago's wit, typified by the lame and impotent conclusion, is used to turn virtue into pitch and lead honest men by the nose as tenderly as asses. Hamlet employs humor in the service of truth, whereas Iago's humor rests primarily upon his ability to lie adroitly. Nevertheless, both use their wit to assert their superiority and impose their particular vision upon the world around them.

The problem of what Iago believes of those around him is exactly the one that Spivack raises most provocatively; the Ancient seems to believe different things at different times. "At one moment all his victims are guilty of moral turpitude and devious faithlessness; at another they are all exemplars of virtue, all honest fools whose simple-minded rectitude and credulity render them his natural prey" (p. 19). However, if the foregoing examination has any validity, this peculiarity should not surprise us; Iago, after all, believes two different things about himself: on the one hand that he is simply the cleverest and most able fellow in the world, and on the other that he is a cuckold, has been slighted by everyone around him, and is made ugly by the beauty in their lives. The empirical construct is built of generalizations, and it is those generalizations he is trying to uphold; in other words, his principal interest is in a theory of men, not in a theory of Othello or a theory of Desdemona. He does not have a concrete notion of what individuals are like, nor does he care. When he is contemplating his grievances, Othello is the lustful Moor; when he is contemplating his superiority, Othello is a credulous fool whose honesty and openness will make him easily victimized. When he is preparing Cassio's murder, he can afford to admit his own envy; when he is preparing to slander Desdemona, Cassio is a rake who may well desire to cuckold his commander. Iago manipulates his own beliefs as subtly as he does the beliefs of others, and the overall cast of his opinion about those around him depends

110

largely upon which half of his bifurcated world he is viewing them from. As I argued in the previous chapter, Shakespeare seemed to have a particular interest in such twofold vision, and indeed it is hardly a quality divorced from human nature. People in real life are seldom as consistent as Stoll and Schücking appear to want dramatic characters to be. Nor is there any need to resort to hybrids to explain the paradoxical attitudes and behavior of Iago; it should not surprise us that inconsistency and paradox in human conduct, along with some insight into the causes, are reflected in Shakespeare's mirror. There is no doubt that Iago's characterization draws upon the tradition of the Vice; if there was ever any doubt of this, Professor Spivack's research has resolved it. But the impish humor and contempt for virtue are not patched on to a partially developed psychological character, but rather fully integrated into a portrait of great intricacy.

I began this study of Iago by asking what the relationship is between the lies Iago tells and the truth he believes, and, specifically, to what extent does he believe the lewd version of Othello's and Desdemona's love that he expounds to Roderigo. The answer, I hope, should now be clear. He believes it in principle; this is really the way love works in the empirical construct.[22] As for Desdemona herself, he has an open mind: "That Cassio loves her, I do well believ't; / That she loves him, 'tis apt and of great credit" (ii.i.280-281). If Desdemona fails to conform to the lewd description he gives of her (ii.iii.14-26), then something drastic is going to have to be done about her, for her presence threatens his world. Her best qualities will have to be inverted—in order to prove how worthless they are:

> So will I turn her virtue into pitch,
> And out of her own goodness make the net
> That shall enmesh them all.
> (ii.iii.343-345)

[22] Schlegel observed: "He does not merely pretend an obdurate incredulity as to the virtue of women, he actually entertains it" (*Lectures on Dramatic Art and Literature*, p. 403).

The remaining views of love are offered by Othello and Desdemona themselves:

> She loved me for the dangers I had passed,
> And I loved her that she did pity them.
> (i.iii.167-168)

> I saw Othello's visage in his mind,
> And to his honors and his valiant parts
> Did I my soul and fortunes consecrate.
> (252-254)

It is fitting, indeed absolutely essential, that we examine these declarations of love together rather than separately, for we are here dealing with the *relationship* of love rather than with two separate characters who say they are in love with each other.[23] Here, as in *Romeo and Juliet* and *Antony and Cleopatra*, Shakespeare treats love not as an abstract quality of which individuals partake, but as a dynamic, multifaceted, ever-changing relationship, an exchange having two sides, both of which continually modify and illuminate each other. When such critics as Robert Heilman claim that either side is deficient, they unwittingly hit upon exactly the point that Shakespeare is at some pains to make. Love is embodied in these plays not in either character, but in the relationship between them, and, when Iago launches his attack, it is not so much an attack on Desdemona's character as against the plausibility of the relationship.

According to Heilman, Othello spins a tale of romance and adventure and is then pleased to find himself the object of an adolescent crush.[24] But Othello, unlike the equally exotic Morocco in *The Merchant of Venice*, does not give a sales talk about himself, boasting of heroic achievements and larding his tale with flattering classical self-comparisons. Othello men-

---

[23] See John Bayley's brilliant analysis of the spaciousness of love's world in *Othello* and the confinement of love in the prison of separate egos (*Characters of Love*, p. 162).

[24] *Magic in the Web*, p. 171.

tions nothing of his victories, nothing which would create a dashing, romantic image of the brave and successful warrior. Rather, what he talks about, what Desdemona responded to, are his defeats, what he has endured:

> Wherein I spoke of most disastrous chances,
> Of moving accidents by flood and field;
> Of hairbreadth scapes i' th' imminent deadly breach;
> Of being taken by the insolent foe
> And sold to slavery; of my redemption thence
> And portance in my travels' history.
>
> (I.iii.134-139)

He wins her by an account not of what he has done but of what he has suffered, suffered with that patience and equanimity reflected by the stateliness of the well-modulated verse. (See Appendix.) In his view, she loves him not for the adventure he has experienced, but for the dangers he has passed, and he loves her not because she adulated his achievements, but because she had pitied his tribulations. It is of the first importance to realize this, not only to avoid getting the speech backward as Heilman has done, but also to understand what happens later in the play. It is a mistake of the most elementary kind to assume that the pronouncements made by Othello and Desdemona in Act I constitute a definition of the relationship between them throughout the play; rather their statements reflect their understanding of that relationship in its earliest stages, and their understanding is incomplete on both sides. Desdemona loves Othello for far more than the dangers he has passed; and, when he speaks about his unhoused, free condition and the absence of passion in his mature, military temperament, he underestimates seriously the hold love has upon him.[25] These statements indicate not a shallow, faulty love, but an incomplete understanding of his own emotions. Only when his love is threatened does he discover how much it means to him, how strong

[25] This point is made by Samuel Kliger in "Othello: The Man of Judgment," *Modern Philology*, 48 (1951), 224.

its hold really is. Desdemona, on her part, has not really seen Othello's visage in his mind.[26] She has perceived only part of him, and her shock and bewilderment upon discovering the more ominous side of his nature are exceeded only by the courage and love which enable her finally to forgive him. Throughout the drama, the love relationship and the two characters' understanding of it, of each other, and of their own emotions undergo a process of continual change, and that change is inseparable from the growth and development of the characters.[27] This is what makes *Othello* such a painful tragedy; love comes to fruition only in the tribulation that destroys it. Desdemona comes to know the full depth of her love only by discovering the powers of loyalty and forgiveness with which it endows her in the face of outrageous wrongs and terrible anguish. Othello learns the power of love and the depth of its roots in his being by the pain it inflicts once he believes it betrayed and, worse still, in the final recognition of how *he* has betrayed it. No man could suffer what Othello suffers unless he not only loved, but had staked everything, his soul itself, upon that love.

The critical question about *Othello*, of course, is why on earth does the Moor believe Iago instead of Desdemona? At the beginning of the famous and oft-analyzed Act III, scene iii, Othello seems to exude the same combination of tenderness and unshakable confidence that has marked all his previous encounters with Desdemona, yet, by the end of the scene, he has vilified her in the coarsest terms, renounced his love with a solemn oath, and is determined to murder her. Not only does Iago secure immediate belief without even circumstantial evidence, but, even more strikingly, throughout their first encounter in III.iii, Othello seems almost to be

---

[26] See Dowden, p. 207.

[27] Barbara Everett has put it perfectly: "Character, in Shakespeare, is what it becomes, but the becoming covers the whole play": "Reflections on the Sentimentalist's *Othello*," *Critical Quarterly*, 3 (1961), 137.

asking to be told something is very much amiss. It is he, not Iago, who first brings up the subject of Cassio's honesty. It is he who first associates Iago's general warning about jealousy with his wife's attractiveness. It is he who first mentions his own "weak merits," and, above all, it is he who first reopens Brabantio's argument that nature could not so err as to make Desdemona love one so different from herself, an opening into which Iago immediately plunges his most effective wedge. In fact, it would not be going too far to say that Iago does not convince Othello of Desdemona's infidelity; rather, he gives the Moor a few suggestive nudges in that direction and lets Othello convince himself. Like Brabantio in the first scene, the Moor already has a predisposition to believe, and that predisposition is not merely an unsettling dream but his world-view itself.

All too often, analyses of III.iii place critical emphasis upon Iago, the intention being to trace the weaving of the diabolical web in which the Ancient ensnares the Moor. But such an approach assumes that Othello is reacting to Iago's tactics and being led by the nose. I propose that the opposite is the case; it is Othello's train of thought that governs the movement of the scene, and Iago, an excellent improviser, takes his cues from his commander. Iago's basic tactic is to make a series of tentative lunges and retreats, each lunge a little bolder than the one before, and in the intervals to allow the increasingly disturbed Moor to raise all the forbidden subjects himself.

Iago brings up the subject of Cassio's relationship with Desdemona, and by his worried "Indeed," indicates there is something on his mind. For the next forty lines he volunteers nothing more, allowing Othello to press him harder for an honest account of what he is thinking.[28] While Iago is thus playing hard to get, these are the Moor's successive utterances:

[28] Spivack notes this tactic of Iago's in *Shakespeare and the Allegory of Evil*, p. 438.

> Discern'st thou aught in that?
> Is he not honest?
>
> (102-103)

> By heaven, he echoes me,
> As if there were some monster in his thought
> Too hideous to be shown.
>
> (106-108)

> And didst contract and purse thy brow together,
> As if thou then hadst shut up in thy brain
> Some horrible conceit.
>
> (113-115)

> Therefore these stops of thine fright me the more.
>
> (120)

> Nay, yet there's more in this.
> I prithee speak to me as to thy thinkings,
> As thou dost ruminate, and give thy worst of thoughts
> The worst of words.
>
> (130-133)

> Thou dost conspire against thy friend, Iago,
> If thou but think'st him wronged, and mak'st his ear
> A stranger to thy thoughts.
>
> (142-144)

Granted, Iago, who has a carefully cultivated reputation for openness and honesty, is purposely leading the Moor to think him reluctant to speak some terrible truth. Still, this emphasis upon "monster," "horrible conceit," "worst of thoughts," "worst of words," and "wronged" indicates a habit of mind already inclined to look for the worst. Iago is not the first to suggest overtly that his thoughts are vile: Othello is.

With the Moor agitated and off balance, Iago is ready to make his next limited sortie: "Good name in man and woman, dear my lord, / Is the immediate jewel of their souls" (155-156). The craftiness of this lies in the "and woman," for it hints, though just barely, that Iago's worst of thoughts involves Desdemona's honor as well as Othello's. As for Othello, the more likely it appears that he is going to hear something terrible, the more determined he becomes to hear it: "By heaven, I'll know thy thoughts!" (162). Another elusive feint on Iago's part produces the ominous "Ha!" and the Ancient is now in a position, under the guise of concerned friendship, to introduce the key words, "jealousy" and "cuckold."

Up to this point, Othello's response has been steadily mounting annoyance and apprehension; nothing irritates him more than not getting a straight answer.[29] But now, at the first clear indication that Iago's thoughts indeed concern Desdemona's faithfulness, Othello once again displays that confidence and self-control which characterized his appearance before the Senate:

> Think'st thou I'ld make a life a jealousy,
> To follow still the changes of the moon
> With fresh suspicions? No! To be once in doubt
> Is to be once resolved.

> (177-180)

This is the dictum of the decisive man of action. Othello is meeting this situation as he customarily meets all situations; he does not yet realize that the situation itself is totally different from any with which he has had to cope. Still, his pronouncement is exactly the kind of rebuff which could nip Iago's scheme in the bud if the Moor could only leave things at that; but, disastrously, he goes on:

> 'Tis not to make me jealous
> To say my wife is fair, feeds well, loves company,
> Is free of speech, sings, plays, and dances;
> Where virtue is, these are more virtuous.

[29] M. R. Ridley, ed., *Othello*, 7th ed. (1958: rpt. New York: Vintage, 1967), p. lv.

117

Nor from mine own weak merits will I draw
The smallest fear or doubt of her revolt,
For she had eyes, and chose me.

(183-189)

Now Iago has mentioned nothing, not even by way of hint, about the differences between Desdemona's youth and courtly accomplishments and Othello's race, age, or occupation. These are Brabantio's arguments, and they are apparently lying dormant in Othello's mind. Though he is here reaffirming what Desdemona had said before the senate, the strength and gratuitousness of his affirmation, preceded and followed by disavowals of jealousy, disavowals in which he declares he would cast off love if he thought it betrayed rather than suffer the degradation of jealousy—all this gives the impression that, like the lady in *Hamlet*, he doth protest too much and protests it more vigorously than he has to:

No, Iago;
I'll see before I doubt; when I doubt, prove;
And on the proof there is no more but this—
Away at once with love or jealousy!

(189-192)

Learning that there is a good deal more than "this" is the first of several painful lessons that lie immediately ahead of him.[30]

Iago is now in a peculiar position: the forbidden subjects —Cassio, Desdemona, good name, honesty, jealousy, cuckold, monstrous thoughts, and the differences between Othello and Desdemona—have all been introduced, some by Othello, some by Iago at Othello's urgent insistence. "Words and thoughts are indeed flung back and forth between them until it would be hard to say whose they first were."[31] But once

[30] See Moody Prior, "Character in Relation to Action in *Othello*," *Modern Philology*, 44 (1947), 232. See also John Money, "Othello's 'It is the cause . . .' An Analysis," *Shakespeare Survey*, 6 (1953), 97.
[31] Granville-Barker, IV, 225.

118

these subjects are out in the open, Othello's self-control and assertiveness threaten to put an end to the matter. It is now possible for Iago to be bolder than he would have dared just minutes before, but by the same token it is *essential* that he grasp the initiative if he is not to lose the gains he has made. So he makes another sally yet more daring than the last, with feigned reluctance and in the spirit of, "I hate to be the one who has to tell you this, but since you insist, it's best you hear it from a friend."

From the beginning of the encounter up to this point, the dialog has been evenly divided between the two (about fifty-five lines apiece), with the Moor clearly taking the initiative; but from the beginning of Iago's speech, "I am glad of this" (193), until his second exit and the beginning of Othello's soliloquy, Iago has fifty-three lines and Othello only fourteen, most of them fragmentary. Iago has clearly seized the initiative and he develops several arguments in quick succession: Othello's trusting, magnanimous spirit renders him vulnerable to abuse; all Venetian women are faithless; if Desdemona is so innocent, how come she deceived her father so adroitly? More telling still is the repeated insistence that Othello is "moved," and, most telling of all, the reverse psychology he uses, cautioning the Moor to move his thoughts no further than suspicion, while intimating that beyond suspicion lie vile truths.

Othello's ominous silence after the "Look to your wife" speech indicates that he is mulling over the probabilities. He shows neither the anger of the man who has heard his wife slandered nor the blunt confidence of the man who believes she had eyes and chose him. He testily rejects the repeated suggestion that he is moved, and is perhaps surprised and troubled by exactly how moved he is. He makes one more affirmation of Desdemona's honesty: "I do not think but Desdemona's honest" (225). The phrasing of his affirmation in the negative intimates his crumbling confidence. Iago shrewdly agrees with him, but with an ambiguous after-thought: "Long live she so! and long live you to think so!"

119

(226). Then comes the turning point of the scene, and indeed of the entire play, as Othello murmurs (to himself, I think), "And yet, how nature erring from itself—"(227). It would be impossible to over-emphasize the importance of this simple, fragmentary line. It is the first overt indication Othello gives that he thinks it possible Desdemona might be false. It is a specific contradiction of Desdemona's assertion before the Senate that she had seen Othello's visage in his mind, and, most significantly, it is the first time the Moor, not Iago, presents evidence against her, convincing himself of her guilt. For an instant, he and the Ancient ironically reverse roles. Moreover, the assertion that nature could not err to such an extent as to make so unlikely a match, or that such a match would *be* an error in nature, has not even been suggested by Iago; he has offered the far more characteristic argument that all women are whores. Othello's utterance is once again a resurrection of Brabantio's case, and Iago, always keen to spot a tactical advantage, grasps it eagerly and recasts Othello's half-spoken thought into his own characteristic terms:[32] nature erring from itself becomes a will most rank, foul disproportion, and thoughts unnatural. The speech is a masterly employment of his basic tactic—thrust, back off, apologize, and then, upon the credit of the apology, thrust deeper. This argument is more devastating than any Iago thought up himself, for it elicits from the Moor the first of many ignominious acts we will see him perform, setting Emilia to spy on Desdemona. Iago shrewdly accepts his dismissal, and, after returning for another game of two steps forward, one step back, he leaves Othello alone to convince himself of Desdemona's faithlessness. In his soliloquy, convincing himself is exactly what Othello does.

Though he has no reason whatsoever to believe Desdemona false, he starts by immediately assuming that his marriage

---

[32] Speaight, in *Nature in Shakespearean Tragedy*, p. 72, notes that Othello makes Brabantio's reasoning his own. "So he ruminates, and Iago is quick to pick up his cue." See also Mercer, "*Othello* and the Form of Heroic Tragedy," pp. 56-57.

was a mistake. Throughout the soliloquy, as in the conversation that preceded it, Othello sees things as worse and
worse the more he thinks about them. He continues to
marshal evidence for the prosecution, citing once again
arguments similar to those offered by Brabantio before the
Senate:

> Haply, for I am black
> And have not those soft parts of conversation
> That chamberers have, or for I am declined
> Into the vale of years—
>
> (263-266)

He resists belief one last time ("yet that's not much—"),
and then surrenders to it completely: "She's gone. I am
abused" (267). From this point on, Othello never frees
himself from the conviction she has been false, until, of
course, it is too late. As I argued in Chapter One, he immediately expands his belief into a view of marriage as
tainted, and expands that into a view of some malignant
destiny which singles out the best for misfortune and
ignominy from the moment of birth:

> Yet 'tis the plague of great ones;
> Prerogatived are they less than the base.
> 'Tis destiny unshunable, like death.
> Even then this forkèd plague is fated to us
> When we do quicken.
>
> (273-277)

Now these are very peculiar lines to be turning up in *Othello*,
which, as everyone agrees, is certainly not a tragedy of fate.
Yet the passage has been generally ignored by critics, and
even those who comment upon it do not attach much importance to it. The anti-Othello critics, predictably, see the hero
striking another of his annoying poses, cheering himself up by
classing himself among the great ones. Perhaps we might
give some credence to this view were this the first or only
reference the hero makes to fate; but, in fact, the part is

121

studded with them, and taken together they delineate a world-view which goes far toward explaning why the Moor is so ready to believe that all is not well with his life. Significantly enough, the first such reference comes from Othello not in his misfortune, but at the height of his success and happiness when he arrives at Cyprus, his enemies defeated and his wife safely waiting for him.[33] The first seven lines of his greeting to her express extravagant joy, couched in the expansive images of the *Othello*-music; but suddenly the speech takes a somber turn, and we hear Othello's first allusion to a fate which is opposed to happiness:

> If it were now to die,
> 'Twere now to be most happy; for I fear
> My soul hath her content so absolute
> That not another comfort like to this
> Succeeds in unknown fate.
>
> (ii.i.187-191)

He again mentions fate when he tells Desdemona of the magic in the handkerchief:

> She, dying, gave it me,
> And bid me, when my fate would have me wive,
> To give it her.
>
> (iii.iv.63-65)

His final and most significant reference to fate occurs in the final act when he abandons his plan to escape, saying:

> Who can control his fate? 'Tis not so now.
> Be not afraid, though you do see me weaponed.
> Here is my journey's end, here is my butt,
> And very seamark of my utmost sail.
>
> (v.ii.266-269)

---

[33] Traversi notes the dark undertone of the greeting in *An Approach to Shakespeare*, p. 138. So do Hugh Richmond in "Love and Justice: *Othello*'s Shakespearean Context," in *Pacific Coast Studies in Shakespeare*, p. 154; and Berry in "Pattern in *Othello*," p. 16.

In addition to these specific allusions, additional speeches make it clear that Othello's mind not only moves on a dark cosmic plane, but also that he sees his own experience as directly connected with cosmic powers. The Moor has adopted (one might better say *adapted*) Christianity, but in his mind the Christian heaven of salvation is transmogrified into another form of an ominous cosmic force that imposes the worst suffering upon the best men:

> Had it pleased heaven
> To try me with affliction, had they rained
> All kinds of sores and shames on my bare head,
> Steeped me in poverty to the very lips,
> Given to captivity me and my utmost hopes,
> I should have found in some place of my soul
> A drop of patience.
>
> (IV.ii.47-53)

Like Hamlet, the Moor appoints himself as heaven's scourge and minister, but the heaven he serves is a hard, almost perverse one:[34]

> I must weep,
> But they are cruel tears. This sorrow's heavenly;
> It strikes where it doth love.
>
> (V.ii.20-22)

Desdemona's death is not only a heavy, insupportable loss for him; in his eyes it shakes the foundation of the universe:

> Methinks it should be now a huge eclipse
> Of sun and moon, and that th' affrighted globe
> Should yawn at alteration.
>
> (V.ii.100-102)

So deep is his conviction that the affairs of man and the universal powers are closely linked that, even on the threshold of unconsciousness, he believes nature is confirming

---

[34] Money, in "Othello's 'It is the cause . . . ,'" notes this, but chalks it up to the Moor's self-delusion (p. 96).

123

Desdemona's infidelity by shaking him with his fit: "Nature would not invest herself in such a shadowing passion without some instruction. It is not words that shakes me thus" (IV.i.39-42). Nor is it primarily Iago's words that shake him in III.iii.

All these allusions tell us nothing about the world of the play, but there are too many of them and they are too consistent with each other for us to shrug off the conviction that they do tell us something about the subjective world of Othello. Moreover, the Moor's belief in a malignant fate and pitiless heavens is quite consistent with the life of broil and battle he has endured. As in the case of Hamlet, and in marked contrast to Lear and Macbeth, Shakespeare has troubled himself to give us substantial background material about the hero's life before the time encompassed by the play. We know that he is descended from men of royal siege and that since his youth he has known the tented field. The background from which he came was dark and perilous, fraught with sybils, magic, and arcane knowledge, and the principal ingredients of his life have been suffering, danger, and disaster. All this information delineates a life which has been exotic and exciting, but also filled with mystery and pain, and Othello's address to such a world has been a self-imposed imperturbability, a stoic patience and absolute self-confidence never more majestically in effect than when we first see him.[35] He imposes emotional distance between himself and his dreadful experiences:

> Can he be angry? I have seen the cannon
> When it hath blown his ranks into the air
> And, like the devil, from his very arm
> Puffed his own brother—and is he angry?
>> (III.iv.134-137)[36]

[35] Julia Wales, "Elaboration of the Setting in *Othello* and Emphasis of the Tragedy," *Trans. of the Wisconsin Acad. of Sciences, Arts, and Letters,* 29 (1935), 335, argues that Othello operates almost by a *theory* of self-control.

[36] Granted, it is Iago saying this, but not everything Iago says is necessarily meant to be taken as a lie. He is depicted saying this in

That Othello can become embroiled in passion comes as a surprise to Desdemona, to Iago, and most of all, to Othello himself.

It is scarcely surprising that Othello should emerge from such a background believing that the best and noblest men are singled out at birth by some malignant power for the worst and most ignominious suffering; such a world-view is simply consistent with his experience—his experience, that is, until the time of his marriage. Hence his comment to himself, "and when I love thee not, / Chaos is come again" (III.iii.91-92), is no hyperbole but a recognition of literal fact.[37] Desdemona's love illuminates his world, redeems his life from chaos, but, beneath the radiance of his new discovery, the old vision lies dormant, like Brabantio's dream, always at the back of his mind, intruding even at the moment of his greatest happiness. Othello's tragedy is that he stakes everything upon a belief that love can transcend the differences of race, age, and custom, but then discovers that he cannot sustain that faith once it is called into question. He ceases to believe that love has such powers because he never did fully believe it in the first place. He had a premonition that life is not constituted to yield such happiness: "It is too much of joy," literally too good to be true.[38] Hence, what we have in III.iii is not a simple, child-like nature entrapped by a diabolically clever schemer, and still less a shallow self-aggrandizer who is more interested in receiving adulation than

---

the presence of Desdemona, who knows Othello's life story, and the allusion is perfectly consistent with the rest of the background which Shakespeare sketched for the Moor.

[37] Gerard notes the significance of the line in "Egregiously an Ass," p. 101.

[38] Maud Bodkin, in *Archetypal Patterns in Poetry*, p. 223, observes that into what Iago speaks are "projected the half truths that Othello's romantic vision ignored, but of which his mind held secret knowledge." J.I.M. Stewart, in *Character and Motive in Shakespeare* (1949; rpt. London: Longmans, 1965), pp. 102-103, states, "Othello hears an inner voice that he would fain hear and fain deny."

in giving love. Rather we have a man whose consciousness is balanced upon a fine edge between a tragic awareness of life as a process of suffering and disaster, and an awareness of the transcendent, joyful powers of love. Iago simply gives the nudge that is needed to upset that balance, and Othello's subjective world collapses.

Now such an interpretation of the Moor's character is a far cry from Bradley's, and even farther from Leavis'. So far as I have been able to determine, no such reading has been suggested before. Yet it explains a good many facets of the play which have been hitherto generally ignored. Why else does Shakespeare depict the Moor's background as consisting entirely of mystery, slavery, disaster, and suffering? Why else the many references to a malignant fate and a pitiless heaven? Why else the dark undertone in the Moor's greeting to Desdemona at the moment of his supreme joy and success? Why else the ominous line, so devastatingly borne out, "and when I love thee not, / Chaos is come again"? And why else does Othello actually seem to solicit bad news in III.iii? Why else does he himself assume the role of prosecutor in his soliloquy, concluding that his worst premonitions about the prerogatives of the great, the malignant destiny fixed at the moment life quickens, were all too true?

Moreover, such an interpretation of Othello's character brings him fully into what I have been arguing is the main thematic line of the play. The tragedy hinges upon belief, and all the other characters believe pretty much what they want to believe, thus isolating themselves and impairing their ability to understand each other. Now Othello is the antithesis of them; because of his tragic predisposition, he rejects a truth he desperately wants to believe and with terrible force embraces an error he does not want to believe but must. Iago wishes to vindicate a world in which he is king; Othello is inwardly impelled to accept a world in which he is victim. The complex, twofold irony of this is what makes the recognition and reversal in Act v almost too much to be borne. Othello is confirmed in the truth which all along he had

126

wanted to believe but could not, confirmed under circumstances of his own making which render the belief of that truth the greatest agony of all.

The second long encounter between Othello and Iago in III.iii is far more than merely a continuation of the first. In the first, the assumptions and assurances upon which Othello's world rests are subtly undermined, while in the second, that world collapses, leaving his mind divided between diametrically opposed beliefs. What happens to Othello in the second encounter is analogous to what happens to Hamlet in the Ghost scene, and though the differences are obvious, the parallel is worth drawing. In each, the hero renounces all past values by which he had formerly ordered his life. Hamlet renounced all past perception of the world and the means of perceiving it. So too, Othello renounces the substance of his past life, his occupation, and the love of Desdemona:

> Farewell the tranquil mind! farewell content!
> Farewell the plumed troop, and the big wars
> That make ambition virtue! O, farewell!
>
> . . . .
>
> Farewell! Othello's occupation's gone!
>
> (348-357)

Here we come, I suspect, to one of the principal difficulties of modern *Othello* criticism; the military temperament and martial virtues have not, to put the case mildly, been widely regarded among twentieth-century intellectuals with unmixed admiration. As Maynard Mack has observed in a different context, our age tends to be "pathologically mistrustful of heroism."[39] In commenting upon Othello's renunciation of his profession, Robert Heilman speaks with a characteristically modern voice, objecting that the Moor sees only half of what he renounces. Shakespeare has given him no awareness of the horror of war, only the tinsel glory of the parade-ground officer. "At his age, and with all his experience, he is still the

---

[39] *King Lear in Our Time* (Berkeley: Univ. of California Press, 1965), p. 84. See also Gardner, *"Othello*: A Retrospect, 1900-67," pp. 5-6.

shiny-eyed novice in war."[40] In the face of this, one must simply point with astonishment to the text and insist that the critic's error is not of interpretation but of fact. Up to this point the *only* allusions Othello has made to war have emphasized its horrors and suffering. The first and only mention he makes of the heroic side of war (a side very much alive for Shakespeare's era, if not for our own) is made in the process of renouncing it. The Moor is here articulating his incalculable sense of loss, and if, in doing so, he stresses the positive values of that which he has lost, one should not see in this ignorance of the other aspects of soldiership with which he is all too familiar. Shakespeare's dramatic viewpoint toward war and warriors is, predictably enough, complementary. It can include a Talbot and a son killing his father and father killing his son; it can include a Prince Hal and a Falstaff, a Hotspur and a Faulconbridge; it could produce, probably within the space of three or four years, *Henry V* and *Troilus and Cressida*. What seems to have interested him particularly in the Jacobean years were the tragic conflicts between the pride, ambition, hardness, and propensity for ruthless action which a great soldier draws from his profession, and those workings of the heart which are part of his heritage as a member of humanity. Thus we have Othello, Macbeth, Antony, and Coriolanus, a formidable succession of soldier tragic heroes, all of whom have to come to terms in some way or another with this conflict.

It is of the utmost significance, moreover, that what Othello first renounces is not pride, glory, pomp, and heroism, but rather "the tranquil mind" and "content." For the remainder of the play he will struggle furiously with his predicament, caught, like Hamlet, in a welter of contradictory beliefs:

> I think my wife be honest, and think she is not;
> I think that thou are just, and think thou art not.
> I'll have some proof.
>
> (III.iii.384-386)

[40] *Magic in the Web*, pp. 185-186.

Hamlet's dilemma, however, arose because the "truth" of anything in the *Hamlet*-world is subject to endless revision, while Othello's even more painful dilemma arises from the conflict between what he wants to believe of Desdemona and what he really does believe, between what he feels for her and what he thinks she is: "A fine woman! a fair woman! a sweet woman! . . . Ay, let her rot, and perish, and be damned tonight" (IV.i.175-179). Such tensions reach their height in the fit, the physical emblem of dissolution, the kind of breakdown which all four of the heroes undergo in one form or another when their subjective worlds collapse.

"Give me a living reason she's disloyal" (III.iii.409), he demands, asking to be told exactly what he is most loath to hear. Now begins what is surely the most incredible search for evidence in dramatic literature, more bizarre in its methods and results than even Hamlet's. There is a definite pattern to Othello's quest for evidence, and it applies to each of the "proofs" Iago offers—Cassio's dream, the handkerchief, and Cassio's "confession." The Moor demands absolute certitude; Iago provides some flimsy circumstance or hearsay which Othello immediately shapes in his own mind into evidence; filled with horror and rage, he flies into a passion, renounces his love, and swears vengeance; but, once the passion is spent, he returns to his wife's beauty and seeming innocence, pulls back from his former conviction, and demands more proof. This pattern persists almost to the moment he strangles Desdemona:

> Therefore confess thee freely of thy sin;
> For to deny each article with oath
> Cannot remove nor choke the strong conception
> That I do groan withal.
>
> (v.ii.53-56)

These lines perfectly capture the paradox inherent in his search for proof. He does not want to be convinced because he is already lethal in his conviction. He is seeking not evidence but congruence between his belief and the external

world, between what she appears to be and what he thinks
she is.

In Othello's predicament, inwardly convinced yet furiously
resisting his conviction, only a confession can restore congruence to the world, and securing one, first from Cassio and
then from Desdemona, becomes his principal obsession. Iago
gamely undertakes to provide something that, in the Moor's
frame of mind, will pass for one. Cassio's "confession" is a
striking example of the way the characters of this play
substitute their own beliefs for objective facts and convince
themselves methodically of their own errors. Othello fills in
the blanks, so to speak, and writes Cassio's confession for
him: "Now he denies it faintly, and laughs it out" (IV.i.112)
. . . "Crying 'O dear Cassio!' as it were. His gesture imports
it" (135-136) . . . "Now he tells how she plucked him to my
chamber" (139-140). Othello manufactures the confession
he was certain he was going to hear to begin with, yet he is
so convinced that he has had objective proof that he can insist
almost to the end of the play, "He hath confessed . . . Cassio
confessed it." Throughout, Shakespeare seems to be exploring
the kind of psychic phenomenon that so interested Montaigne,
particularly in "Of Imagination." The central problem is the
relationship between the subjective world and the objective
one, the implication being that if ignorance, resignation, or a
mistaken belief can make the tribulations of the objective
world negligible ("He that is robbed, not wanting what is
stol'n, / Let him not know't, and he's not robbed at all"
[III.iii.342-343]), on the other hand a passionately held belief,
however groundless, can make the objective world a hell.
"Reality" to the individual depends less upon objective fact
than on subjective interpretation, and there is nothing good
or bad but thinking makes it so.[41]

"If she be false, O, then heaven mocks itself! / I'll not
believ't" (III.iii.278-279). This line establishes the inner

[41] This theme, like so many of importance, was first introduced
in connection with Brabantio. See his exchange of sentences with the
Duke (I.iii.199-220).

conflict with which Othello will struggle for the remainder of the play.[42] As in *Hamlet*, the problem can best be understood in the light of the Neoplatonic doctrine that the order and benevolence of heaven necessitate that a beautiful exterior must denote a virtuous soul; if not, then the natural and divine orders are perverted in a manner bordering on sacrilege.[43] If Desdemona thought she had seen Othello's visage in his mind, he no doubt believed he had seen her mind in her visage. His former view of her has been shaken, and yet the goodness and love he had seen in her remain to torment him as something holy and beautiful that has been lost—and not just lost but desecrated. Othello agonizes over the discrepancy between her beauty and her "vice," and it is finally her "hypocrisy" far more than her "infidelity" that infuriates him.

Throughout all of their encounters in the second half of the play, Othello and Desdemona are invariably talking to each other without understanding what the other means. In *Hamlet*, the major characters were all, in one way or another, trying to mislead those around them; what makes *Othello* so much more painful a tragedy is that the Moor and Desdemona are desperately trying to tell one another the truth as they see it, but she cannot comprehend his "truth" and he cannot believe hers. Hence their attempts to communicate only drive them further apart, worsening their terrible isolation. As Othello demands more and more vehemently to see the handkerchief, Desdemona simply has no idea what on earth can be bothering him. This is a side of Othello she had not seen in his mind; so, because she cannot fit what he is saying into her conception of him or of the world, she concocts a version of what is transpiring that makes sense to her. In a manner completely characteristic of the *Othello*-world, she makes a disastrous, unwitting blunder: "This is a

---

[42] Winifred Nowottny, in "Justice and Love in *Othello*," *Univ. of Toronto Quarterly*, 21 (1952), 333-337, perceptively analyzes Othello's plight, torn between two views of the woman he loves.

[43] See Hawkes, *Shakespeare and the Reason*, pp. 114-115.

trick to put me from my suit: / Pray you let Cassio be received again" (III.iv.87-88). As Othello demands the token, she pleads all the more strongly for Cassio, and we see a grotesque tableau of two people laboring under errors, pressing mistaken beliefs with greater and greater heat, working at cross-purposes to themselves and each other, until even this parody of communication breaks down.

In the "brothel" scene, isolation and estrangement reach their bleakest limits. I know of no other scene in drama which so vividly and painfully portrays two people trying desperately to talk *to* each other, but who, because of mutual incomprehension and error, are able only to talk *at* each other. The process of communication has become absolutely impossible, and at the end of the scene each is utterly alone and utterly aware of it. The scene is so powerful and so painful because both give poignant expression to their individual suffering in terms that are comprehensible to us, but not to each other.

The dreadful interview consists primarily of questions that go unanswered:

> Upon my knees, what doth your speech import?
> I understand the fury in your words,
> But not the words.

> (IV.ii.31-33)

Because Othello believes this bewilderment to be just more hypocrisy, he does not answer her question but asks one of his own, a question he himself has already answered in his own mind: "What art thou?" (34). When she answers this truthfully, "Your wife, my lord; your true / And loyal wife" (34-35), he again equates her "hypocrisy" with a mockery of heaven. "To whom, my lord? With whom? How am I false?" (40). It is a fair and reasonable question, but Othello cannot answer it because her "obstinacy" and "dissembling" shatter his composure (such as it is), and he is overcome by weeping. But even if he had made an outright accusation at this point, as he does just before strangling her,

132

what difference could it make? Such is belief in the *Othello*
world that her denials only add blacker sins to her guilt and
arouse his ire more. It is difficult to imagine anything that
Cassio might say, were Othello to send for the man and ask
him, that would not simply add to the Moor's conviction and
fury. Even if Emilia were to confess the theft of the handkerchief, it could make no difference, since he now believes her
to be an accomplice in the adultery. The tragic irony of this
play is that truth can be believed only after it has lost its
power to save and has assumed devastating power to torment.

> If haply you my father do suspect
> An instrument of this your calling back,
> Lay not your blame on me. If you have lost him,
> Why, I have lost him too.
>
> (44-47)

This is Desdemona's last attempt to cling to the belief that
something trivial and unconnected with their love is at the
bottom of Othello's passion, though by this time she has good
enough reason to know otherwise. At the same time, the
speech reflects her growing, apprehensive sense of her own
isolation: she had forsaken everything for Othello, and now
he is forsaking her. Once again, pain and erroneous belief
render communication impossible; Othello seems now not
even to be listening to her. Instead he communes with his
own lonely, unendurable grief in a speech which can best be
interpreted as a soliloquy, and a very great one. He has
borne all the hardships of war, and, even if they had been
worse, he could have found the patience to bear all with
equanimity. Enduring the ignominy of the cuckold comes
harder, but even this he could steel himself for.

> But there where I have garnered up my heart,
> Where either I must live or bear no life,
> The fountain from the which my current runs
> Or else dries up—to be discarded thence.
>
> (57-60)

133

These lines better than any other in the canon express the devastation of the subjective world, the attack upon life through those elements that are most essential to it, the undermining of values at their most fundamental, most vulnerable level. The lines that follow capture perfectly the characteristic problem of the Shakespearean tragic hero after his personal world has been destroyed, how to endure what is, for him, simply unendurable:

> —turn thy complexion there,
> Patience, thou young and rose-lipped cherubin!
> Ay, there look grim as hell!
>
> (62-64)

I have never been wholly satisfied with the nickname "brothel" scene for iv.ii. Undeniably, the imagery of the bordello permeates the episode, yet to place exclusive emphasis upon the degradation of Desdemona misses the true pathos of the encounter. Othello's summons to Emilia contains a more appropriate epitome:

> You, mistress,
> That have the office opposite to Saint Peter
> And keep the gate of hell!
>
> (90-93)

It is the hell most characteristic of the *Othello*-world, the isolation of both parties from each other and from all that had constituted the happiness of their lives; the hell of solitary suffering. It is the same hell into which Othello will plunge even deeper when, in the final scene, his crime is revealed and he is left alone with the body of Desdemona.

As in the aftermath of the handkerchief episode, Desdemona's bewilderment goes far beyond perplexity as to why she has been treated thus, and involves the very identity of the man she thought she had known. But whereas before she had tried to assuage harsh reality with a rationalization, to "cheer herself up," to use the term Mr. Eliot offered in such a different context, she is now quite beyond self-delusion,

134

and when Iago offers her her old rationalization (Othello is merely upset by matters of state), she refuses it. Completely cut off from all that constituted her life, she has only her own inner resources to fall back on, and they rise to the occasion in a sudden blossoming and enrichment of the character. Othello in Act I was an easy man to love; Othello in Act IV is impossible to love, but she loves him, nonetheless.

Desdemona's awareness of her own loss, isolation, and vulnerability makes her one of Shakespeare's most moving heroines; yet, I do not think that the remainder of her part is simply the panegyric to the power of love that it has been taken to be, for the inner beauty and selflessness of her character are exactly what render her most vulnerable to the fate that overtakes her. Throughout the last two acts, her character is continually sharpened by contrast with Emilia (whose part grows in direct proportion to the diminishing importance of her husband), and with Bianca. Both the latter are quite capable of dealing with men whom they believe guilty of wrong-doing or duplicity. Desdemona may arraign Othello's unkindness in her mind, but Emilia makes no bones about telling him exactly what she thinks, even at the risk of her life. In the willow scene, Emilia's speech about the relationship between husbands and wives is a side of love Desdemona does not see, a kind of running battle between men and women in which the wives assert their will no less than the husbands, a view used elsewhere by Shakespeare and many others as the basis of comedy. Desdemona's reply, "God me such usage send, / Not to pick bad from bad, but by bad mend!" (IV.iii.103-104), makes her far more moving than Emilia, but also far more fragile. The complementary contrast accounts in part for the pathos of the willow scene, one of Shakespeare's finest lyric accomplishments; that which is of highest value is most easily destroyed, that which is most unselfish is most outrageously violated. Emilia and Bianca are better able to cope with the world, but only by taking part in its coarseness and cynicism. Desdemona steadfastly refuses to do this, placing all her faith in the love that

135

will not alter where it alteration finds, even though she has some premonition what the outcome of such love can be—for Barbary or for herself.

When next we see Othello, he has composed himself so completely as to assuage Lodovico's earlier doubts about his sanity. There is a deadly calm in the way he gives his orders to Desdemona before leaving the house, a calm born of the absolute conviction that what he is about to do must be done. His brief appearance in v.i is a masterful dramatic stroke to maintain continuity and build dramatic tension toward the final scene, even though there is a good deal of complicated business which must be gotten through before the action switches to the chamber.

> 'Tis he. O brave Iago, honest and just,
> That has such noble sense of thy friend's wrong!
> Thou teachest me. Minion, your dear lies dead,
> And your unblest fate hies. Strumpet, I come.
> Forth of my heart those charms, thine eyes, are
>   blotted.
> Thy bed, lust stained, shall with lust's blood
>   be spotted.
>
> (v.i.31-36)

This remarkable speech concentrates in six lines all the erroneous beliefs which govern Othello's conduct—belief that Iago is honest, that Desdemona is a strumpet, that his cause is just, that he can renounce his love and act dispassionately—all this plus one new error: he now believes, contrary to the readily ascertainable facts, that Cassio is dead, and the discovery to the contrary will be the first of many stones from heaven that will fall on him. The speech is a kind of compendium of error and prelude to disaster, couched in deep, stately verse similar to that of the opening soliloquy in v.ii. This combination of calm, sure resolve with multiple error contributes to the dread of the impending catastrophic mistake that is about to be made irrevocable.

136

It is the cause, it is the cause, my soul.
Let me not name it to you, you chaste stars!
It is the cause.

(v.ii.1-3)

Critical interpretation of these lines has generally polarized around either of two possible readings. One interprets "cause" to mean that which produces an effect, i.e. Desdemona's "adultery" is the cause of his doing what he is about to do. The second line of the speech supports this reading strongly: as in iv.ii, he cannot bring himself to name her deed before the chaste natural elements. Other critics, however, interpret "cause" to mean a worthy enterprise which must be championed, and this reading seems in perfect accord with the Moor's insistence that he is proceeding not from a desire for revenge but as heaven's minister of justice. Though I favor the former reading, I do not think we are forced to make an either-or choice between the two. All along, Othello has universalized the implications of Desdemona's "adultery," seeing it not merely as an individual sin but as an affront to nature and heaven. In these lines he is surely speaking of her "adultery" as the cause of his actions; the second line admits no other plausible interpretation. But he is speaking of it in a universalized, abstract sense. He believes that the natural elements and heaven share his repugnance for the vice; hence it is the nature of her "sin" that requires this drastic action. Under no other conceivable circumstances, for no other kind of offence, could he be brought to harm her. In other words, it is not necessary in this case to make a distinction between the universal and particular, the abstract and the concrete meanings of "cause," since the distinction is not present in Othello's own mind. As he sees it, the "cause" of his actions and the "cause" of nature are identical: the abhorrence of beauty in the service of vice. The word "cause" is being used here to serve a double function, to express two meanings so closely related in the mind of the speaker as to be mutual reflections of each other.

137

The insistent repetition portrays a man steeling himself to do what he cannot bear to do.[44] Particularly significant is the line "Should I repent me" (10). Othello not only realizes the finality of his act but also anticipates his own loss and grief once it is consummated: "I will kill thee / And love thee after" (18-19). It is an acceptance of an unendurable lot, to love after he has killed what he loved, yet he feels that it must be so. Furthermore, like "the pity of it, Iago," the line has a gruesome twist of dramatic irony: Othello *will* kill Desdemona and love her after, but in a far different way from how he thinks. The speech is a final recognition on Othello's part of the futility of all his previous renunciations of love. His love for her and his conviction that she must die must coexist, yet the private agony which their coexistence causes momentarily undermines his self-control and elicits from him a reference to the cruelty of the general order of things, of heaven itself.

Of course, no explication of this soliloquy can account for its dark, horrific beauty or haunting power. Othello is summoning the best that is in him and dedicating it to the commission of a ghastly crime, consecrating himself almost ceremonially to error. The magnitude of his error is exceeded only by the terrible intensity with which he believes it and struggles with it. Too often, because Othello is wrong about the basic fact of Desdemona's faithfulness, we tend to dismiss as erroneous everything he says from III.iii until the discovery of the truth late in Act V. This, I feel certain, is a mistake. Othello's suffering and the suffering he imposes is needless and has no foundation in fact, but that only makes it more painful to behold. Moreover, the problems which proceed from his initial mistake are very real problems indeed—problems of belief, order, patience, beauty masking evil, seeming versus being, endurance—in short, all the problems that consistently turn up as the crucial issues of mature Shakespearean tragedy.

[44] See Bayley, *Characters of Love*, p. 169.

138

One significant character trait that Shakespeare has given to Othello is that he always reacts with strong emotion to the immediate and the tangible. As long as he can think of Desdemona's "infidelity" in abstract terms, he can impose upon himself a deadly calm and lethal resolve, but as soon as he is reminded of the physicality of adultery, and the conflict between her beauty and her "lust," he loses control immediately. Thus he has repeatedly renounced his love for her in her absence, but the sight of her is always enough to plunge him back into the torment of loving her though he considers her an adulteress and a hypocrite. In the present scene, as long as she is asleep, he can objectify his predicament and see himself as acting from detached motives of justice, but, as soon as she awakens and pleads her innocence, his composure crumbles and he returns to his principal fixation, obtaining a confession. Even Desdemona's tears become, in his mind, grief for her dead lover. His last attempt to impose emotional distance between himself and his situation fails, and he kills her in a savage burst of passion.

Four and one half acts have now been used to build an amazing construct of errors, lies, blunders, and misunderstandings. Once the tragedy has become irreversible, less than 150 lines suffice to bring the entire structure down in a recognition and reversal unparalleled for power in English drama, or indeed in world drama save only *Oedipus the King.* Othello's discovery of what he has done is reinforced by various mirroring devices—the discovery of the murder, Cassio's discovery of what has been going on all around him without his slightest awareness, Emilia's discovery of her own unwitting complicity in the crime, and everyone's discovery of what "honest" Iago is really like. But in Othello's case, it is not simply *dis*covery of the truth but *re*covery of the truth. He had had the truth at the beginning and had needlessly abandoned it for a passionately held delusion. Now he must face not only the heinousness of what he has done but the needlessness of it as well; having steeled himself to face the worst and deal with it, he discovers he had not even dreamed of what the worst could be. This discovery entails a second devastation of his personal world, the world in which he was a minister of justice eliminating an outrageous insult to nature and heaven. He must not only face a great error and greater loss, but he must come to a completely new evaluation of himself and where he stands in the *Othello*-world. As always at the crucial juncture in mature Shakespearean tragedy, when the hero must make a complete reappraisal of himself and the world, when he discovers that things are the exact opposite of what he thought them to be, there is a period of inner division and confusion, vacillation, and sudden changes of attitude as new values struggle with old for possession of the mind.

Othello's conduct throughout the play has been characterized by total acceptance followed immediately by total recoil, and the fifth act extends that pattern. In attempting to champion honesty, he has destroyed the epitome of honesty, and lost his own honor. His initial reaction is bleak despair, a renunciation of everything: "But why should honor outlive honesty? / Let it go all" (246-247). I think we are to understand this early in the scene that Othello is depicted as resolved upon suicide. Certainly his references to his journey's end and the happiness of dying make it clear that killing himself is not a spur of the moment impulse that occurs to him toward the end of his final speech. Yet no sooner is one course resolved than its opposite asserts itself. Othello's old values of heroic action and martial prowess emerge again from sheer force of habit. "I have another weapon in this chamber" (253), he recalls and challenges Gratiano. We do not need a critic to tell us this challenge is a vain boast; Othello tells us so himself. At the very moment that escape becomes a concrete possibility, its futility becomes apparent, for what he must cope with now, for the first time, is not an armed foe who can be vanquished, but his own enormous guilt. Othello's moment of truth is similar to Oedipus' in that he must cease to regard himself as judge and executioner and see himself as condemned criminal. Moreover, both had exerted

their utmost energies to struggle against what they conceived
to be a malignant fate decreed for them at birth, only to
discover that all their efforts had all along been impelling
them *toward* a fate even more terrible than the one they had
been trying to avoid. It is the devastating irony of this,
coupled with the completeness of the reversal in each case,
that makes the peripeteia of both plays so overwhelming.

Abandoning a clear avenue of escape, Othello resolves to
face not only ignominy and certain death, but also what he
believes to be inevitable damnation. He embraces his own
damnation with ferocious intensity. His despair is not the
chill spiritual atrophy of Macbeth, not even despair at all in
the usual sense. He does not simply lose hope for salvation;
rather he wills his own damnation as the only punishment
commensurate with his guilt.[45] Damnation comes almost as a
relief to Othello; no gulfs of liquid fire could be worse for him
than the sight of Desdemona dead, and it is in that context
that I think we must interpret his remark to Iago: "I'ld have
thee live; / For in my sense, 'tis happiness to die" (v.ii.289-
290). It is also the context in which we must interpret his
actions after the return of Lodovico with Iago. At this point,
all Othello's assumptions have been demolished, and all his
beliefs about himself are shattered. He has lost his love, his
life, and his soul; he has betrayed all the values he sought to
champion; he has literally lost everything that once constituted his world. Moreover, he already thinks of himself
as a dead man. Hamlet had started his final speeches with the
realization, "I am dead," and had then addressed himself to
the problem of perpetuating order and avoiding misunderstandings in the world of the living. Othello, too, is virtually
speaking from the grave, addressing himself to a world of
which he is no longer a part. The story of what has tran-
spired will have to be told in the Venetians' letters, not in
his account of himself during a trial. In Act I, he had

---

[45] Wilson makes a similar point in his introduction to the play:
John Dover Wilson and Alice Walker, eds., *Othello* (Cambridge,
Eng.: Cambridge Univ. Press, 1957), pp. liv-lv.

specifically refused to defend himself privately before Brabantio, preferring to make his explanations to the full Senate. Now he exactly reverses his previous course, preferring to give his account of himself to a small group still shocked by his act, the grisly evidence of which is before them. These two aspects of the Moor's condition—having literally lost everything and already considering himself a dead man—give him a kind of terrible, lonely freedom and detachment from a world of which he is no longer a part. Thus, he is as far from cheering himself up as he is from the previous orgies of self-castigation.[46] It is simply all over.

> LODOVICO: O thou Othello that wert once so good,
>   Fall'n in the practice of a damnèd slave,
>   What shall be said of thee?
>
> OTHELLO: Why, anything:
>   An honorable murderer, if you will;
>   For naught did I in hate, but all in honor.
>   (291-295)

This is grim paradox, not shallow self-justification. It is absolutely essential to keep our attention focused upon both sides of Othello's oxymoron, "honorable murderer," something difficult to do since the noun ironically undercuts its own modifying adjective.[47] The lines epitomize the discrepancy between intention and result which I have argued is essential to the workings of the *Othello*-world. The Moor's reply is bitter self-mockery, not *bovarysme*, and its ironic tone is unmistakably established by the cutting, "Why, anything."

The same kind of bitter retrospection permeates the Moor's final definition of himself in his last speech: "Then must you speak / Of one that loved not wisely, but too well" (343-

[46] Levin effectively refutes Eliot's interpretation of the last speech: "*Othello* and the Motive Hunters," pp. 7-12.

[47] Robert Hapgood, "The Trials of Othello," in *Pacific Coast Studies in Shakespeare*, p. 146.

344). That Othello's conduct was unwise scarcely needs demonstration, but the essence of his unwisdom was not simply gullibility, but rather that, having staked everything upon love, he himself did not have sufficient faith in its power to overcome the obvious obstacles between him and Desdemona. Othello became jealous only when Iago was able to dislodge his confidence in those assumptions upon which his love, his world itself, was founded. "Jealousy and violence are mere indications of the crash of his universe," Julia Wales has observed.[48] Iago's sole genius at intrigue was that he displayed an uncanny ability to search out and exploit exactly those premonitions, doubts, and insecurities which were most vulnerable, those beliefs and confidences which were most tenuous. Iago's ruse would not have deluded any other man, but even an infinitely more intricate and airtight case would not have shaken Othello had not those basic assumptions been undermined and those specific doubts catered to.

The phrase "too well" lies at the heart of the play's complementary thematic structure. It is because Othello staked so much upon love that he reacted so intensely to the belief that love had been betrayed. Jealousy as extreme as Othello's would not have been possible without love as extreme as Othello's. Though love is certainly presented in this play as the most positive and transcendent of all human values, it also, paradoxically and tragically, can provide fuel for the most abhorrent passions once its energies have been perverted. "So sweet was ne'er so fatal" (20), is a complementary phrase that echoes through every line of the tragedy.[49] As with "honorable murderer," the two branches of "not wisely, but too well" must be considered not sequentially but simultaneously, each reflecting upon the other. Had Othello loved more wisely, tragedy could have been averted, but,

---

[48] "Elaboration of the Setting in *Othello*," p. 337.

[49] See Franklin Dickey, *Not Wisely But Too Well* (San Marino, Calif.: Huntington Library, 1957), esp. Chapter II, "The Divided Nature of Love," pp. 19-27. See also Richmond, "Love and Justice," pp. 169-172; and Gardner, "*Othello*: A Retrospect, 1900-67," pp. 9-10.

even in the presence of unwisdom, love could not have plummeted so inexorably into tragedy had it not been for the intensity of the passion and completeness of the hero's involvement in it from the first. In Act I, Othello had felt love, but had incompletely understood what he felt and had underestimated the degree of his own involvement. He had believed Desdemona loved him, but had not grasped the power or durability of her love. Now, surveying these values from the vantage point of having irrecoverably lost them, he understands them only too well:

> . . . of one whose hand,
> Like the base Judean, threw a pearl away
> Richer than all his tribe; of one whose subdued eyes,
> Albeit unused to the melting mood,
> Drop tears as fast as the Arabian trees
> Their med'cinable gum.
>
> (346-351)

Jealousy in Othello is not the antithesis of love so much as it is a dark potentiality of love; what jealousy *is* antithetical to is the affirmation and expansiveness which are also potentialities of love. Jealousy in the *Othello*-world does not destroy love, but rather twists and inverts its energies, transforming it from the most ample of joys to the most abysmal of miseries, from the marriage of true minds to dissolution, isolation, and death.

FOUR

KING LEAR: THE TEMPEST IN THE MIND

FROM the earliest days of his career, Shakespeare appears to have been fascinated by the problematic relationship between the power and powerlessness of the monarch, between the king's divine office and the king's mortality. Reflections upon that conflict constitute the only memorable speech of Henry VI; the insubstantiality of kingly power is Richard II's favorite subject and Henry IV's most unsettling worry; thoughts of his own frailty trouble even the redoubtable Harry the Fifth on the eve of his greatest triumph. Shakespeare renders his definitive treatment of the theme in *King Lear*. In the history plays, however, the struggle for power—its ins and outs, its changing fortunes, personalities, stratagems, machinations, and ultimate outcome—is of paramount interest. In *Lear*, on the other hand, the struggle becomes almost incidental to the real business of the tragedy: the crude wresting of power from the weak by the strong provides the context in which men of extraordinary passion and commitment confront the possibility, indeed the inescapability, of a violent, anarchic universe, wholly without a stable, inherent structure and utterly devoid of meaning. Faced with such a possibility, Lear is forced to ask himself and the cosmos a series of questions, the answers to which hold terrible implications. If the hierarchy of state and family is not real, then what is? If he is not the king, then who or what is he? If the bonds of nature are not sanctioned by divine ordination, then what holds the world together? If the trappings of civilization are superfluous "lendings," then what differentiates man from the animals? If the heavens are indifferent, if they do not love old men, if their sweet sway does not allow—*demand*—obedience, if they themselves are not old except in the myths

145

of a collective imagination, if they do not send down and take the part of outraged kings and wronged fathers, then what becomes of justice and morality? If kingship itself is not a divinely established office, then what is the great image of authority?[1]

More than any other of the mature tragedies, *King Lear* has conveyed the unmistakable impression of creating the unique universe in which it takes place. Critics as far removed from each other in time, technique, and point of view as A. C. Bradley, G. Wilson Knight, and Maynard Mack have all analyzed the universe of *Lear*, and terms such as "*Lear*-world" or its equivalents occur again and again in the work of dozens of commentators.[2] Perhaps the reason for the ubiquitous feeling that the world of *King Lear* is self-created and self-defining is that life in that world is so far removed from literal experience not only of Shakespeare's England but also of any historical period which he might have thought he was recreating. In *Hamlet* and *Othello*, the dramatist relied heavily upon the conventions and trappings of life in Renaissance Europe, but, in *King Lear*, he seemed expressly to avoid transposing the old legend into contemporary times, in contrast to the author of the probable source play, *The True Chronicle History of King Leir*. Nor do I think he was attempting to recreate the atmosphere and life style of an ancient civilization, as he so manifestly was in the Roman plays. Rather, it seems to me, the setting of the *Lear*-world is an amalgam in which borrowings from several different eras and civilizations are fused for particular dramatic purposes, the two most important epochs being the Middle Ages and Shakespeare's own time. *King Lear* is, among many other things, a paradigm of the waning medieval hierarchy confronting the onset of pragmatic materialism. As John Danby has pointed out, it reflects Hooker while anticipating Hobbes.[3]

[1] See Mack, King Lear *in Our Time*, p. 106.

[2] Bradley, pp. 261-273; Knight, pp. 194-226; Mack, King Lear *in Our Time*, pp. 83-117.

[3] *Shakespeare's Doctrine of Nature* (London: Faber and Faber, 1949), p. 18.

In no play since *Richard II* did Shakespeare so conspicuously incorporate the forms, conventions, and ideas of medieval times. The most obvious examples are the pomp and pageantry of the distinctly feudal court in the first scene and the trial by combat in the last, both of which have close parallels in *Richard II*. Far more significant, however, is the inclusion of so many medieval attitudes and ideas, beginning with the idea of kingship itself. When he first appears, Lear is an openly absolute monarch of the kind England had not seen in centuries (if, in fact, it had ever seen one). Claudius, like his Tudor counterparts, had to submit his judgments to a privy council, being careful not to bar their better wisdoms, and the Duke of Venice, like the Stuarts, had a legislative body to deal with. But Lear's word, like Richard's, is absolute law, no matter how rash or foolish that word may be. To disobey, or even to disagree, is tantamount to treason and risks the gravest consequences. Hence there is no middle ground between acquiescence and usurpation, a fact as instrumental to Lear's tragedy as to Richard's.

Moreover, the court which Lear convenes is unmistakably medieval and feudal. References to feudal bonds and the dues of hospitality abound throughout the play, and the concepts of familial, political, and social order reverenced by Lear, Cordelia, Gloucester, Edgar, Kent, and Albany are all firmly rooted in the world-picture of medieval times. In style and manner, too, the court of Lear has none of the elegance and polish which characterize a Renaissance court such as Claudius'. Kent is hardly depicted as having mastered the intricacies of Castiglione, and the principal nobles are warriors rather than courtiers. Moreover, the world outside Lear's court has a distinctly medieval cast, lacking the urban society and middle classes so prominent a part of subsequent civilizations.[4] There are no capitals, no universities, no strolling players, no wealthy centers of commerce in *Lear* as there are in *Hamlet* and *Othello*. The indoor action is set in that bastion of feudal society, the castle-fortress, "this hard house /

---

[4] Noted by Knight, p. 197.

147

More harder than the stones whereof 'tis raised" (III.ii.63-64). We are told that there is a town of Dover, but we never see it; action which is not set in a castle is set in wild, rustic fields, isolated heaths, in hovels, or in the tents of military camps.

Though Shakespeare drew heavily upon the Middle Ages for the setting of *King Lear*, he did not, as in *Richard II*, attempt to give a literal depiction of feudalism in action. Rather, starting from a medieval base, he made certain crucial additions and subtractions. The most significant of the subtractions is, of course, the deletion of the Christian orthodoxy from which the medieval hierarchy had drawn both its rationale and its viability. Instead, the *Lear*-world posits a dubious set of pagan gods drawn anachronistically from Greek and Roman mythology, and an anonymous though energetic principle of Nature. By removing the theological underpinnings of the family and the state, Shakespeare opens for exploration the possibility that such institutions rest not upon immutable order and objective truth, but upon purely human assumptions which sway not as they have power but as they are suffered.

If the removal of the theological basis of hierarchy is Shakespeare's principal subtraction from the basically medieval setting of *Lear*, his most significant addition is the inclusion of an approach to life more characteristic of Renaissance political philosophy than of the court of Edward the Confessor. This view, much in the air in Shakespeare's day, is preached by Edmund and practiced by him, Goneril, Regan, Cornwall, and Oswald. The conflict between good and evil characters is in large measure a conflict between medieval idealism and Renaissance pragmatism. The good characters are deeply concerned about the way things should be, while the wicked ones keep an unblinking eye upon the way things are. Moreover, most members of the good faction, especially Lear, begin with an assumption that there is no discrepancy between the way things should be and the way things are,

148

while the wicked ones, especially Edmund, are acutely aware of the discrepancy and alert to turn it to their advantage.

An understanding of the setting of *King Lear* as an amalgam of medieval and Renaissance cultures and world-views points the way to the definition of those qualities of the *Lear*-world which, for purposes of this study, loom most important. I would summarize them as follows:

The *Lear*-world is very basic.
It is charged at every level with an often ferocious primal energy.
It tends always toward violently opposed extremes.
It is a world of constantly shifting identities.
The *Lear*-world is complementary.

"Basic" is perhaps a peculiar word to apply to the world of a play, but I can think of no other which better describes the way that all things in this tragedy, including the dramaturgy itself, have been stripped down, literally, to the essentials.[5] The conflicts and issues are of the most basic kind, centering on the two most fundamental units of society, the family and the state. Moreover, the conflicts which break out within these two basic units are not merely disruptive but tend to annihilate the institutions themselves. The sources of conflict are essential to the human condition and transcend particular details of time, place, or systems of social organization: age versus youth, individualism versus communality, order versus anarchy, moral significance versus emptiness and absurdity, supernaturalism versus empiricism, wealth versus poverty, justice versus injustice, endurance versus despair or rebellion, reverence for tradition versus scorn for convention—the list could be considerably lengthened. Everything is reduced to the lowest denominator for presentation with the utmost clarity and power. From the first scene onward, the

[5] See L. C. Knights, "*King Lear* as Metaphor," in *Myth and Symbol*, ed. Bernice Slote (Lincoln: Univ. of Nebraska Press, 1963), pp. 28-29.

action strives relentlessly to peel away layer upon layer of all that is incidental or merely assumed, and to arrive at the bedrock of absolute reality—the true identity of man, the real nature of society, the cause of evil, the value of existing at all. Nothing, absolutely nothing, is given or assumed in the *Lear*-world.[6] Any course of action is judged not upon the correctness of its principles, but upon the consequences it produces. Each belief, system, and individual identity must stand the proof of action, and if it cannot stand that test, not even its right to exist is granted.

The basicness of the *Lear*-world is everywhere evident in the dramaturgy. If the action of *Hamlet* may properly be called elliptical, *King Lear* is unstintingly linear, proceeding without digression or abatement from its startlingly abrupt beginning to its apocalyptic end. Time and space are drastically compressed so that incidents which would require many months seem to take place in a matter of days or even of hours. As if driven by storms and demons, the action plunges headlong to its conclusion. So economical is the dramaturgy of *Lear* that many of its most memorable points are made not through spoken words but through a series of intense visual images.[7] The action is ingeniously wrought to produce situations which I think may be properly called visual metaphors, situations which assume emblematic meaning and communicate directly through the eye, largely bypassing language. For example, there is the mock trial in which a madman, a naked beggar, and a fool sit in judgment on a joint stool, or the image of the madman leading the blind man. Tom O'Bedlam himself becomes such a visual metaphor in Lear's eyes, and in ours, when the King asks us to consider him well. The image of a mad king outlandishly decked and crowned with

[6] L. C. Knights, "*King Lear* and the Great Tragedies," p. 232.

[7] For an interesting discussion of Shakespeare's use of the visual dimension of theater, see Inga Stina Ewbank, " 'More Pregnantly Than Words': Some Uses and Limitations of Visual Symbolism," *Shakespeare Survey* 24 (1971), 13-18, esp. 17-18.

wild flowers, presiding over a wholly imaginary kingdom is another such metaphor which conveys at least as much meaning visually as by what is spoken. And in the final scene, the stage-direction, "Enter Lear, with Cordelia in his arms," says all that can be said, leaving as the only possible elaboration Lear's inarticulate "Howl, howl, howl!"

In the *Lear*-world, nothing is done either in leisure or in moderation. Violent energy charges the action, the characterization, and the imagery, and is apparent at all levels—in human affairs, in the natural elements, and in the heavens as variously envisioned by Lear, Edmund, and Gloucester. More often than not, the enormous energy of the *Lear*-world is expended in disruption and upheaval. Of course, the most obvious manifestation of violent, primal energies is the storm which rages throughout six of the central scenes; no ordinary tempest this, it seems almost to possess the apocalyptic qualities Lear demands of it. Something of the same energy seems to charge every one of the major characters, conferring upon them extraordinary strength either to inflict or to endure. Edmund pursues his intrigues with a ferret-like busyness that exceeds even Iago's. Goneril and Regan also go promptly and swiftly about their devastating business, moving on a tight schedule, impelled by the feeling that there is not a moment to lose. "We must do something, and i' th' heat," Goneril urges her only slightly less energetic sister (I.i.306). Edgar practices his disguise with manic intensity, pursuing or fleeing from his imaginary fiends. Kent from the first has too much energy for his own good. Cordelia, we are told, is always queen of her passion, which seeks to be king of her; but beneath the gentleness and compassion which come as such a relief in Act IV pulses the vital energy of the *Lear*-world. Her will is the equal of her father's, she is no less prompt than Kent to speak her mind, and, in Act V, she becomes one of three ladies we see going off to war with the men. "Shall we not see these daughters and these sisters?" (V.iii.7), she asks when she is taken prisoner. One can indeed

151

imagine that she has a word or two to say to them. Even suffering, that most characteristic activity of the *Lear*-world, is imbued with the energy of the *Lear*-world. Gloucester's despair is extraordinarily vigorous; rather than quietly stab or hang himself, he will walk to Dover, climb a hill, address the gods, and hurl himself from a cliff. When he has been half-cozened and half-cajoled out of this course of action by Edgar, his resolution embraces an almost superhuman ideal of endurance:

> Henceforth I'll bear
> Affliction till it do cry out itself
> 'Enough, enough, and die.'
>
> (IV.vi.75-77)

The metaphysical universe of *King Lear* is also imbued with the primal force we find in the natural elements and in the characters. In marked contrast to *Othello* and *Macbeth*, there is no clearly defined metaphysical system presumed in the world of *King Lear*; rather, each of the major characters attempts to project upon a neutral and inscrutable universe a particular concept of the forces which presumably govern it.[8] Each defines the universe differently, but they all impute to it the energy and force so characteristic of the play. The King's gods, like the rhetoric of his invocations to them, have a distinctly Old Testament character, despite the surface trapping of classical paganism. They are gods and wrath and judgment who will seek out their enemies for swift and terrible vengeance, and will inundate ungrateful man in a second deluge. The gods that Gloucester ultimately comes to believe in torture and kill men for their savage sport. The goddess Nature, to whom Edmund's services are bound, is cast in his own energetic image:

[8] See Danby, *Shakespeare's Doctrine of Nature*, p. 181. Also Robert Heilman, *This Great Stage* (1948; rpt. Seattle: Univ. of Washington Press, 1963), p. 115; Dowden, pp. 239-240; Knight, pp. 204-209.

Who, in the lusty stealth of nature, take
More composition and fierce quality
Than doth, within a dull, stale, tirèd, bed,
Go to th' creating a whole tribe of fops
Got 'tween asleep and wake?

(I.ii.11-15)

As far as he is concerned, it is the very energy of nature that renders him superior to his conventional, legitimate brother. The values of Christianity—charity, forgiveness, compassion—we identify with Cordelia, but in her they are raised to the status of heroic virtue, the stuff that martyrs are made of. And, of course, towering over all this turbulent and energetic world is the titanic energy of Lear himself—Lear, with his implacable "constant will," vehemently insisting that things be as he demands or cease to be at all; Lear, flying into apocalyptic rages, thundering at the elements, in madness marshalling imaginary forces and furiously indicting his imaginary subjects, and finally, at the threshold of death, killing the rugged soldier Edmund has bribed to hang Cordelia and bearing her body from the prison.

Because the issues of the *Lear*-world are the most basic in human experience, and because the exploration of these issues is animated by surging, primal energy, all elements in the world of the play seem to be pushed almost from the outset to violently conflicting extremes. The middle-ground, which forms so much of life in even turbulent or disruptive times, is eliminated entirely, and life seems to be lived at one or another of its outermost limits. For instance, one main line of development is the conflict between youth and age, and the *Lear*-world seems to be populated largely by people who are either very old or fairly young. Among all the major characters, only Kent is depicted as being of middle years, and, indeed, his stated age of forty-eight conflicts so noticeably with certain aspects of his character that Bradley envisioned him as much older (pp. 308-309). While I think

153

we must take Shakespeare at his word about Kent's age, still it is undeniable that by the end of the play the Earl has aged considerably from the vigorous ruffian of Act I to a tired old man longing for death.

So intent was Shakespeare upon emblemizing the conflict between youth and age by pushing both to extremes and eliminating the middle that he presented us with a rather peculiar family. Lear is over eighty, yet he has only three daughters, the youngest of whom is not yet married and the eldest of whom has not yet borne children. That is, we may assume the dramatist intended them to be played as ranging in age from the late teens to perhaps the middle twenties. While such a situation is not impossible, it is most certainly not usual, especially in royal families. This is not in the least to worry the question of how many wives had King Lear, a question the play does not encourage or permit us to ask. The point is that Shakespeare has set young daughters against a father easily old enough to be their great-grandfather in order to sharpen the basic conflict by pushing it to its extremes. There is a parallel example in *Timon of Athens*, a play close to *Lear* in chronology and themes. In the great tirade outside the walls of the city, Timon rants:

> Son of sixteen,
> Pluck the lined crutch from thy old limping sire;
> With it beat out his brains!
>
> (IV.i.13-15)

Now sons of sixteen do not usually have fathers quite so decrepit, but the purpose here, as in *Lear*, was not to render the typical but to find in the extreme an emblem of the basic conflict.

Though the pattern of conflict between a very old king and the very young daughters was part of Shakespeare's inheritance from all his probable sources, he has intensified it by doubling it: white-bearded Gloucester has two sons who are obviously portrayed as very young, perhaps not having reached their majority. Moreover, throughout the world of the play, there is none of the balanced gradation of ages we find not only in real life but also in the worlds of *Hamlet, Othello,* and *Macbeth.* No specific ages are given for Albany and Cornwall, and while neither impresses us as a beardless youth, there are indications in the text that Shakespeare intended them to be cast as relatively young men. Cornwall addresses Kent as "old fellow," and "You stubborn ancient knave, you reverent braggart" (ii.ii.80,121), scarcely terms which one middle-aged man would be expected to use to another. Edgar's "we that are young" (v.iii.326) presumably includes Albany (since it can scarcely include Kent), and there is just a possibility that this speech may actually have been delivered by Albany since the Quarto text assigns it to him. The Fool is essentially ageless, though throughout he is addressed and treated as a child. Even many of the anonymous functional characters are portrayed as very old or very young. Oswald can best be imagined as a young man out to make a career for himself by whatever means prove expedient. Cornwall's servant is younger than Cornwall, while Gloucester's tenant is the second octogenarian we see in the play.

The same emphasis upon extremes characterizes the social situation of the *Lear*-world. The two boundaries of the social scale are the absolute top and the absolute bottom, royalty and penury, the king and the naked beggar. Toward one or another of these extremes every one of the major characters is inexorably drawn. Goneril, Regan, Edmund, Cornwall, and initially perhaps Albany are locked in a life and death struggle for possession of no less than all. Conversely, when Lear, Cordelia, Gloucester, Kent, and Edgar fall upon ill fortune, they are all reduced, in one way or another to

> the basest and most poorest shape
> That ever penury, in contempt of man,
> Brought near to beast.
>
> (ii.iii.7-9)

Vulnerable, despised, humiliated, and homeless, they all at one time or another possess "nothing," that word that echoes so sepulchrally throughout the world of the play. The epitome of these extremes is Lear himself, who goes with dizzying speed from the pomp and power of the first scene to the desolation of the heath, where he attempts to rip off his "lendings" and become the thing itself, thus traversing the whole social spectrum of the *Lear*-world.

As with the conflict between youth and age, the middle ground of the social spectrum, which might lend some balance and normalcy to the *Lear*-world, has been almost entirely omitted. The nobles are shut up in their castles and the beggars are shut out on the heath. The minor characters, who in the histories and comedies, and in such tragedies as *Hamlet*, lend balance and proportion to the play-world, are kept nameless and faceless in *King Lear*—a gentleman, an officer, servants to Cornwall, an old man, a doctor, a herald. Their appearances are brief and their roles are transparently functional; they are not individuated by the quirks their counterparts so frequently display in the rest of the canon. They are given no opportunity to distract our attention from the conflict between the two significant extremes, king and beggar.

As I suggested at the beginning of this chapter, the two concepts of social and political organization depicted in *King Lear* are also extreme examples of the political outlooks which coexisted in an uneasy and doomed compromise in Shakespeare's England. In the early scenes of the play, the older hierarchical system is pushed to its extreme and falters. Age and position are given absolute sway, and act with incredible folly. Conversely, in the later scenes, the new order of individualism and ruthless opportunism is also pushed to its extreme, and it, too, falters. Neither the old nor the new can stand the proof of action: when their principles are followed with single-minded determination to their logical conclusions, both finally destroy themselves.

156

The emotions and attitudes which the various characters register also shun moderation to epitomize extremes. Thus we have the bestial cruelty of Cornwall against the angelic kindness of Cordelia, the apocalyptic rage of Lear against the superhuman patience of Edgar. Kent's loyalty is completely without reservation while Edmund's opportunism is utterly without scruple. Gloucester's despair is abysmal and unmitigated, yet hope is indomitable and unquenchable in the *Lear*-world even at its worst. Joy, what there is of it in this play, is ecstatic, almost celestial, while the sorrow which inevitably displaces it is such as flesh and blood should not be called upon to bear. Frequently the two are placed in stark contrast within a single scene or even within a single speech, as in Lear's comparison of Cordelia to a soul in bliss while he is bound upon a wheel of fire, or in the description of Gloucester's death, or in Lear's final agony where illusory joy is juxtaposed against the all too factual sorrow.

Many critics, most notably Danby, Heilman, and Mack, have pointed out the importance of relatedness in the play; but, as Mack has observed, the problem of identity precedes the problem of relatedness.[9] The basic question is not "how is this related to that," but rather, "exactly what is it that is related to what?" What is a king? What is a father? What is "natural"? Who is a madman? Who is blind? Who is a fool? Is identity fixed and immutable or is it arbitrary and fragile, built from the curiosity of nations and plague of custom and resting upon a foundation of nothing? What is man himself? These questions underlie the rapid, frequent shifts of identity and the search for the bedrock of identity which form such an important part of the action.

Edmund's identity, for instance, is self-defined and self-imposed, and depends upon his ability to manipulate external circumstances to his advantage. He means to become a self-made man in the most literal sense of the term. Man, in his

[9] King Lear *in Our Time*, pp. 109-110; Danby, pp. 43-46; Heilman, *This Great Stage*, pp. 117-123.

view, starts out with what nature has given him, and what he makes of it is entirely in his own hands. Edmund considers himself distinctly superior raw material, but the identity which the curiosity of nations and the plague of custom have assigned him is wholly unsatisfactory. He makes a steady climb up the social scale of the *Lear*-world, and throughout his changes in fortune, his sense of his own identity never falters as long as his theory of self-definition works out well. But the trial by combat, if it does not prove that the gods are just, at least does prove that physically Edgar is the better man, a direct negation of Edmund's initial contention that he had drawn better parts and fiercer qualities from the lusty stealth of nature. His confidence in his own nature crumbles, and he undergoes a startling reversal, accepting that to show mercy might be "some good," an idea he had contemptuously rejected during his meteoric rise. Still, Edmund's self-made identity is one of the more stable in the play, so stable, in fact, that his sudden conversion is, if not unconvincing, at least not very compelling either in the text or in the theater.

Edgar's career is the opposite of his brother's. He plummets from the rather comfortable position of heir to an earldom to that of a hunted criminal, and rises again agonizingly back to the earldom and perhaps to the throne itself. Superimposed upon this quick fall and slow rise in fortunes is a startling progression of disguises and incognito appearances. Muriel Bradbrook has pointed out that disguise in Elizabethan-Jacobean drama, far from being merely a device to advance plot, is primarily "the substitution, overlaying or metamorphosis of dramatic identity, whereby one character sustains two roles."[10] Edgar, then, can best be regarded as multiple personae rather than a single characterization.[11] As Edgar, son of Gloucester, he is important to the play, but rather un-

[10] "Shakespeare and the Use of Disguise in Elizabethan Drama," *Essays in Criticism*, 2 (1952), 160.

[11] Kirschbaum provides a detailed analysis of Edgar and his disguises in *Character and Characterization in Shakespeare*, pp. 59-75.

interesting in himself. His disguises, however, are extraordinary both in conception and execution, and the first identity he assumes, the bare, forked animal, unaccommodated man, becomes a central image of the play. After his meeting with his blind father, his personae progress through peasant, soldier, knight incognito, and perhaps to king. The rapid fall and slow rise of his fortunes suggest that the *Lear*-world, having been dismantled from the top down, must be reassembled slowly and painfully from the bottom up. Moreover, the progression of assumed identities portrays the narrow distance between nobleman and beggar, accommodated man and the forked animal, and provides the context for the most sweeping question of identity which the play poses: "Is man no more than this?" (III.iv.97-98). When Lear asks us to consider him well, what we see is not a disguised noble whom the King mistakenly thinks a real Bedlam beggar; we see what Lear sees, man stripped of all his sophistications.

For Gloucester, the problem of identity is twofold, discovering his own identity and correctly identifying the world around him. When we first see Gloucester, he fairly exudes self-satisfaction, making jokes about his earlier exploits and congratulating himself on his own magnanimity. After the agony of his ordeal, however, he redefines the man he was as "the superfluous and lust-dieted man . . . that will not see / Because he does not feel" (IV.i.67-69). His failure to correctly perceive the true natures of his sons leads to the necessity of asking the identity of everyone he encounters. He must redefine not only himself but also the gods whom he has always felt to be in such immediate and influential contact with the affairs of men. In Act IV, they appear alternately to be the "kind gods" who, despite their manifest unkindness, must still be venerated and obeyed, and the "wanton gods" whose vindictive sport makes man's life a cruel joke. The problem of correctly identifying external reality is brilliantly dramatized by the conjunction of Gloucester's blindness and Edgar's disguise. Throughout his search for the correct identity of things, Gloucester takes the man who guides him for a

159

naked beggar, one whose speech is suddenly improved, a grotesque fiend, a poor man made tame by fortune's blows, and a trusty peasant, before correctly perceiving him as the man whom he had wanted to encounter more than anyone in the world. So, too, in the great meeting between Lear and Gloucester, blindness, madness, and the inversion of values are all focused upon the problem of perceiving the true identity of those in the *Lear*-world, of seeing how the world goes and being able to distinguish which is the justice and which the thief.

The problem of identity receives its fullest treatment in the main plot, centering on the figure of Lear. "He hath ever but slenderly known himself" (i.i.292-293), we are told of him early in the action. Yet, when he first appears, Lear is absolutely certain about who he is: he is *The King*. That the king may be a thing of nothing would never occur to him, and, when it proves to be the case, his identity, which he has defined largely in terms of his place in a supposedly immutable hierarchy, begins rapidly to disintegrate. "Who am I," he asks Oswald facetiously, confident that the only possible reply is the one he has always received: "His Majesty, the King!" When the servant pipes back, "My lady's father," Lear is thunderstruck (i.iv.75-76). It is the first of many times that Lear will pose the question in one form or another, and the first of many unsettling replies he will receive. The Fool has a good deal to say on the subject of Lear's identity, and saying it is one of the principal functions of this fascinating character. Lear has made his daughters his mothers, the Fool informs him in an image both comic and cruel; he has exchanged his position as parent for that of a child awaiting chastisement. The King is by turns a bitter fool, Lear's shadow, a shealed peascod, and, finally, nothing. The destruction of Lear's subjective world, so overwhelmingly complete, begins with the destruction of his identity.[12]

[12] See Manfred Weidhorn, "The Relation of Title and Name to Identity in Shakespearean Tragedy," *Studies in English Literature 1500-1900*, 9 (1969), 303-319, esp. 306-310.

The final quality of the *Lear*-world which I propose to consider here is its complementarity, the way in which Gloucester's "And that's true too," sounds a note which reverberates throughout the length and breadth of the drama.[13] There is no more striking evidence of the complementarity of *King Lear* than the remarkable division of the criticism into two mutually exclusive factions. Of course, all the plays of Shakespeare engender varying interpretations, and there seem to be as many readings of *Hamlet* as there are critics who have commented upon it. But only in the case of *Lear* is criticism so sharply divided between an interpretation which sees it as the most glorious and transcendent dream of human redemption ever conceived, and one that sees it as the most unstintingly pessimistic indictment of the absurd human condition ever written.[14] In reviewing the peculiar critical history of the play, John Rosenberg has remarked, "each assertion in the play confronts a counter-assertion, and all interpretations contain the seed of their refutation."[15] It seems to me that the only plausible reason for this phenomenon is that *King Lear* embodies two views of life's potentials, and that these views or attitudes are diametrically opposed in such a way that each must logically exclude the other. Yet, there they exist together, side by side, in perfect artistic unity and

[13] The duality of the play has long been recognized, though perhaps no subsequent critic has ever equalled Dowden's comment (p. 230). Bradley suggested that the *Lear*-world is Empedoclean (p. 263), an idea expanded by E. Catherine Dunn in "The Storm in *King Lear*," *Shakespeare Quarterly*, 3 (1952), 329-333. See also Heilman, *This Great Stage*, pp. 178-179; John Lothian, King Lear: *A Tragic Reading of Life* (Toronto: Clark, Irwin, 1949), p. 35; George Duthie and J. Dover Wilson, eds., *King Lear* (Cambridge, Eng.: Cambridge Univ. Press, 1960), pp. xliv-xlvii; Rabkin, *Shakespeare and the Common Understanding*, pp. 10-11.

[14] Nicholas Brooke presents an excellent survey of the divided opinion in "The Ending of *King Lear*," in *Shakespeare 1564-1964*, ed. Edward Bloom (Providence, R.I.: Brown University Press, 1964), pp. 71-78.

[15] "King Lear and His Comforters," *Essays in Criticism*, 16 (1966), 144.

161

harmony in the play. The dreadful way things have of working out in the *Lear*-world never allows us to dismiss the possibility that the world as seen by Edmund and Cornwall, by Gloucester in despair and by Lear in madness is, in fact, the *Lear*-world as it really is. Yet, at the same time that this abominable vision is being forced upon us most relentlessly, we are also kept aware of the intrinsic values represented by Cordelia, Edgar, Kent, and by Lear after the reconciliation.

If in one sense *King Lear* is the confrontation between order and chaos, between age and youth, between the waning Middle Ages and ascendant modernism, in a much more fundamental sense it is the confrontation between ethics and experience. Ethics and experience are the two principal poles of the *Lear* dialectic, and that dialectic is complementary in that both elements have inexorable demands to make and there is no resolution or meeting ground between them. As the play clearly demonstrates, there must be ethics if life is to continue, let alone be endurable. But the play no less clearly demonstrates that at every turn experience is an overmatch for ethical values. Though Edgar does kill Edmund and the wicked characters do prey upon themselves like monsters of the deep, yet a dog, a horse, a rat *has* life and Cordelia no breath at all. The *Lear* dialectic forces us at once to assent to both the necessity and intrinsic worth of ethical values, but at the same time to contemplate the utter inability of such values to cope with experience. Thus it seems to me that "optimism" and "pessimism" as terms to describe the vision behind *Lear* are wholly beside the point. Neither one is capable of including the whole picture. O. J. Campbell and Jan Kott demonstrate between them that one can posit a wholly redemptive or wholly absurdist interpretation of this tragedy only by ignoring at least half of it.[16]

[16] O. J. Campbell, "The Salvation of Lear," *ELH*, 15 (1948), 93-109; Jan Kott, " '*King Lear*' or *End Game*," in *Shakespeare Our Contemporary*, trans. Boleslaw Taborski, 2nd ed. (London, Methuen, 1967), pp. 100-133.

A comparatively minor incident demonstrates, perhaps even better than Gloucester's "And that's true too," the complementary mode of vision which underlies the tragedy. I refer to the scene in which a messenger reports to Albany the death of Cornwall:

MESSENGER: O, my good lord, the Duke of Cornwall's dead,
Slain by his servant, going to put out
The other eye of Gloucester.

ALBANY: Gloucester's eyes?

MESSENGER: A servant that he bred, thrilled with remorse,
Opposed against the act, bending his sword
To his great master; who, thereat enraged,
Flew on him, and amongst them felled him dead;
But not without that harmful stroke which since
Hath plucked him after.

ALBANY: This shows you are above,
You justicers, that these our nether crimes
So speedily can venge. But, O poor Gloucester,
Lost he his other eye?

MESSENGER: Both, both, my lord.

(IV.ii.70-81)

There is justice in Cornwall's death, though it is achieved not by the supernatural forces envisioned by Albany, but by the common humanity of the servant, thrilled with remorse and opposed against the deed, an opposition which we have no alternative but to admire and share. Yet Gloucester lost both eyes. The promptings of outraged humanity and the ineffectuality of those promptings in experience are the poles of the *Lear* dialectic. From the tension between them arise other complementary oppositions, all centered upon the principal problem of the *Lear*-world, how is existence to be endured.

163

Having sketched in what appear to me to be the essential qualities of life in the *Lear*-world, I turn now to direct analysis of the action and of its central facet, the destruction of the hero's subjective world. The startlingly abrupt first scene of *King Lear* has engendered an enormous amount of critical commentary, much of it centering upon the kind of dramaturgy Shakespeare employed, for it is clearly different from his usual methods of beginning a tragedy and introducing the hero. From his earliest plays onward, Shakespeare usually constructed characterizations sequentially; that is, the character unfolds before our eyes gradually, and we get to know a fair amount about him before he performs his most crucial actions. Thus, Hamlet soliloquizes, philosophizes, and discourses upon a variety of subjects, including himself, before he confronts the Ghost. We see Othello before he is jealous, and are shown Iago's plot developing gradually in his mind from its first inception. Nothing of the kind occurs in *King Lear*. The old monarch walks out, sits down on the throne, and without preliminaries proceeds to commit several of the most astounding blunders anywhere in world drama. At this point in the play, we know nothing of what is going on inside his mind, nothing of what the declarations of love mean to him or why he chose this particular contest when he has obviously determined beforehand what each of his daughters will receive. It is only *after* the irrevocable action has been consummated and the King has exited that we begin to get essential information about him, starting with the crucial "He hath ever but slenderly known himself." If Lear's initial action startles and nonpluses us when it occurs, when we look back on it from the vantage point of Act III or later, knowing what we do by then of Lear and his world, his idiosyncrasies and irascibilities of Act I are perfectly consistent with his character and world-view. Lear's world makes sense to him, but we do not find out what kind of sense until by his own actions he has undermined its foundations. The kind of reason, or more exactly, the specific kind of unreason behind his early blunders becomes gradually more

164

clear and convincing as we come to understand the terms in which he uses the world in which he lives. This delay in presenting what would ordinarily be antecedent information is, so far as I can see, the only departure Shakespeare has made from his usual dramatic practice. Apropos of this, we may note that, increasingly in the Jacobean plays, Shakespeare unveiled his main characters fully formed and of a single piece without much in the way of preliminaries or self-revelation. Antony, Cleopatra, Coriolanus, Timon, and Leontes all burst upon the scene fully developed and swing right into action. What we find out about their internal complexities, we find out after they have completed the startling initial actions that lead directly to their misfortunes. Moreover, Lear is markedly different from the other Shakespearean tragic heroes in that he is initially defined almost entirely in terms of his misconceptions about himself and those around him.[17] Our knowledge of him increases as he learns about himself, and hence we are more intimately involved in the process of his self-discovery.

But what, ultimately, *are* we to make of the love contest and parceling out of the realm? The text makes clear that the King has already divided the realm and reserved the fairest portion for Cordelia, who will speak last.[18] Obviously, then, what the three daughters say will have no effect upon what they are to receive, as long as all three are willing to obey their father's command that they make a formal declaration of their love to him. The emphasis of the entire contest is not upon loving but upon *saying*, beginning with Lear's opening inquiry, "Which of you shall we say doth love us most" (I.i.51). The words "say" and "speak" are reiterated again and again throughout the scene: "Goneril, / Our eldest-born,

[17] See Warren Taylor, "Lear and the Lost Self," *College English*, 25 (1964), 509-511.

[18] Dr. Johnson thought this fact "an obscurity or inaccuracy in this preparatory scene" (*Johnson on Shakespeare*, p. 659). Coleridge discusses its significance (*Coleridge's Shakespearean Criticism*, I, 55), and Bradley elaborates on Coleridge (pp. 249-251).

speak first" (53-54). "What says our second daughter" (67). "What can you say to draw / A third more opulent than your sisters? Speak" (85-86). "Nothing will come of nothing. Speak again" (90). "Mend your speech a little" (94). The protestations of Goneril and Regan do not smack of the oily hypocrisy which Shakespeare could portray so subtly when he wished. Rather, they are formal set pieces which give the distinct impression of having been memorized for the occasion.[19] They have the inflated cadence of court ceremony, and their extravagant compliments are like the comparisons of courtly poetry, expected by convention but hardly taken literally—at least not by Lear. He receives each of the two declarations without comment, delivering the goods he had already set aside once the formalities are dispensed with. What Lear is indulging in is not a sentimental desire for flattery, but rather a determination to have his exalted position venerated. In the love trial, as in so many medieval ceremonies, the act of saying is itself the significant gesture by which obligations under a stratified system are formally fixed and acknowledged.[20] Lear's final court ceremony is to be a demonstration and celebration of his position as king and father, as well as a formal, public acknowledgment of what is owed him. Indeed, what is owed him is a major preoccupation of Lear throughout the first three acts of the tragedy. The difficulty is that he has not only a wildly extravagant notion of what is owed him but also a naïve assumption that his due will be paid after the real basis of his power has been given away.

Cordelia's actions in the first scene are even more perplexing than her father's. Once again, we know nothing

---

[19] Simon O. Lesser records a similar feeling about these speeches in "Act One, Scene One, of Lear," *College English*, 32 (1970), 161. Beyond this, similarities between Professor Lesser's reading and my own emphatically end.

[20] For a full discussion of Shakespeare's use of ritual in *King Lear* and elsewhere, see William Frost, "Shakespeare's Rituals and the Opening of *King Lear*," *Hudson Review*, 10 (1958), 577-585.

about the character before she performs what proves to be a crucial action; she speaks a scant three lines before she utters the fateful "Nothing" which will launch the play upon its increasingly turbulent course. Like Goneril, Regan, and Edmund, she is less a psychological study than a principle or point of view carried to its conclusion; she does not compromise her principles in this scene because to a large extent she *is* her principles. The characterization operates along a few simple but rigorously consistent lines with all superfluities removed; it shares in the basicness, energy, and extremism of the *Lear*-world. Her actions are grounded upon love that springs not from obligation but from spontaneous human impulses, and expresses itself not in words but in actions. In her speeches throughout the scene, the tension between speech and act is almost as prominent as the tension between seeming and being in the early lines of Hamlet; she can scarcely open her mouth without referring to it. As Muir has suggested, the tardiness in nature, which often leaves the history unspoke that it intends to do, is a constant of the characterization.[21] "Love and be silent," could well serve as an epigraph for the role. When Lear demands an acknowledgment of what is owed him, she pays him in his own coin: "I love your Majesty / According to my bond, no more nor less" (92-93). However, when Lear is in need of succor, she loves far beyond the bond; ironically enough, she leaves her husband to love her father all.

The argument that it would not have hurt her to bend a little and humor an old man's whim misses a major point about the nature of the world in which *King Lear* takes place:[22] the middle ground, the only natural habitat of compromise, has been eliminated with respect to all characters and virtually all issues. Words mean one thing to Lear and quite another to Cordelia, because he defines his world al-

[21] Kenneth Muir, "Madness in *King Lear*," *Shakespeare Survey*, 13 (1960), 38.

[22] Coleridge suggests this attitude (I, 60-61), and Bradley elaborates it (pp. 320-321).

most exclusively in terms of a given hierarchy in which his own position is peerless, whereas she defines hers by the strength and immediacy of her emotions. If, in refusing to do as she is told, she is striking a blow at the basis of his identity, in asking her to make love a formal political act, he is tampering pretty drastically with the basis of hers. Goneril, always a shrewd tactical judge, sizes up the situation correctly: "You have obedience scanted" (278). Moreover, her father is scarcely less clear-headed about what Cordelia's "Nothing" means. When Kent says, "Thy youngest daughter does not love thee least" (152), he is not telling Lear anything that Lear does not know already. As I say, love has very little to do with the goings on in the play at this early stage. Before long we will see a Lear who *does* become convinced his daughters do not love him, a Lear whose wrath is choked with tears and laced with self-pity. There is none of that in the present scene: "Let pride, which she calls plainness, marry her" (129). Moreover, his treatment of Kent is exactly the same as his treatment of Cordelia, because he believes them guilty of the same sin, strained pride that comes between his sentence and his power, which neither his nature nor his place (as he conceives them at this point) can bear.

All of the foregoing is certainly not to say that Lear commits no errors in scene i; it is to say that the errors he commits have nothing whatever to do with sentimental self-indulgence, susceptibility to flattery, or the inability to discern the true nature and degree of his daughters' devotion. Lear's misconceptions are more deep-seated than that, misinterpretations of the nature of reality as a whole, rather than isolated mistakes about an individual character or situation. The delusions under which the King is laboring when he first sets foot on stage are legion, but they all stem from two false assumptions: first, that identity is inherent in an individual, is stable and immutable, and is defined largely by one's place in a fixed hierarchy; second, that the forces of nature and his own indomitable will are in such close harmony as to be practically synonymous. Lear has a great deal to learn about the facts of life in the *Lear*-world, but what gets him into trouble initially is not what he does not know but what he mistakenly thinks he does know.

In the first place, he is under the impression that his proclamations are permanent, that what he decrees must remain in effect until he himself revokes it. A preoccupation with permanence, a conviction about the durability of the arrangements he is making, runs through his speeches. Bestowing upon Goneril her share of the kingdom, he says, "To thine and Albany's issues / Be this perpetual" (66-67). To Regan he says, "To thee and thine hereditary ever / Remain this ample share of our fair kingdom" (79-80). Cordelia's rejection is also in perpetuity: "And as a stranger to my heart and me / Hold thee from this for ever" (115-116). Kent's banishment has the same ring of finality. Lear fails to see the political unwisdom of what he is doing because he thinks that future strife may be avoided now: no son-in-law or daughter could conceive of violating an arrangement settled for once and for all by his royal word.[23] Of course, in the reality of the *Lear*-world, the dukes have hardly returned to their respective castles before they are rumored to be casting predatory eyes upon each other's portion.

Lear divides more than a kingdom; he divides kingship itself by distinguishing between the name and the addition to a king, and the sway, revenue, and execution of the rest.[24] That the former may be wholly dependent upon the latter never occurs to him because his false assumptions are so

[23] John Holloway, in *The Story of the Night* (London: Routledge, 1961), p. 80, points to parallel divisions in *Gorboduc, The Misfortunes of Arthur, Selimus, Woodstock,* and *Locrine,* noting that parceling out a kingdom was always regarded as an unwise move that either threatened or precipitated disaster.

[24] Josephine Bennett, in "The Storm Within: The Madness of Lear," *Shakespeare Quarterly,* 13 (1962), 151-153, discusses the incongruity of Lear's desire to be king in honor but not in responsibility.

169

fundamental to his world-view that he never even thinks to question them.[25] He does not see, as his elder daughters (and in another way, his Fool) plainly do, that a king who has given away his power and wealth is simply no king at all, but an idle old man, a shealed peascod, or nothing. Lear assumes that his kingship, virtually the entirety of his identity at this point, rests upon his "nature" and his "place," while in the reality of the *Lear*-world, which takes nothing for granted, it rests upon his power.[26] The one vestige of real power which Lear retains for himself is a small private army, and it is no accident that the retinue of knights immediately becomes the main bone of contention between him and his daughters.

Furthermore, Lear's world-picture as it stands in scene i embodies a crucial paradox, whose incongruity he alone misses. On the one hand, he considers that the system of nature with himself at the apex is inviolable, and he takes for granted that all others must abide by its relationships simply because it *is* reality. There is no other way for reality to be. On the other hand, so closely does he identify his own constant will with the will of nature that he assumes nature endorses his actions, how ever much they may controvert the most fundamental natural obligations, the spoken and unspoken agreements by which order and degree are able to exist at all. Throughout the first three acts, he never fails to call upon nature to witness, endorse, and even be accomplice in his threats, furies, and outrages. He repeatedly insists that nature countenance unnatural events—sterility, the birth of deformed infants, the severing of natural bonds—because they are what *he* wills at the moment. The first of his tirades, the remarkable speech in which he disowns Cordelia, juxtaposes images of immutable powers presumed to control nature with images of deeds as unnatural as anything Othello could have

[25] Ivor Morris, in "Cordelia and Lear," *Shakespeare Quarterly*, 8 (1957), 153, makes a similar point.
[26] Lothian, in *King Lear: A Tragic Reading of Life*, pp. 47-48, makes a similar point.

witnessed among the Anthropophagi.[27] Similarly, he banishes Kent unjustly in the name of those very values which he presumes define the relationship between them: "Hear me, recreant, / On thine allegiance, hear me!" (166-167). Thus he begins the process dismantling the *Lear*-world from the top down, a process that will with incredible speed reduce all order to chaos. The king unkings himself, the father nullifies all property and propinquity of blood, providing the precedent and incentive for his elder daughters to do the like. The lord dispossesses the vassal, setting the pattern of broken oaths and usurped titles that will transform the *Lear*-world into a jungle of predators. In sum, the first scene, through use of a specialized dramaturgy in which psychic antecedents of action are withheld until after the action has been performed, depicts a feudal court in the midst of a feudal ceremony. One of the participants, for private and compelling reasons, refuses to play her assigned part, whereupon the man who stands at the top of the natural order in both family and state, who believes implicitly that the established order is the only conceivable system of reality, and who defines himself almost exclusively in its terms, invokes the forces presumed to control nature, and, in a final exercise of power, destroys the basis upon which order was permitted to exist.

The almost palpable sense of dissolution in *King Lear* is a carefully wrought cumulative effect, the end result of a series of increasingly potent blows against the principles upon which order rests. One by one, each of the characters is pushed further and further from what had constituted his or her normality, the final effect being nearly total disorientation from the secure and familiar world. The betrayal of Edgar, the appearance of banished Kent in disguise, the violent rift between Lear and Goneril, the hasty, confused midnight journeys ending at Gloucester's castle, the rumor of war between the dukes, Gloucester's persecution of his son, the latter's flight and disguise, the brawl between Oswald and

[27] Noted by Danby, pp. 175-176.

Kent, the stocking of the disguised nobleman, Lear's rage at discovering how his messenger has been treated, the arrival of Goneril, the systematic reduction of Lear to destitution, the approaching storm—all these piled one on the other lead inexorably to the chaos of the storm-lashed heath, populated by the mad King, the mad beggar, the Fool, and the frantic well-wishers, whose best efforts only make the situation worse. The good characters are completely isolated and estranged from one another, while the evil characters are perfectly united, treating one another with a deference and courtesy, even affection, which throws into gruesome relief the brutality of what they are doing. All bonds save those of mutual self-interest break down until at last the extraordinary energy of the play seems to be bent wholly upon anarchy and cruelty in both the macrocosm and the microcosm. The tremendous impact of the storm scenes in Act III depends in no small measure upon the cumulative force achieved in Acts I and II.

It is significant that, in the first two acts, Goneril, Regan, and Cornwall attack only Lear's *position* as king and father; the violence and cruelty against his person and Gloucester's begins only in the closing moments of Act II. Moreover, their acts alone—ordering an old man to behave himself and reduce the size of his train, stocking his exceedingly unruly servant, and refusing to compromise on any issue—may be harsh, but they scarcely plumb the depths of human depravity and evil. Their actions become heinous only when juxtaposed against what Lear considers his due as king, father, generous patron, and honored guest. To us, those actions present shocking examples of greed, ingratitude, and implacable lack of feeling, but to Lear they suggest the appalling possibility that the inviolable order upon which both his position and his identity rest is merely a figment of his imagination.

Three scenes, I.iv, I.v, and II.iv, present with exceptional force and clarity the destruction of all Lear's assumptions about himself, those around him, and the cosmos. Yet even before Goneril and Regan begin the process of mercilessly

172

stripping him of his illusions, he is already aware, or half-aware, of certain unsettling facts.[28] First of all, he knows that his eldest daughter's hospitality is not all that could be desired; the Knight's observation reminds him of his own conception, and he himself has perceived Goneril to be too much in the frown of late. He also knows, though he will not fully admit even to himself, that he wronged Cordelia. The mere mention of her name unsettles him, and when Goneril's brutal determination to bring him to heel makes itself clear, his first thought is of his youngest daughter. His cry, "O Lear, Lear, Lear!" echoes not a little of Othello's "O fool, fool, fool!" Thus the quiet but deep "I did her wrong" at I.v.21, is not a fresh insight but a culmination, bringing to the forefront of his mind a guilt which he had been determined to keep buried. Finally, he has a dim awareness that his own position is both ludicrous and dangerous: "If thou be'st as poor for a subject as he's for a king, thou art poor enough" (I.iv.20-21). The larger questions of his own identity, his relation to nature, the true state of reality, and the composition of the cosmos do not occur to him yet, but they are just around the corner.

Lear, however, has a variety of ways to avoid acknowledging those truths that hold threatening implications for him. Throughout the first two acts, a tremendous tension builds up between the implacable realities of the *Lear*-world and the King's determination to resist them. The more relentlessly the facts press in on him, the more desperate and violent is his insistence that things cannot possibly be as they so manifestly are. His simplest and generally least effective method is evasion; he denies or minimizes the importance of those facts he does not wish to see: "I have perceived a most faint neglect of late, which I have rather blamed as mine own

[28] William Elton, King Lear *and the Gods* (San Marino, Calif.: Huntington Library, 1966), p. 261, describes Lear's mind as caught in "that tension between belief and fear not to believe." See also Paul Jorgensen, *Lear's Self-Discovery* (Berkeley: Univ. of California Press, 1967), pp. 70-72.

jealous curiosity than as a very pretense and purpose of unkindness" (i.iv.65-67). The facts of the *Lear*-world, however, cannot be so easily dismissed, and, when they assert themselves relentlessly, his most characteristic reaction is sputtering rage: "My lord's knave, you whoreson dog, you slave, you cur!" (77-78). In Lear's scheme of things, it is simply inconceivable that a daughter and a subject would presume to give the king, her father, a stern dressing down. His claim to respect is based upon "sovereignty, knowledge, and reason," and it is quite inconceivable that such a claim should be worthless. The very term "daughter," which he repeats compulsively, carries with it implicit obligations, and a refusal to meet them is tantamount to subverting the relationship itself. When Cordelia had refused to conform to his idea of filial obedience, he had severed the bonds of nature. Now he denies that such bonds ever existed between him and Goneril. (Gloucester does the same with Edgar, and Lear later makes similar glances at Regan's legitimacy when he begins to doubt her "kindness.") He would prefer to think himself a cuckold than to think his idea of nature could be wrong.

Lear also tries at several junctures to outscorn the facts of the *Lear*-world with heavy-handed irony: "Your name, fair gentlewoman?" (226), he asks Goneril, pretending not to know her, and, in ii.iv, he attempts to shame Regan by offering a broad parody of his situation:

> Do you but mark how this becomes the house:
> 'Dear daughter, I confess that I am old.
>   [*Kneels.*]
> Age is unnecessary. On my knees I beg
> That you'll vouchsafe me raiment, bed, and food.'
>   (ii.iv.148-151)

But Lear's irony invariably rebounds upon him; he is not parodying his situation, but giving a most precise statement of his daughters' position.

174

But when it comes down to the wire, Lear places his fullest
faith in the consonance between his will and the powers of
nature. As in the first scene, he calls upon the vivifying and
ordering forces of nature to perpetrate unnatural deeds on
his behalf:

> Hear, Nature, hear; dear goddess, hear:
> Suspend thy purpose if thou didst intend
> To make this creature fruitful.
>
> (I.iv.266-268)

If at this point Lear can still presume that the forces of nature
are at his beck and call, the emotional and intellectual foundation upon which so mammoth a presumption has been
built is clearly beginning to crumble. In contrast to his implacable fury in scene i, his rage is now mixed with tears,
more of frustration, I think, than grief. Lear resists them
furiously, seeming to sense that tears only dramatize the
impotence of his rage: "Life and death, I am ashamed / That
thou hast power to shake my manhood thus!" (287-288).
As at so many junctures in the play, when Lear is faced with
unacceptable and frightening facts, when the situation has
passed completely beyond his control, he responds by insisting ever more vehemently that nothing has changed and his
position is as strong and inviolable as ever:

> Thou shalt find
> That I'll resume the shape which thou dost think
> I have cast off for ever.
>
> (299-301)

This is perhaps the epitome of Lear's self-delusion, betraying
a complete misunderstanding, or, more exactly, a vehement
refusal to understand, what he is and what he is not.

If by this point tears are making inroads into the emotional
basis of Lear's self-assertion, doubts are also beginning to
erode the intellectual foundation of his world-picture. At the
back of his mind are not only half-awarenesses of the folly

175

of his past actions and the grim reality of his present situation, but also terrifying glimpses into what the future may hold. The tension between what Lear knows to be true and what his position can permit him to admit informs the compact but powerful I.v. The prattle of the Fool is juxtaposed against the monosyllabic responses of Lear. The King seems hardly to be listening, absorbed in his own ruminations; the scene provides one of several instances in this play where silence speaks louder than the thunder. The fragmentary thoughts that break into his self-absorption depict a mind being dragged unwillingly through a world it is no longer sure of, pushed toward consequences it can foresee but not forestall. Here, as elsewhere, his state of mind is characterized by alternation between various different approaches to the situation, the kind of fragmentation which, in Shakespeare's mature tragedies, is synonymous with the destruction of the subjective world. At one moment he openly recognizes his own guilt, but then retreats into the wilfull self-delusion that he can take back his kingdom by force. Then in the next breath he yields to shock and self-pity before the very possibility of such things happening as have happened. Such reflections, mixed with his absent responses to the chatter of the Fool, lead directly to the terrible anchor of the scene: "O, let me not be mad, not mad, sweet heaven! / Keep me in temper; I would not be mad!" (I.v.40-41). At this point, we are reminded that self-knowledge and tragic self-awareness are not necessarily the same thing. Lear still has a great deal to learn about himself, but just as he had previously been aware of himself as the apex of a hierarchical structure, so now he is aware of himself as a man being pushed irresistibly over the brink of an abyss. Lear's plunge from greatness into madness is so powerful not only because of the degree and duration of his agony, but also because he himself is fully capable of comprehending what is happening to him, though powerless to avert the horror of what he sees.

Act II, scene iv, presents us with an increasingly desperate man exploring one blind alley after another in a frantic

attempt to salvage what had been his secure and meaningful
world. The first part of the scene, before Goneril's entrance,
employs an almost patterned repetition of all Lear's previous
responses to the rapidly decaying situation: evasion, vehement insistence that things cannot possibly be as they obviously are, sputtering rage, insistence that his own position
has not changed, slights at his daughters' legitimacy, bathetic
self-pity, heavy-handed irony, and imperious commands to
nature to come down and take his part. Though the responses
are the same as in Act I, the voltage has been stepped up
considerably, since Lear knows that in appealing to Regan
he is playing his final card. His determination to believe what
he would believe is indefatigable, but the facts of the *Lear*-
world are implacable: Kent sits in the stocks, the bitter Fool
prattles the truth while Gloucester hedges, and Lear's rising
heart swells toward the bursting that is to come.

When he discovers that Regan is indeed as similar to
Goneril as a crab is to a crab, Lear changes his approach to
the situation: previously he had *demanded* absolute sway
because he thought it the inviolable due of his position as
king and father. Now he implies that respect and obedience
are owed to him out of *gratitude* for his generosity. It is the
first visible crack in his monumental pride, and it places him
only a step away from the outright begging to which he will
be reduced before the scene is over.

The entrance of Goneril and her kind reception by Regan
provides the penultimate blow to Lear's crumbling world.
At her appearance, he once again addresses heaven, but this
time in the form of a plea rather than a command. As Elton
has observed, "for the first time the great word 'if' enters his
prayers" (p. 189).

> O heavens!
> If you do love old men, if your sweet sway
> Allow obedience, if you yourselves are old,
> Make it your cause.
>
> (II.iv.184-187)

177

As happens so frequently in *King Lear*, pleas to heaven for mercy or justice are followed immediately by fresh disasters, as if to underscore the futility of supplication to whatever violent powers hang fated o'er men's heads in the *Lear*-world.

It was a dramatic master-stroke on Shakespeare's part to delay Cornwall's admission that he stocked Kent until immediately after Goneril's arrival. Together the events are a rapid one-two punch, shattering the last of Lear's delusions and breaking the back of his determination to believe that things are other than they are. He now begins a hasty retreat from all his former positions. Where before he had called Goneril "degenerate bastard" and willed her annihilation, he now affirms her legitimacy and proposes peaceful coexistence. Where before he had called down all the stored vengeances of heaven upon her, he now assures her that he will not tell tales of her to high judging Jove nor bid the thunderbearer shoot. "I can be patient" (225), he assures her, introducing a theme which is to become the major dialectic of both the plot and the subplot for the remainder of the play. Heretofore, Lear could not even imagine a situation in which patience might be required of him. Yet at this point, his patience is based upon a self-delusion to which he clings tenaciously in spite of the most self-evident facts: "I can stay with Regan, / I and my hundred knights" (225-226). When Regan loses no time in setting him straight on that score, he can only reply with the outraged "I gave you all" (245), which meets with the implacably true "And in good time you gave it." Like Edmund's reflections upon aged tyranny and the Fool's quips about being old before one is wise, the sisters' arguments throughout the scene carry the weight of unfeeling logic and heartless truth.

Abandoning his former position entirely, Lear now attempts a series of desperate compromises with his situation. But if the facts of life in the *Lear*-world cannot be evaded, cannot be shouted down, and cannot be outscorned, neither can they be compromised. The ruthless whittling down of Lear's retinue is symbolic not only of the destruction of his

illusions and the devastation of his subjective world, but also
of the way in which life itself is being stripped down to its
basics, shorn of all accommodations until it stands denuded,
the thing itself. "What need one?" Regan asks (258), and
concludes the process of dismantling which Lear himself had
initiated in scene i. His great reply to her question points the
play in a new direction:

> O reason not the need! Our basest beggars
> Are in the poorest thing superfluous.
> Allow not nature more than nature needs,
> Man's life is cheap as beast's.
>
> (259-262)

With these four lines, Lear expands his situation to embrace
the *Lear*-world itself; it is the first generalization he has made
thus far, and the first awareness he has shown of anyone's
distress except his own.[29] These lines prepare for his realization that man without accommodations is nothing but a poor,
bare, forked animal; yet at this point, his grasp of the lot of
unaccommodated man is faulty. He has still to meet a beggar
who is superfluous in absolutely nothing.

Face to face at last with the reality of his situation, Lear
once again turns to heaven, but it is now a heaven populated by ambiguous and ominous gods who, far from coming
down to take his part, may actually be the instigators of his
torment:

> If it be you that stirs these daughters' hearts
> Against their father, fool me not so much
> To bear it tamely.
>
> (269-271)

In the course of a single speech, he prays first for patience
and then for fury: patience is the only alternative to madness,

[29] This point is well made by Norman Maclean in "Episode,
Scene, Speech, and Word: The Madness of Lear," in *Critics and
Criticism*, ed. R. S. Crane (Chicago: Univ. of Chicago Press, 1952),
pp. 600-601.

but rage is the only alternative to humiliating helplessness. Both his prayers, like all prayers in the *Lear*-world, go unanswered. Hardly has he prayed for patience when tears begin to choke him, and, when he asks that tears give way to fury, the answer is not the noble anger which he had sought, but impotent, sputtering rage, which, even more than the tears, underscores his powerlessness in a world he can no longer control or even comprehend:

> I will have such revenges on you both
> That all the world shall—I will do such things—
> What they are, yet I know not; but they shall be
> The terrors of the earth.
>
> (274-277)

The speech concludes as he is pushed inexorably toward exactly what he has dreaded most: "O fool, I shall go mad!" (281).

King Lear presents an exceptionally clear and powerful example of the collapse of the subjective world as a central facet of tragic experience in Shakespeare. When Lear rushes out of Gloucester's castle, he is entering a dark, chaotic world which is the diametrical opposite of the structured hierarchy he had presumed to be the immutable basis of reality, and in Tom O'Bedlam he will meet the extreme antithesis of the man he had conceived himself to be. The failure of the scheme of relationships he had considered inviolable and the loss of his power as both king and father have led to the loss of all those bearings and reference points by which he had identified himself and defined the world around him.[30] He has been shorn of everything that had previously constituted the foundation of his world.

But dissolution in this tragedy is by no means limited to the microcosm. One reason *Lear* is so much more comprehensive in scope than *Othello* or even *Hamlet* is that the *Lear*-world is uprooted in a way that the worlds of the other two

---

[30] See Elton, King Lear *and the Gods*, p. 220.

plays are not. The familial and societal institutions of the *Hamlet*-world may be corrupt and ailing, but they are not annihilated, and, in *Othello*, tragedy occurs precisely because the hero believes the world to be worse than it is. But the first half of *Lear* presents a terrible vision of dissolution in the macrocosm, terrible not only because it is complete but even more because it is so plausible. The empowered rule so badly, the aged are so rash, the cherished institutions are so patently preposterous, the kind gods are so conspicuously absent or indifferent that the pragmatic world of Edmund and Goneril, however much it may repulse us, makes a much better claim to credibility than the top-heavy hierarchy of Lear or the fretful superstition of Gloucester. The world of Lear deserves to perish, but, in perishing, it takes with it the only fixed system of values by which human conduct may be limited or guided. The presentation of the *Lear*-world in the first two acts convinces us that Lear's version of reality is false; and if the heaven-sanctioned system he espouses is indeed the foppery of the world, then there is no absolute basis for rejecting the world envisioned by Goneril, Regan, Cornwall, and Edmund—except, of course, that it is un-inhabitable, but that demonstration must wait until the second half of the tragedy.

With his previous vision of reality shattered, Lear now faces the problem I have suggested is common to all four Shakespearean tragic heroes: how to endure what is, for him, simply unendurable. He has resisted with all his enormous strength a world in which such things as have happened could happen, but, when he does accept it, he confronts it with more of the same titanic power so characteristic of the play. But, as yet, it is strength without a single sure direction. We have seen in both *Hamlet* and *Othello* that, when the subjective world of the tragic hero is destroyed, he plunges into a state of confusion in which fragments of his former world-vision fly almost randomly through his mind, inter-mixed with new and more ominous perceptions which he had never before taken into account. In *Lear*, this chaotic state is depicted by the tempest in the mind, culminating in the King's spectacular plunge into madness. Faced with such a world as the *Lear*-world, he vacillates among a variety of ways of responding to it, all of which prove equally untenable. First, there is apocalyptic rage which would have all things change or cease, preferably the latter. Barbara Everett has aptly observed: "In the storm scenes Lear is at his most powerful and, despite moral considerations, at his noblest; the image of a man hopelessly confronting a hostile universe and withstanding it only by his inherent power of rage, endurance and perpetual questioning, is perhaps the most purely 'tragic' in Shakespeare."[31] But juxtaposed against Lear's noble anger is its exact opposite, a determination to endure all with silent patience: "No, I will be the pattern of all patience; / I will say nothing" (III.ii.37-38). Set against both patience and rage is bathetic self-pity, and in the course of a single speech he lurches almost incoherently from one to another:

> But I will punish home.
> No, I will weep no more. In such a night
> To shut me out! Pour on; I will endure.
> In such a night as this! O Regan, Goneril,
> Your old kind father, whose frank heart gave all—
> O, that way madness lies; let me shun that.
> No more of that.
>
> (III.iv.16-22)

So, too, his attitude toward humanity in general sways between compassion for the lot of the helpless, and fathomless loathing which can be satisfied only by the annihilation of the species. His attitude toward the deity similarly moves between two extremes: on one hand he acknowledges that the forces of nature owe him nothing, and then a moment later can call upon the storm to punish the crimes of humanity. But it is in the area of redefining himself that Lear explores the widest range of conflicting possibilities.

[31] "The New *King Lear*," *Critical Quarterly*, 2 (1960), 333.

Paradoxically, during this period of mental chaos Lear begins to exhibit most clearly and forcefully those qualities which I have suggested are common among all four of the mature Shakespearean tragic heroes. Lear has had many of these qualities *in potentia* all along, but they were necessarily limited by his unconditional acceptance of a fixed, hierarchical universe with himself at its apex. For instance, he has always shown a penchant for seeing individual events in cosmic terms, but only those terms that conformed to his narrow and absolutely fixed notion of reality. His attention in Acts I and II seldom wandered far from those persons or actions which immediately affected him. In Act III, with the basis of his world-view undermined, the horizons of his perception vastly widen. Mankind is evil not only because his daughters have abused him, but because all men abuse and prey upon each other. His daughters have taught him something about the human capacity for rapaciousness, and he now dilates that lesson into a universal picture of mankind receiving just punishment for the crimes committed against one another. On the other hand, the compassionate side of his attitude toward humanity as victim is founded not only upon his own suffering, but upon his realization for the first time of the universal suffering of humanity. In the midst of the tempest, he can deliver one of the most serene and beautiful speeches in Shakespeare, as he begins to see feelingly.

Lear's self-awareness, too, has been acute in degree but limited in scope; he had never ventured outside the fixed system for terms in which to define himself. He was eminently aware of himself as king and father, but now, shorn of these two roles, he becomes aware of himself as a man among suffering humanity, beneath cruel and implacable skies. The need to reestablish an identity is the most pressing problem he faces in the chaotic *Lear*-world, and, both in and out of madness, he explores a multitude of frequently contradictory possibilities. On the one hand he is a man more sinned against than sinning, the more or less innocent victim of hard-heartedness and ingratitude, but on the other hand he

183

is also a man who, through luxury and indifference, has caused the suffering wrongly imputed to heaven. At one moment he sees himself marshalling an army of ten thousand to execute terrible vengeance, while at another he is a poor, weak, infirm, despised old man. In madness he is every inch a king, and, returning to sanity, he is a foolish, fond old man. But throughout all the various identities he tests, his heightened sense of self-awareness, the basis of his monumental pride earlier in the play, remains with him in adversity to make him fully able to comprehend both his guilt and his suffering.

Lear's self-awareness and his search for his true identity are closely linked to a third quality of the Shakespearean tragic hero, the desire for consonance with a wider dimension of reality. In fact, the search for consonance is the substance of his search for identity. Initially, Lear's most monumental error had been to assume that nature and the gods would conform themselves to his will. When no gods came down to take his part, that mammoth presumption was shattered. For the remainder of the play, he sees the gods in almost as many guises as he sees himself. First there is the distinctly Old Testament power of wrath and vengeance, inundating the world in a second deluge. Then there are the indifferent gods who watch the corruption of mankind and take no action whatsoever. Finally, there are the gods who throw incense upon such sacrifices as Cordelia's. So too, he views the world at large through very different eyes, at one point seeing the grotesque, inverted world of his madness, at another the golden world which he and Cordelia will enjoy in the solitude of their prison. The significant point is that, though he defines himself and the world from shifting perspectives, he is constantly trying to bring his identity and conduct into register with the world he sees. Convinced that man is a forked animal, he attempts to tear off his clothes and become the thing itself.[32] Later, when he believes that

[32] Heilman, *This Great Stage*, p. 77, observes: "So the Lear who

human society is totally engulfed by evil and that the heavens watch indifferently, he attempts by royal decree to abolish entirely the spurious concept of ethics: "None does offend, none—I say none! I'll able 'em" (IV.vi.165). Still later, he accepts forgiveness from Cordelia on his knees, humbling himself so much that it pains her. Then he anticipates his imprisoned life with a sort of ecstatic fervor. Finally, he faces her death with rage and grief that would crack heaven's vault if they could. In Acts I and II, Lear's exacerbating personality was always the same, and his actions always predictable. However, in each of his four appearances after the storm scenes, he is a remarkably different man. In each case he is seeing the world differently and acting in consonance with the world that he sees.

Another trait possessed in common by all four tragic heroes is a hatred of hypocrisy. In Acts I and II, hypocrisy was very little on Lear's mind. Obedience was the thing, and those two cornerstones of Shakespearean ethics, love and honesty, had little significance for him. But as soon as he rushes from Gloucester's castle, he becomes obsessed with misrepresentation throughout the whole gamut of human affairs. The withering indictments he delivers in Acts III and IV are all linked by the same basic charge, covering real vice with artificial virtue. The murderer practices upon man's life under covert and convenient seeming. The incestuous man perjures himself and simulates virtue. Guilts are pent up in concealing continents that must be riven by apocalyptic justice. The robes and furred gowns hide a justice as corrupt as the thief he condemns. The lascivious woman seems chaste while the beadle lusts in the very execution of his office. The crafty politician seems to see what he does not. With Lear, as with Hamlet and Othello, plating sin with the gold of apparent virtue is more heinous than the sin itself.

---

is in effect naked wants to be naked in fact; the passion for harmonizing of inner and outer belongs to his bitter enlightenment."

The final quality which the tragic heroes share is a vulnerability to having their subjective worlds undermined at the level of their most basic assumptions. Of this, in Lear's case, enough has already been said. His private universe, built entirely upon a few false assumptions, crashes resoundingly, and he plunges first into confusion and finally into madness. To Shakespeare, mental disintegration seemed to suggest the perfect dramatic emblem for the destruction of the personal world, the total disorientation from reality as the hero had conceived it to be. As I have argued, Hamlet, Othello, and Macbeth all experience psychic disturbance at the moment when their most fundamental assumptions about themselves and the world are rudely yanked from under them. These disturbances manifest themselves in outbursts of hysteria in which the hero lapses from the mental coherence we usually recognize as sanity. I use the word "coherence" here in its most exact sense, the quality of holding together. For the tragic hero in Shakespeare, the subjective world quite literally falls apart, is reduced to disconnected fragments which must be individually tested and reassembled upon some new basis. In Lear's case, the fear of madness first arises as soon as he has reason to believe that things are not as he supposed them to be. His actual plunge into madness occurs at exactly that point where his former ideas of man and nature become wholly untenable. The process is longer and more complete than in *Hamlet* or *Othello*, extending even to the reordering of his personal world. The Prince and the Moor reshape their worlds during protracted struggles during which they are deeply disturbed, but certainly not mad. Lear, on the other hand, reorders his world into a grotesque madman's vision, which he unfolds to us in a way that suggests that for purposes of the drama his madness is far more than just a manifestation of his personal mental collapse. Madness in this play becomes a mode of commentary upon the supposedly sane world.

The madman is totally disoriented from what is ordinarily understood by the sane characters as reality. It is the very

186

otherness of his perspective which frequently, in Shakespearean drama, makes the lunatic's observations about the activities going on around him so pertinent. He can see, and, even
more important, he can *admit* he sees, things which prudent
men with vested interests in the "real" world must turn away
from. The actions of Goneril and Regan have brought Lear
to a vision of humanity as corrupt and brutal, vicious and
contemptible, deserving only immediate, final annihilation.
With the appearance of Edgar as Tom O'Bedlam, this vision
is supercharged with the obsessive intensity of madness. Lear
does not decline into madness; he embraces the inverted madman's vision with the savage energy typical of the character
and the play, and from the center of that vision sends out
scathing indictments of the supposedly sane world around
him.[33] By the time he has arrived at Dover in Act IV, his
madness has become a comprehensive way of seeing, a
coherent and lucid reading of experience. Hence, his imaginary court is harrowingly vivid, and his imprecations seem to
encompass not only the *Lear*-world, but our own.

Moreover, in *King Lear*, the actions and fantasies of the
mad become an inverted paradigm of all human conduct. The
Third Act presents a world in which all are blind men, fools,
and lunatics. All human institutions and activities rest upon
a foundation of madness and madly pursue hallucinatory
conclusions. The philosopher is a madman whose study is
how to kill vermin and prevent the foul fiend. The judicial
process consists of two madmen and a fool presiding over an
illusion. The yeoman is mad, the trusting man is mad, the
gentleman is mad, and, in a world of madmen, the maddest of
all is "A king! A king!" Madness in *Lear* provides the ultimate reduction of humanity itself, and does so in a way that
has particularly captured the modern imagination.

Of course, such sweeping effects are not achieved through
Lear's madness alone, but depend upon the superb coalescence between events and their context that is one of the hall-

[33] As Maclean puts it in "Episode, Scene,": "the mind now revels
in what the mind once knew it could not endure" (p. 607).

marks of this tragedy. As in Acts I and II, events combine to produce an overwhelming cumulative effect. The most spectacular ingredient, of course, is the storm, which time and again is equated with mental turmoil. All restraints upon nature are broken, as if some mindless cosmic fury has been unleashed, and threatens to upset all balances and crack the molds of nature. Less spectacular, but no less essential than the storm, is the use of secondary characters, especially the Fool and Tom O'Bedlam.

In Acts I and II, the main topics of the Fool's prattle were Lear's folly, the relationship between folly and knavery, and the nature of service. His wit applied the *reductio ad absurdum* to good men and knaves alike, and met the panorama of vice and self-seeking with derisive gaiety. The Fool sees how this world goes, and what he sees is not much different from what Lear will see by Act IV; the Fool, however, responds not with rage, but with laughter. But Act III has brought the introduction of physical cruelty, and, in the face of man's pain and vulnerability, the Fool's detached, sardonic viewpoint is simply not possible. Pain is too serious and too real to be mocked indefinitely. The Fool himself suffers pitiably from exposure to the storm, and his first pronouncement in Act III clearly indicates that the joke is no longer a joke: "O nuncle, court holy-water in a dry house is better than this rain-water out o' door. Good nuncle, in; ask thy daughters blessing. Here's a night pities neither wise men nor fools" (III.ii.10-13). Moreover, the subject of his quips changes to sexuality, a topic of no importance in the earlier scenes, but which looms large in Acts III and IV. His many references to sex invariably depict it in grotesque, denigrating terms, with the emphasis on cod-pieces, prostitutes, bawds, old lechers, and venereal disease. The introduction of bawdry into the Fool's discourse coincides with the emergence of the seamiest side of sex elsewhere in the play. The culmination of disgust with carnality is Lear's diatribe against sex in general and women in especial, a denigration anticipated by the Fool's "For there was never yet fair woman but she made mouths in a glass" (III.ii.35-36). As in *Othello* and *Hamlet*, the vitriolic revulsion is not so much against sex itself as against the hypocritical and rapacious behavior that accompanies the pursuit of sexual pleasure.

Throughout the mad scenes, the Fool enters into Lear's fantasies, yet at the same time stands apart, mocking them with cruel parodies. When Lear attempts to tear off his clothes and become the bare, forked animal (an action already sufficiently grotesque in itself), the Fool quips, "Prithee, nuncle, be contented; 'tis a naughty night to swim in" (III.iv. 104-105). So too, when the King transfers the cause of his distress to Tom O'Bedlam, the Fool enters into the delusion just far enough to mock it:

> LEAR: Has his daughters brought him to this pass?
> Couldst thou save nothing? Wouldst thou give 'em all?
> FOOL: Nay, he reserved a blanket, else we had all been shamed.
>
> (III.iv.61-64)

The same pattern is repeated in the trial scene. The spectacle of the Fool in cap and bells seated upon the bench of justice is itself a visual parody, and the Fool plays his part in Lear's hallucination up to a point, beyond which point he mocks it bitingly:

> FOOL: Come hither, mistress. Is your name Goneril?
> LEAR: She cannot deny it.
> FOOL: Cry you mercy, I took you for a joint-stool.
>
> (III.vi.49-51)

But by far the most important use of the Fool in Act III is to epitomize, along with Tom O'Bedlam, the weakness, vulnerability, and pitifulness of mankind. All along there has been something child-like about the Fool, and the spectacle of him shivering and unprotected first awakens in Lear the stirrings of compassion. There is awesome majesty in Lear's suffering, and Gloucester's agony has some dignity since it brings him to a knowledge of himself and awakens in him generosity, compassion, and endurance quite beyond anything in the smug man of scene i. But the suffering of the Fool, like that of Tom, is without dignity or compensation. The viewpoint he had earlier represented is whittled away by the brutal fact of physical pain. His detached amusement at the antics of knaves and fools crumbles before the enormities of the *Lear*-world, to be replaced by the fathomless disgust of the title character in Act IV, scene vi. It seems to me that the Fool does not abruptly vanish after III.vi; rather, he and the viewpoint he represents are worn down by brutality until there is virtually nothing left of them.[34]

Tom O'Bedlam, even more than the Fool, dramatizes human suffering which is utterly pointless in origin and degrading in effect. Shakespeare has spared nothing to make us, along with Gloucester, think a man a worm. Tom is one of the visual metaphors which I discussed earlier, suggesting by his mere appearance one of the extremes which the play contemplates as the basic nature of humanity.

It is odd that Shakespeare, having carefully avoided introducing Christian references to the deity, should go to a contemporary tract to dredge up a tribe of imaginary but distinctly Christian devils to haunt Poor Tom. Yet his reasons for ransacking Harsnett appear evident enough. Seldom has the grotesque strain of the human imagination manifested itself more bizarrely than in the demonology of medieval Christianity, a tradition still very much alive in Shakespeare's time:[35]

> As I stood here below, methought his eyes
> Were two full moons; he had a thousand noses,
> Horns whelked and waved like the enridgèd sea.
> (IV.vi.69-71)

[34] Cf. Roger Ellis' original and perceptive study, "The Fool in Shakespeare: A Study in Alienation," *Critical Quarterly*, 10 (1968), 245-268, esp. 264-266.

[35] See Walter Clyde Curry, *Shakespeare's Philosophical Patterns* (Baton Rouge: Univ. of Louisiana Press, 1937), p. 61.

Tom's devils, with their grotesque, semi-comic names, torment him in a variety of singularly undignified ways: "Hop-
pedance cries in Tom's belly for two white herring. Croak
not, black angel; I have no food for thee" (III.vi.30-32).
Moreover, though the introduction of Harsnett's demons
into the *Lear*-world may be a theological anachronism, it is
quite in keeping with the poet's usual practice: Shakespearean
tragedy consistently presents us with a world in which God's
presence is hard to discern, though the devil's is everywhere
apparent.

Tom's presence offsets the madness of Lear in that the
madder Lear becomes, the saner and more normal Tom
appears to him. Edgar's appearance, heralded by the terrified
Fool, marks Lear's final plunge into a world of hallucination;
yet, initially, the King is able to recognize Tom as an extreme
and abnormal case. A moment later, however, having considered him well, Lear no longer finds him an aberration, but
the thing itself, quintessential human nature. From that point
on, a deepening inversion occurs until Tom appears to be
first a philosopher, then a learned judge, and finally one of
the King's knights, though a bit too lavishly dressed. Casting
mad and naked Tom in these roles provides a visual parody
of the "sane" functions of philosopher, judge, and knight,
and makes a stinging comment upon the "sane" world such
exalted men inhabit. Tom's injunction at the imaginary trial,
"Let us deal justly" (III.vi.40), taken in its visual context, is
one of the bitterest lines in the play.

The storm and the use of no less than three highly abnormal characters all help delineate a macrocosm itself gone
mad; a further device used for the same effect is the elaborate
confusion of identities which prevails throughout Acts III and
IV. Partially, such confusion is caused by the storm; benighted
and tormented by wind, rain, and lightning, the characters
grope through chaos seeking one another out:

LEAR: What's he?
KENT: Who's there? What is't you seek?
GLOUCESTER: What are you there? Your names?
(III.iv.118-120)

Fundamental questions of identity abound in the storm scenes, and the situation is further complicated by the fact that two of the characters are in disguise while a third is experiencing hallucinations. Gloucester does not know who either Kent or Edgar is. Edgar knows who Gloucester is, but does not know who Kent is, and Kent does not know who Edgar is. Lear's idea of who anybody is depends upon the particular hallucination going through his shattered mind at any given moment. Shakespeare uses this extraordinary situation to play dazzling variations upon the theme of identity, frequently underscoring the cruel comedy so prominent in the central scenes of the play. Lear insists that nothing but unkind daughters could reduce a man so low as Tom, when in reality it is a father who has done so. When Gloucester enters, preceded by the Fool's quip about fire in an old lecher's heart, Edgar characterizes him as the foul fiend Flibbertygibbet and later compares him to Goneril and Regan. Gloucester, in a single speech, extolls Kent's foresight to the disguised Kent and bewails his son's treachery in the presence of his disguised son. The cruelest of such mix-ups occurs in iv.vi, when Lear declares:

> Let copulation thrive; for Gloucester's bastard son
> Was kinder to his father than my daughters
> Got 'tween the lawful sheets.
>
> (113-115)

He is, of course, saying this in the presence of blind Gloucester, who now knows that Edmund betrayed him, but does not know that his guide is his beloved Edgar. Such multiple confusions are not set straight until Gloucester is on the verge of death and Lear's mind is too numbed with grief to comprehend anything further.

There is, however, a crucial difference between Lear's madness in Act iii and his madness in Act iv, and it is in part a difference in context. In Act iii, the world itself is mad, but, in Act iv, it has started to mend. One of the most effective strokes in the play is having Lear vanish for an extended

192

period after the storm scenes and then reappear toward the end of Act IV in a completely different context. By that time, the *Lear*-world, though terribly scarred by its ordeals, is making a concerted effort to right itself. Chaos and darkness have yielded to calm and fair daylight. Cordelia has returned to relieve her father, and Edgar, no longer the bare, forked animal, has taken charge of Gloucester's rehabilitation. Cornwall is dead, Albany has sided with Lear against Goneril, and the two sisters are wrangling bitterly over Edmund. In such a context, Lear's madness becomes not part of an overall picture of dissolution, but a devastating critique of the supposedly sane world around him. His madness itself has undergone a marked change in character: in Act III, his mind lurched from one hallucination to another, but, in Act IV, his madness has settled into utter lucidity, and his momentary delusions of catching a mouse or having his boots pulled off are almost incidental to the coherent reading of experience he unfolds. He has constructed a new subjective world in madness, and it is, amazingly, the same world Edmund had seen to begin with, a world in which, as Maclean puts it, "man is leveled to a beast and then raised to the most fearful of his kind: the source of man's power, as with the beast's, is sex and self, but above the girdle which the gods inherit is the special gift of reason; only it is a kind of sadistic ingenuity by which man sanctifies his own sins—the universally inevitable sins of sex and self—by declaring them anathema for others."[36] Edmund, however, cheerfully accepts the world he sees because he thinks himself uniquely gifted to prosper in it. But Lear has arrived at the world of sex and self via the destruction of his world-vision, his identity, and his sanity itself. Experience forces him to acknowledge the world envisioned by Edmund, but he does so with boundless loathing.

[36] Pp. 599-600. The critic says that Lear's shift in perception is as radical as if the tortured came to have the inquisitor's estimate of the rack. This provocative analogy ignores the fact that, while Lear sees the same world as Edmund, his attitude toward what he sees is directly opposite.

193

Lear's meeting with Gloucester is among the most powerful scenes Shakespeare ever wrote. The two old men, meeting now after all they have endured, become emblematic of human experience at its worst: mutilated, blind, bitter, suffering, and mad. But beyond this, much of the unique effect of the meeting depends upon the tension between abysmal contempt for a mankind who has made such a world and pity for a mankind who must endure such a world. As in the storm scenes, man is at once loathsome and contemptible, but also victimized and pitiable. This dualism toward human nature accounts for the strange mixture of the grotesque and the pathetic which intermingle to create the basic dramatic tone of the encounter. Shakespeare seems at one moment to be offering a spectacle of extreme pathos, and then at the next presenting a cruel parody of human suffering, engaging our compassion for human misery, and then taunting us with its ludicrous indignity.

The great tirades of Lear gather together with particular force and emphasis many of the central preoccupations of the play—the real source of power, the animalism of human nature especially as evinced by sexuality, the ever-present discrepancy between appearance and reality, the futility, even nonexistence of ethics, and the solidarity of humanity in ubiquitous suffering. Lear presents us with a grotesquely distorted parody of his own kingdom and kingship; in fact, one might say he has gone mad because only in madness has it been possible for him to sustain the illusion that he is still king. He repeatedly imagines himself raising, training, and leading an avenging army; he extends royal clemency to adulterers because they provide him with soldiers; he will prove his gauge upon a giant, asks Edgar for a password, and tells Gloucester to mark the penning of a challenge. But if on the one hand his favorite image of himself is as a king engaged in that most kingly activity, waging battles, on the other hand his new insight into the operation of the *Lear*-world suggests to him that there is an even more potent source of power than the sword: allusions to money dot the scene almost as

194

frequently as military references. He enters insisting upon his
royal prerogative to coin money, and proceeds to make no
fewer than four imaginary disbursements: he raises his army
by paying press money, buys an ounce of civet to sweeten his
imagination, bribes a corrupt official to seal an accuser's lips,
and, finally, offers ransom to his imagined captors. The army
may stand for the heroic ideal and the glory of kingship, but
money is what gets things done in the new order, and to be
without it is to be utterly powerless: "O, ho, are you there
with me? No eyes in your head, nor no money in your purse?
Your eyes are in a heavy case, your purse in a light" (IV.vi.-
143-145). The subjects in Lear's imaginary kingdom, in contrast to the subjects we have seen in his real court, are strikingly middle class, and their sins are the bourgeois vices of
chiseling and venality. The tension between the old chivalric
ideal and the new order of materialism and graft is embodied
in a single striking image: "Plate sin with gold, / And the
strong lance of justice hurtless breaks" (162-163).

A significant difference between Lear's madness in Act III
and his madness in Act IV is that in the latter scene he is
firmly convinced at all times that there is no remedy for
human vice and cruelty. He no longer believes that the great
gods will seek out their enemies now—or later. The usurer
hangs the cozener in a moral vacuum and the heavens are
empty or indifferent. There is no longer any point in arraign-
ing Goneril and Regan before a tribunal, for such tribunals
are themselves corrupt, and the great image of authority, far
from being the inherent nature of the king, is a dog obeyed in
office. In such a world, the very idea of ethics is preposterous,
and, with obsessive insistence, Lear pronounces the abolition
of ethics as if by royal decree; none can offend if there is
nothing real to offend against.

As with Hamlet, once Lear comes to see man's basic nature
as vicious and corrupt, everything connected with humanity
acquires a stench, and all appearances of virtue become
masks for loathsome realities. Sex, divorced from the capacity
to love, becomes lust in action. The pretenses of civility and

restraint are cast to the winds in the pursuit of sexual pleasure, and nowhere in Lear's mad vision does man seem to be an animal, and nothing more, than in his sensuality. Since, as Maclean has observed (p. 606), Lear has converted everything, even white-bearded Gloucester, into his daughters, it is against female sexuality that he delivers his most withering diatribe. His revulsion, like Hamlet's and Othello's, arises from the discrepancy between the pretensions to virtue and the reality of vice, between the appearance of civility and the actuality of rapaciousness. But sex is only one facet of life which comes under the taint of Lear's vision of man as predatory animal; social institutions are merely convenient instruments for the exploitation of the poor and defenseless by the rich and powerful; the family operates by flattery and deception; flesh smells of mortality, and the robes and furred gowns that clothe it merely hide the festering corruption. Lear has implicitly answered his earlier question, "Is there any cause in nature that makes these hard hearts?" (III.vi.75-76). There must be, for hardness of heart is universal as nature itself, and there is nothing to be done about it.

However, juxtaposed against the violent misanthropy of his diatribe is an acute awareness of man as victim, of weakness and suffering as the true common denominators among men. The simple thief, the hounded beggar, the lashed whore —all are poor naked wretches whipped from tithing to tithing to support the shibboleths of order and morality, property and power. Moreover, Lear himself has learned to feel what wretches feel and knows now that he is not ague-proof. The turning point of the scene occurs when the King recognizes Gloucester; prior to that, Lear's speeches have consisted largely of the most scathing indictments of humanity ever committed to paper. But in the second part of the encounter, he offers bitter, weary consolation to his blind vassal, and preaches upon the universal misery of mankind. Now Gloucester, too, has learned to see feelingly, and what he has seen has not been the abysmal vision Lear showed him, but the wretchedness of the King himself: "O ruined piece of nature"

(133). It is finally Gloucester's tears of fellow-feeling that bring the mad King somewhat to himself:

> If thou wilt weep my fortunes, take my eyes.
> I know thee well enough; thy name is Gloucester.
> Thou must be patient. We came crying hither.
>
> (173-175)

Patience has been crucially important as a theme throughout the play, because it directly confronts the central problem of the *Lear*-world, how is experience to be endured? Gloucester has vacillated between patience and despair while Lear has been torn between patience and rage. Patience is necessary for the survival of both, since Gloucester's despair leads directly to suicide, while rage for Lear is the path to madness, as he himself realized early in the play. But patience in the *Lear*-world simply is not possible; the outrages are too enormous and the pain too excruciating. Each and every time that Lear, Gloucester, or Edgar makes a heroic resolution to patiently endure the worst, a fresh disaster breaks to convince them they did not even know how bad the worst could be.[37] Patience is absolutely essential but absolutely impossible, and there is no resolution, just as there is no conclusion to Lear's sermon on the subject. "When we are born, we cry that we are come / To this great stage of fools" (179-180): the speech begins as if it were going to be one of the greatest in Shakespeare. Surely this is the place for the play to "make its ultimate statement," were Shakespeare interested in anything so simplistic as making a statement. But the sermon ends on a non sequitur almost as soon as it has begun; Lear's next comment is not upon the universal condition of mankind, but upon the quality of his hat, and from there he drifts into a grotesque fantasy of shoeing a troop of horses with felt and stealing noiselessly upon his sons-in-law. Within a few lines of counseling patience in the face of man's ubiquitous

[37] See Elton's chapter, "Irony as Structure," in King Lear *and the Gods*, pp. 329-334.

197

suffering, he falls into a paroxysm of savagely vindictive rage: "Then kill, kill, kill, kill, kill, kill!" (184).

It is signal of the complementarity of *Lear* that in the immediate wake of the King's abysmal vision, a diametrically opposed view of the world should develop in both the macrocosm and the microcosm. The forces of good have not been absent from the *Lear*-world; rather, they have been present but ineffective, which is much worse to witness. As early as ii.ii, Kent's perusal of Cordelia's letter has paved the way for the counter-movement, and his subsequent conversations with the anonymous gentleman, as well as Gloucester's information about the impending invasion, have kept us mindful that there is an alternative in the *Lear*-world to the unfeeling ruthlessness of Goneril, Regan, and Edmund. But, throughout the first three-and-a-half acts, the efforts of Kent and Gloucester to improve the situation have succeeded only in making the situation worse for Lear and for themselves. Cordelia's appearance offers, for the first time, a viable alternative to the world that Lear has seen in madness; it offers hope at exactly that juncture where all hope had been abandoned. The compassionate forces have managed to rally, while the conspiracy of opportunism has lost its all but invincible effectiveness.

But even more important, Cordelia restores us to the world of feeling, and that, I think, is what makes her reappearance such a welcome relief. Throughout the action, it has been abundantly evident that, if there are to be ethical values, they must be based not upon the hierarchy of a given system, nor upon an external set of immutable principles, but upon spontaneous promptings of compassion, love, and pity, which are generated not in the macrocosm but in the microcosm.[38] Cornwall's servant strikes the first effective blow against the conspiracy because his common humanity cannot endure the outrage perpetrated by his master upon the aged Gloucester,[39]

[38] See Elton, p. 97. Also Kenneth Muir, ed., *King Lear*, 8th ed. (1952; rpt. London: Methuen, 1963), pp. lv-lvi.

[39] Both Kirschbaum, in *Character and Characterization*, p. 72, and

198

and his fellow servants risk their lives to comfort the blind
Earl because they are totally unwilling to accept a world
dominated by the principles of Regan and Cornwall. Albany
finds his manhood in his capacity for moral outrage, and
Edgar, beginning his long and painful ascent from the state
of the forked animal, describes himself as:

> A most poor man, made tame to fortune's blows,
> Who, by the art of known and feeling sorrows,
> Am pregnant to good pity.
>
> (IV.vi.217-219)

The introduction of feeling and the values of pity, love, and
compassion that arise from the capacity to feel, suggest an
alternative to the problem of how experience in the *Lear*-
world is to be endured. That world cannot be changed, and
patience is unequal to its enormities; but there is now the
possibility of retreat from the macrocosm into a private world
of feeling, a world which is impervious to the blows of the
external world because it is generated from within.

The idea of subjective escape from objective pain is first
introduced by Gloucester toward the end of IV.vi:

> The King is mad. How stiff is my vile sense,
> That I stand up, and have ingenious feeling
> Of my huge sorrows! Better I were distract;
> So should my thoughts be severed from my griefs,
> And woes by wrong imagination lose
> The knowledge of themselves.
>
> (274-279)

Gloucester may envy the "oblivion" of Lear's insanity, but
we know well that, for Lear himself, madness holds an awareness of the world more painful than anything he perceived

---

Derek Traversi, in *"King Lear," Scrutiny*, 19 (1952), 141-142,
discuss the significance of this anonymous servant. So does Paul
N. Siegal in *Shakespearean Tragedy and the Elizabethan Compromise*
(New York: New York Univ. Press, 1957), p. 167.

while sane. The King must find comfort in a return to sanity, stripped of everything that had formerly constituted his pride and power; but before this can happen, he, too, must find some relief from the pain which recognition of the way things are in the *Lear*-world has caused him.[40] The Doctor advises Cordelia:

> Our foster nurse of nature is repose,
> The which he lacks. That to provoke in him
> Are many simples operative, whose power
> Will close the eye of anguish.
>
> (IV.iv.12-15)

As the sleeping potion wears off, Lear first believes that the eye of anguish is being reopened. As he revives somewhat, he wants to be assured of his condition, to test the physical reality of his own body and of Cordelia's. He does so by looking for those ubiquitous facts of life in the *Lear*-world, pain and tears: "I feel this pin prick" (IV.vii.56); "Be your tears wet?" (71). But the world to which Lear awakens is far different from the one he had expected to find; the reconciliation scene, for all its simplicity, depicts nothing less than the synthesis of a new subjective world. All along, Lear has been primarily concerned with what is owed him, and madness came when the system which had guaranteed his claims proved figmental. But now Lear knows that nothing is owed him, except perhaps punishment for the wrong he did Cordelia; expecting nothing, he finds himself restored to kingship and fatherhood on a completely new basis, a basis of values not imposed from without by some given structure, but which spring from within. The revelation opens up a new world for him, impervious to even so great a disaster as the sudden defeat of Cordelia's forces. He greets that reversal of his fortunes not with howls of indignation or cries to heaven, but with a transcendent description of the subjective world he now believes possible. Though a helpless prisoner, he

[40] See H. A. Mason, *"King Lear* (III): Radical Incoherence?," *Cambridge Quarterly*, 2 (1967), 222.

taunts his captors with their powerlessness to enter or corrupt
that private world he and Cordelia will inhabit together.

But, of course, the *Lear*-world offers no such solutions.
An outlandish but all too credible combination of vindictiveness, negligence, and wanton chance combine to destroy the
basis of Lear's new world. He is brought back to the old
one, now far more terrible than before because it finally had
seemed to offer hope, but the hope proved false. The truth
is simply too terrible to be faced, and yet too overwhelming
to be evaded. Lear's mind vacillates between anguished recognition and vigorous rejection:

> I know when one is dead, and when one lives.
> She's dead as earth. Lend me a looking glass.
> If that her breath will mist or stain the stone,
> Why then she lives.
>
> (v.iii.261-264)

I think Bradley was unquestionably right when he said the
actor playing Lear should die with an expression of joy on
his face, but that joy scarcely makes *Lear* a drama of personal redemption and fulfillment.[41] Quite the contrary; Lear's
joy is far more painful to witness than despair could possibly
be. His joy is based upon hope, but his hope is groundless.
He *knows* it to be groundless, but must cling to it desperately
because the alternative is too terrible to be accepted.[42] Lear
in his final agony becomes emblematic of the human capacity
to hope when there is nothing left to hope for. His is the hope
which seeks from life that which life is unwilling to yield;
it is hope that breaks the heart.

What makes the ending of *Lear* so excruciating is not

[41] P. 291. It is difficult to tell exactly what Bradley meant by the
phrase "unbearable joy." Unbearable to whom? Lear? Us? Both?

[42] Arthur Eastman, in "King Lear's 'Poor Fool,'" *Papers of the
Michigan Acad. of Science, Arts, and Letters*, 49 (1963), 537, has
described Lear's final moments superbly. See also Judah Stampfer,
"The Catharsis of *King Lear*," *Shakespeare Survey*, 13 (1960), 2-3.

simply that the forces of good fail, but that they fail after having come within an ace of succeeding. Cordelia and Kent, Edgar and Albany, by the exertion of their best qualities under the worst and most unpromising conditions, have wrenched control of the *Lear*-world from the forces of self-seeking and amorality. Yet the entrance of Lear with Cordelia dead in his arms seems to drain their heroic accomplishment of all value even in their own eyes. What, then, is the point of the struggle to generate values? No point, certainly, if the utlimate object of ethics is to mitigate suffering, to give men the wages of their virtue and the cup of their deservings. Yet, at its low point, the play presents us with Tom O'Bedlam and asks us "Is man no more than this?" In the *Lear*-world, nothing, not even man's humanity is given; he must earn it from instant to instant by the heroic assertion of all that is best in him, even if his only reward is to suffer as a man rather than as a beast. His best efforts are absolutely futile in achieving his desired goals, but they are nonetheless what define his humanity. His capacity to feel is his capacity to generate ethical values and differentiate himself from the beasts, but it is also his capacity to suffer.[43] Those characters who are devoid of feeling suffer very little; Edmund goes to his death with gallant equanimity. But both dual protagonists literally die of their feelings, and the same fate seems in store for Kent: "His grief grew puissant, and the strings of life / Began to crack" (217-218). The accommodations which separate men from beasts are not the robes and furred gowns as Lear had thought, but sentient human nature, though the inescapable corollary is his capacity to suffer. Tom's breath was qualitatively no different from that of any other animal, but Lear's mourning for Cordelia affirms the quality of human life, though it is an affirmation made in agonizing knowledge of its loss and of the injustice of the loss: "Why should

---

[43] See Maynard Mack, "We Came Crying Hither," *Yale Review*, 54 (1964), 185-186. Cf. Morris Weitz, "The Coinage of Man: *King Lear* and Camus' *L'Etranger*," *Modern Language Review*, 66 (1971), 31-39.

a dog, a horse, a rat, have life, / And thou no breath at all?" (307-308).

Critics who would offer a totally nihilistic or absurdist reading of *King Lear* point to the ending and tell us that our hopes, and Lear's, have been raised so high only so that they may be more devastatingly smashed. The "statement" of the play is a "bare iteration of an unredeemed negative."[44] Critics of a more optimistic bent usually skirt quickly around the apocalyptic ending and point to the regeneration of Lear before his death—his discovery of life and the salvation of his soul. I do not think the play yields willingly to either embrace. It is perfectly true that Lear is regenerated, but it is also perfectly true that Cordelia is hanged, and that her death devastates the new spirit she had built upon compassion and love. Yet *King Lear* does not make us feel like *End Game*, even when a clever director and a great actor try to convince us that it does. The final agony of Lear expands rather than diminishes man's proportions.

The critical problem, then, is how can a play be both optimistic and pessimistic at once, or more exactly, how can a play which deals with such basic human issues be neither optimistic nor pessimistic without being detached and noncommittal—two things that *Lear* decidedly is not. When we are faced with a work that appears to be saying a variety of contradictory things, the rational tendency is to resolve the tension by building a case for one side or the other, or working out some sort of compromise. But art is not necessarily rational, and, when we resolve its tensions, we may be undermining exactly what makes it art. All too often critics on both sides of the fence seem to proceed on the assumption that buried somewhere in the convolutions of the text is a "statement" which the play somehow "makes."[45] But it seems to me

---

[44] Brooke, "The Ending of *King Lear*," p. 75. See also Carol L. Marks, " 'Speak What We Feel': The End of *King Lear*," *English Language Notes*, 5 (1968), 163-167.

[45] E.g., Heilman, *This Great Stage*, pp. 178-179: "By such means the play moves toward its final statement."

that Shakespeare's plays consistently present us not with statements but with points of view.[46] If Shakespeare conceived of himself as holding a mirror up to nature, it was distinctly his own mirror, with its own unique configuration of concavities and convexities, which shape and modify the image given back. Now a statement and a point of view are two decidedly different things. A statement should be concise, cogent, and consistent, and should lend itself to paraphrase in any number of other more or less satisfactory formulations. But a point of view resists such reduction to exactly the extent that it is complex, variegated, and all-inclusive. I have been arguing throughout this study that the viewpoint underlying all four of Shakespeare's mature tragedies is complementary in Rabkin's sense of the term, and nowhere is that more true than in the final scenes of *King Lear*. If a concept as simplistic as pessimism can be applied at all to *Lear*, it must be applied to the play's attitude toward the world man must inhabit:

> He hates him
> That would upon the rack of this tough world
> Stretch him out longer.
>
> (314-316)

But toward man himself, the play expresses a much more complicated attitude captured in Keats's brilliant phrase, "impassioned clay": clay, certainly, because of his mortality, his vulnerability, his utter failure to triumph over his circumstances; but "impassioned" calls to mind the greatness of Lear, his capacity to fly in the face of the elements, his capacity for moral indignation and for love. Above all, the very prime matter of the tragedy, again to use Keats's words, is a *fierce dispute*—the dialectic between the macrocosm and the microcosm, the conflict between man and his condition, a conflict whose awesome scope transcends even its dismal outcome.

I have suggested that a central theme of Shakespearean tragedy is how the unendurable is to be endured. *King Lear*

[46] See Mack, King Lear *in Our Time*, p. 117.

is Shakespeare's most titantic tragedy because its central postulation is that the unendurable is not a particular situation, as in *Hamlet* and *Othello*, but the human condition itself. Hamlet, by a personal catharsis of rage and bitterness, can come to ultimate terms with his world. Lear seems about to do the same, but the *Lear*-world grants neither quarter nor asylum. What the play establishes, however, is the unique and differentiating capacity of human beings to experience a whole gamut of feelings which are distinctly and characteristically human, having nothing to do with the predatory world of animals: love, fidelity, compassion, hope; but also outrage, despair, spiritual anguish, and final heartbreak.

FIVE

MACBETH: THE TORTURE OF THE MIND

In *Macbeth*, Shakespeare focuses his attention fully upon a problem he had dealt with peripherally in *Hamlet* and *Measure for Measure*: that of the criminal who is deeply aware of his own criminality, is repulsed by it, but is driven by internal and external pressures ever further into crime. What differentiates such villains as Claudius, Angelo, and Macbeth from Richard III, Iago, and Edmund is that the former fully admit the validity and worth of the moral laws they violate, while the latter dismiss the ethical standards of the world as so much folly and delusion. The latter three relish their superiority over their victims, while the former judge themselves from the same ethical perspectives as their victims. The descendants of the Vice believe in what they do, while the conscience-stricken criminals are in the agonizing position of being committed by their actions to one set of values while committed by their beliefs to quite another. *Macbeth* dramatizes this predicament as experienced by a man who possesses the fundamental qualities of the Shakespearean tragic hero.

For all its emphasis upon blood and violence, *Macbeth* is the most completely internal of all Shakespeare's tragedies. It presents us with a man who has a clear conception of the universe and his own proper place in it. But, when confronted with the possibility of committing a daring though criminal act, he wilfully deceives himself for a short time and embraces an opposite view of the world. In the aftermath of an irrevocable act, he finds himself irrevocably committed to a world-view in which he does not believe. The key to his savagery, and, even more, to the soul-sickness that elevates him to tragedy, is that he must proceed as if the self-delusion were true, when in his mind and heart he knows that it is not. This constant lying to himself, and the discrepancy between his beliefs and the world that he has chosen for himself, produce the self-loathing and the numbing sense of loss that are the essence of his tragedy.

The *Macbeth*-world is one of the most distinctive Shakespeare ever created, having an atmosphere very much its own, upon which almost all extensive commentaries have remarked. Like the *Hamlet*-world, the world of *Macbeth* can be divided into three spheres or loci—the court over which Macbeth gains bloody sway, the world outside that court from which the forces of retribution issue, and a metaphysical sphere which intrudes physically upon the action. But the *Macbeth*-world has none of *Hamlet's* variegation; it is all very much of a piece, and the same nightmarish qualities of violence, fear, equivocation, and diabolism permeate every corner of it. The metaphysical realm seems scarcely more than an extension of the dark recesses of the hero's mind, a projection of his own inner promptings and fears. The consistency and intensity of the *Macbeth*-world have given rise to the widespread impression that this play is the most unified product of Shakespeare's art, that it issued as if a single breath from the most profoundly disturbing recesses of his imagination.[1]

The world Macbeth sees corresponds in striking detail to the world that the play presents us. Indeed, when the Thane describes his microcosm on the eve of the murder, he presents us with a most haunting delineation of the macrocosm, the world of the play:

Now o'er the one half-world
Nature seems dead, and wicked dreams abuse
The curtained sleep. Witchcraft celebrates

[1] Knight gives a particularly good account of this view on p. 155. Paul A. Jorgensen's fine study, *Our Naked Frailties* (Berkeley and Los Angeles: Univ. of California Press, 1971), appeared too late to be of use to me in writing this chapter. The similarities and ultimate differences between his thinking on this play and my own will be apparent to anyone familiar with his book.

Pale Hecate's offerings; and withered murder,
Alarumed by his sentinel, the wolf,
Whose howl's his watch, thus with his stealthy pace,
With Tarquin's ravishing strides, towards his design
Moves like a ghost.

(II.i.49-56)

Because of this coalescence between the macrocosm and the microcosm, Macbeth's own words provide us with the most useful index to the salient qualities of the *Macbeth*-world.

Nature seems dead. In the world of *Macbeth*, the inverted and the unnatural constitute the normal state of affairs. Paradox, antithesis, and equivocation are the characteristic idiom of the play.[2] The word "strange" and its derivatives appear twenty times, far more often than in any other tragedy by Shakespeare, and more often than in any other of his plays except *The Tempest*. All the characters, young and old, good and bad, are troubled by a sense of being estranged from the "natural touch," of being surrounded by conditions which are " 'gainst nature still." Disruptions in the natural order occur everywhere, from the firmament to the stables, "even like the deed that's done." Darkness at noon, predatory animals, night's black agents, murdering ministers, crying orphans, weeping widows, and innumerable other large and small touches all combine to delineate a macrocosm which, like the microcosm of the hero, has suffered the death of nature. As if to underscore the ubiquitousness of the strange, the weird, and the inverted in Macbeth's Scotland, the one presentation of the benificent face of nature occurs in a context of extreme irony. The temple-haunting martlet may seem to approve by his loved mansionry that the heavens' breath smells wooingly around Macbeth's castle, yet we know from the previous scene that it is the raven, not the martlet, which

[2] For detailed analysis see Margaret Burrell, "*Macbeth*: A Study In Paradox," *Shakespeare Jahrbuch*, 90 (1954), 167-190. Also George Duthie, "Antithesis in *Macbeth*," *Shakespeare Survey*, 19 (1966), 25-32.

208

croaks the fatal entrance of Duncan under those grim battlements.

Wicked dreams abuse the curtained sleep. The *Macbeth*-world is predominantly nocturnal, and the aberrations that can occur in sleep are central to the play. Though this has been amply pointed out, what has not received sufficient attention is the nightmarish quality of the *Macbeth*-world itself. Like *The Winter's Tale*, *Cymbeline*, and *The Tempest*, *Macbeth* is in a sense a dream-play; that is, its world is informed by the same meaningful distortions which, in universal human experience, characterize the world seen in dreams—the same combination of the real and the unreal, the logical and the absurd, the probable and the fantastic, the frightening and the grotesque.[3] Like a dream, the play seems both to rush forward with inexorable speed and yet to move with the agonizing slowness of stupor. The two main characters engage in swift, violent action, yet their lives wind down to absolute stasis, the frozen horror of Lady Macbeth's nightmares and the bedrock of Macbeth's despair. The *Macbeth*-world is a projection of Macbeth's mind in exactly the way the world seen in dreams is a projection of the mind of the dreamer. Like a dream-world, the *Macbeth*-world is filled with symbols, both obvious and obscure, which portray to Macbeth's mind the essential qualities of his thoughts and acts. Like the world of nightmare, the *Macbeth*-world is oppressive, airless, and claustrophobic, a quality suggested by "curtained sleep," and made explicit by Macbeth's feeling of being "cabined, cribbed, confined." Memories are filled with rooted sorrows, the stuffed bosom is fraught with perilous stuff which weighs upon the heart, and the imagination quails before nameless terrors. Even the good characters describe their native country in terms which, like the world of night-

---

[3] "He is living in an unreal world, a fantastic mockery, a ghoulish dream: he strives to make this single nightmare to rule the outward things of his nation. He would make all Scotland a nightmare thing of dripping blood" (Knight, p. 170).

209

mare, embody at once distortion and reality, exaggeration and absolute conviction:

> Where signs and groans, and shrieks that rent the air,
> Are made, not marked; where violent sorrow seems
> A modern ecstacy. The dead man's knell
> Is there scarce asked for who, and good men's lives
> Expire before the flowers in their caps,
> Dying or ere they sicken.
>
> (IV.iii.168-173)

As in the world of dreams, the boundaries between what is and what is not are thin and flexible. That the witches are real seems pretty clear, since Banquo sees them, but, like the contingent "realities" of dreams, they are as insubstantial as breath or bubbles, and they can melt into the wind, leaving their astonished interlocutors wondering, "Were such things here?" There has been no unanimity in either the theater or in criticism about whether Banquo's ghost, the air-drawn dagger, and the disembodied voices that haunt Macbeth are strictly the products of his imagination or manifestations of the supernaturalism of the *Macbeth*-world. Shakespeare seems to have left the matter purposely vague; Macbeth is tortured by both external and internal "sights," symbolic manifestations both in the macrocosm and the microcosm, and it is not always possible for him to say where one leaves off and the other begins.

'Twere best not know myself. In the *Macbeth*-world, characters are constantly turning their eyes toward the innermost recesses of nature, especially their own natures, and they are invariably appalled by what they find there. Macbeth, in his first appearance, is horrified by his own propensities, and, as the play progresses, an unstintingly negative appraisal of himself and of life in general becomes the substance of his tragedy. But he is not the only one who is repulsed by what he sees within himself. The discreet Banquo can keep his mind under control when he is awake, but is shaken by nameless "cursed thoughts" that nature gives way to in re-

210

pose. Lady Macbeth, too, can cope with the waking world by embracing the worst she sees there with ferocious assent and enthusiasm. But in sleep, with her defenses—her rationalizations and ruthless will—in abeyance, she is brought to a horrified recognition of herself. Watching her, the Doctor cries, "God, God forgive us all!" (v.i.70), which could well serve as an epigraph for the play. Both the young Lennox and the Old Man are appalled by natural aberrations and the deeds which initiate them. Ross delivers the nightmare description of Scotland quoted above. The Porter sees Macbeth's courtyard as the entrance to hell. Both Lady Macduff and her son paint a glum picture of the relation of innocence and experience, a picture that proves all too accurate in their case. Even Malcolm recites a whole catalog of fictitious vices of which he is supposedly guilty. The constant discernment of evil supports the play's overall impression that both microcosm and macrocosm are vast repositories of the unspeakable, that the serpent lurks beneath every innocent flower, readily apparent to anyone who has the nerve or misfortune to look.

Witchcraft celebrates. Whatever one may make of the reality of Banquo's ghost, the witches most certainly have a more vivid dramatic reality than Banquo living. The problem that their presence poses is central to the tragedy, for it involves the degree of freedom Macbeth exercises in committing his succession of crimes. If the witches can accurately foresee the future in the instant, then the future must be fixed. If the future is fixed, had Macbeth any real choice? If he had no choice, what becomes of the moral significance of his actions? The quest for a solution has run the gamut from the venerable Kittredge, who saw the sisters as Norns who could not only see the future but could determine it, to Stoll, for whom the problem scarcely existed, since the witches are primarily devices intended to sustain an illusion.[4] Walter Clyde Curry

[4] George Lyman Kittredge, ed., *Macbeth* (Boston: Ginn, 1939), pp. xviii-xx; Elmer Edgar Stoll, *Art and Artifice in Shakespeare* (Cambridge, Eng.: Cambridge Univ. Press, 1933), pp. 87-88.

attempted to steer a middle course, pointing out that in the mainstream of theology in Shakespeare's England, evil was both subjective and objective, existing both in the mind of man as a result of the Fall, and also in a whole realm of devils, imps, and spirits, whose existence was in no way dependent upon the human mind.[5] The degree of their influence upon human actions, he tells us, depended largely upon how a given individual was disposed at the time of temptation. The critic suggests that Macbeth had free will to begin with, but appears to have forfeited it after the crime. "We have a passage from strict indeterminism to apparent determinism" (p. 105). The insight is valuable insofar as Macbeth, as he himself realizes, does drastically circumscribe his range of possible choices after he commits regicide. Yet, when Curry attributes to the witches "a dignity, a dark grandeur, and a terror-inspiring aspect" (p. 77), he commits the same error Kittredge had before him, placing more confidence in exhaustive research among arcane books on witchcraft than in the witches Shakespeare has given us in the play. Far from being awesome demons or implacable Norns, they are filthy old hags who possess very little grandeur of any kind; when not trifling with the destiny of kings, they seem to derive equal pleasure from killing swine, cadging chestnuts, collecting thumbs, and gathering from ditch and gibbet the loathsome ingredients of their brew.[6]

Besides, to attempt a cogent theological explanation of *Macbeth* is almost as grave an error as to seek one for *Hamlet*. For one thing, the doctrine of free will itself has always been a particularly controversial and ambiguous one in Christian theology, resting upon the essentially paradoxical formulation that God's foreknowledge of the future, even though infallible and at one with His omnipotent will, is not the cause of the future.[7] Ultimately, the whole matter was

[5] *Shakespeare's Philosophical Patterns*, p. 58.

[6] See Robert Reed, *The Occult on the Tudor and Stuart Stage* (Boston: Christopher, 1965), pp. 168-171.

[7] See Roland M. Frye, *Shakespeare and Christian Doctrine* (Princeton: Princeton Univ. Press, 1963), pp. 147-148, 157-165.

usually presented as a mystery beyond the full understanding of the finite intellect, a seeming contradiction which had to be accepted on faith. Shakespeare, for the purposes of this play, seems to have accepted it on exactly those terms. The sisters can indeed look into the seeds of time, and their predictions are always right. The play accepts a central paradox of Christian thought; though the future is foreknown, it is not fixed. Macbeth himself alternately trusts the prophecies completely and ignores them entirely; more precisely, he attempts to skirt around those prophecies he does not want to believe, as when he plans the murders of Banquo and Fleance so that the prediction about Banquo's issue will never come true.[8] Shakespeare, in contrast to Milton, does not even explore the problem of foreknowledge and free will directly; he takes it for granted and goes on to those aspects of man and evil that interested him more.

The witches are not instruments of a power that *causes* destruction and suffering; they are instruments of a power that *enjoys* destruction and suffering. They go about their work with gusto and enthusiasm, inverting values, reporting their exploits, and gleefully anticipating fresh trouble. Their principal function in the drama is to embody a supernatural order which desires suffering and evil, does what it can to promote them, and finally exults in the destruction that follows. As such, they have more to do with the tone and atmosphere of the work than with the metaphysics of the *Macbeth*-world. Shakespeare could have chosen to omit them entirely and still have written essentially the same kind of play about the same characters. What would have been lost, however, is the haunting sense that the center of the universe depicted in *Macbeth* is not heaven but hell. They serve not so much to tempt Macbeth as to tantalize him; they do not so much impel his deed as insure that it will be as bitter as possible to him. When they first encounter him, they

---

[8] Wilbur Sanders, in *The Dramatist and the Received Idea* (Cambridge, Eng.: Cambridge Univ. Press, 1968), pp. 280-281, analyzes Macbeth's complex reaction to the prophecies.

whet his appetite for the crown, but then in the next breath predict that Banquo's issue, not his own, will be the ultimate beneficiaries of disruption in the royal line. More prudent tempters might wish to conceal this, for it could deter Macbeth from regicide. But, characteristically, Macbeth defers recognition of all that does not immediately suit his bent of mind. It is only after he has killed the king that he turns to the second prophecy, and then the prospect of Banquo's heirs enjoying his spoils becomes the source of unbearable torment to him, torment which the sisters increase by showing him Banquo's successors triumphantly crowned. So, too, they produce spirits to instill in him a false sense of confidence, and the bursting of that bubble of imagined security is Macbeth's final agony. The witches, then, are not on hand to make wounds, but to rub salt in them and relish the howls that follow. They do not cause Macbeth's fall; they do not even contribute much to it; rather, their most characteristic function is to exacerbate it, to revel in it, and profanely celebrate it: "Show his eyes, and grieve his heart! / Come like shadows, so depart!" (IV.i.110-111).

This even-handed justice. Perhaps the most extraordinary thing about the *Macbeth*-world is that it contains a strong, effective principle of retributive justice in operation throughout the play. This is not something which our experience with the worlds of Shakespeare's tragedies would lead us to expect. In *Hamlet*, to be sure, there is a heavenly inclination toward justice, but, like all things in the *Hamlet*-world, it works in obscure and devious ways. In *Othello*, there is only that justice which the characters can make for themselves— too late. In *King Lear*, tragedy occurs finally because there is no justice, no way to make ethics and experience congruent. But in *Macbeth*, the title character describes a verifiable phenomenon when he observes:

> But in these cases
> We still have judgment here, that we but teach
> Bloody instructions, which, being taught, return

214

To plague th' inventor. This even-handed justice
Commends th' ingredience of our poisoned chalice
To our own lips.

(I.vii.7-12)

Paradoxically, it is the presence rather than the absence of
justice in the *Macbeth*-world that gives the tragedy its particularly grim and futile outlook. The forces of conventional
good triumph completely, but their triumph is strangely
hollow, almost devoid of any power to mitigate the reality of
evil or reconcile humanity to its condition. Justice in the
Macbeth-world gives the impression of being less real and
significant than the problems it successfully confronts.[9] That
evil exists is the essential fact in the world of the play; that, in
the face of its existence, there is nothing to do but punish it
is the essential futility. It is at the moment of justice's complete triumph that the most famous statement of futility
echoes sepulchrally from the depths of Macbeth's world and
from the *Macbeth*-world itself. It will not do to say that
"tomorrow and tomorrow" are the embittered words of a man
who has lost his humanity, for they carry far more weight
within the context of the play than does anything spoken by
the lackluster defenders of right. Justice is necessary, and we
greet its reestablishment with a sigh of relief; but to say that
justice is necessary is not the same as to say it is meaningful.
When Macbeth commits his crime, he seems to embody a
dimension of mankind left quite untouched by Macduff's
and Malcolm's vengeance upon the individual man. It is almost as if Shakespeare were taking the most optimistic
theological explanation of the operation of divine justice
and demonstrating that it, too, contains the seeds of tragedy.

No other Shakespearean hero faces so pallid an array of
antagonists. Hamlet must deal with the cunning and capable
Claudius; Othello faces the super-subtle Iago; and Lear is
pitted against a conspiracy of no less than four ruthless and
determined predators. But whom does Macbeth face? Ban-

[9] See Sanders, p. 275.

quo, Malcolm, and Macduff. Bradley's futile attempt to build a character for the first shows effectively how little the progenitor of kings is fleshed out, while Wilbur Sanders has effectively refuted those who would make a heroic, saintly king figure out of Malcolm.[10] Macduff is more sympathetic and impressive than the other two, but, by the time he becomes a significant figure, his motivation rests more upon personal grief and thirst for vengeance than upon the desire to reestablish justice:

> If thou beest slain and with no stroke of mine,
> My wife and children's ghosts will haunt me still.
> I cannot strike at wretched kerns, whose arms
> Are hired to bear their staves. Either thou, Macbeth,
> Or else my sword with an unbattered edge
> I sheathe again undeeded.
>
> (v.vii.15-20)

Macduff's grief does not animate the new order which is established at the end of the play; Malcolm's cautious politics do, and they loom much smaller in our imagination than the bloody criminal whom they supplant.

By pitting Macbeth against a combination of forces whose sum total is so much less compelling than himself, Shakespeare emphasizes that in this play, the protagonist is his own most formidable adversary. As I say, *Macbeth* is the most private and internal of Shakespeare's tragedies, and the tragic suffering that occurs is the torture of the mind that goes on within the hero and heroine. But, further, the comparatively pallid nature of the hero's opponents is essential to the complementary tension of the play, a tension that accounts for the deep ambivalence of feeling which the tragedy prompts

---

[10] Bradley, pp. 379-387; Sanders, pp. 258-263. Nevil Coghill, who brings to the play the experience of both critic and director, also finds Malcolm a lightweight: "Listening to Shakespeare," in *Stratford Papers on Shakespeare, 1962*, ed. B. W. Jackson (Toronto: Gage, 1963), pp. 25-32. On the matter of Banquo, see Kirschbaum, *Character and Characterization*, 52-58.

toward its title character.[11] The central question to which almost all critics have addressed themselves is, "How can anyone who does what Macbeth does command not only our interest but our awe and empathy throughout the play? How can a man who violates his humanity tell us so much about what humanity is?" There is no doubt that Macbeth is wrong, but in his mammoth wrongness he completely over- shadows the pint-size rightness of Malcolm and is much closer to realizing the outer limits of human potential than the even-handed characters who remain cautiously in the center. Like many tragic protagonists from Oedipus and Orestes to Kurtz and Raskolnikov, he is a lone voyager into the forbidden, who severs his ties with the comfort and security of the community. Such mythic figures do not merely circumvent conventional moral judgment; they pass through and beyond it. Throughout the play, Macbeth is surrounded by men who accept the limitations imposed upon them by the world, and he, too, initially considers his extraordinary pow- ers to be "children and servants" to his king. He transgresses all the bounds that others accept, and in doing so he becomes evil and must be destroyed. But at the same time, in trans- gressing, fully aware of the enormity of his transgression, he assumes awe-inspiring dimensions quite beyond Duncan, Malcolm, Banquo, and Macduff. Humanity as Macbeth is terrible, but humanity as Malcolm is merely insipid.

Over the years, a theatrical tradition has sprung up, en- couraged by much of the critical commentary, which casts Macbeth as a gruff, burly character of no mental prowess, one who is distinguished from other roughnecks only by his

[11] Willard Farnham, in *Shakespeare's Tragic Frontier*, p. 10, notes the duality of feeling Macbeth prompts, and makes that duality the basis of his study (pp. 79-137). Sanders also analyzes "the essential ambivalence of our reaction to the 'criminal' Macbeth," on pp. 292ff. Sanders seems to have arrived independently and almost simultane- ously at a reading of the play somewhat similar to Rabkin's idea of complementarity in *Shakespeare and the Common Understanding*. Cf. Sanders, p. 299; Rabkin, pp. 12-13.

hyperactive imagination.[12] Such an interpretation, I feel certain, falls far short of the intricate characterization Shakespeare created. Macbeth's imagination is fired by a mind of considerable power and discernment; his imagination is the violent instrument by which his intellect attempts to make itself heard over the all but indomitable voice of his will. No other Shakespearean hero has so firm and correct a sense of self-knowledge, nor so fully developed a concept of the universe and his place in it. Macbeth has a unique ability to foresee both the practical and the ethical outcome of his actions.[13] Lear, in contrast, starts off with a completely mistaken notion of who he is and what the world is like; he blindly pulls down tragedy upon his own head and is shocked and outraged when disaster strikes. Othello, because of his predisposition, convinces himself of a falsehood upon virtually no evidence. Hamlet, for all his mercurial brilliance, is hopelessly inept at foreseeing the logical outcome of his actions. But Macbeth suffers from none of these perceptual shortcomings. The most terrible thing about his tragedy is that he goes to it with his eyes wide open, his vision unclouded, his moral judgment still in perfect working order. He wilfully disregards his own best perceptions and intuitions, but he is never rid of them. More than any other Shakespearean hero, he has a perfectly clear concept of who he is and where he stands—and it is exactly this perception that torments and spiritually destroys him.

In the opening scenes, Macbeth's mind is already under that kind of tension which we have seen to be so characteristic of mature Shakespearean tragedy, the tension that precedes the collapse of the personal world. The opposites are basic and the opposition is total. Macbeth is the most honored peer in the realm, but his honor is based upon incongruous and irreconcilable qualities; on the one hand, he

[12] See esp. Bradley, pp. 352-358; and J. Q. Adams, ed., *Macbeth* (Boston: Houghton Mifflin, 1931), p. 135.

[13] Robert Pack, "*Macbeth*: The Anatomy of Loss," *Yale Review*, 45 (1956), 536-537.

is able and willing to dare anything and fear nothing, but, on the other, he accepts limits and boundaries which cannot under any circumstances be transgressed. Gory descriptions of his individual fearless deeds alternate with praise of him as a loyal subject who curbs the lavish spirits of those who dare to rise against their king. The tension of Macbeth's position in the macrocosm is reflected by a corresponding tension in the microcosm, the tension between a deeply moral intellect and an utterly amoral will.[14]

> The service and the loyalty I owe,
> In doing pays itself. Your Highness' part
> Is to receive our duties, and our duties
> Are to your throne and state children and servants,
> Which do but what they should by doing everything
> Safe toward your love and honor.
>
> (i.iv.22-27)

These are not the oily words of a political intriguer.[15] Macbeth really believes this version of his position in life, or at least a part of him believes it. But another part is impelled with terrible force to the ruthless action of the man for whom bounds do not exist, the man who dares to do anything.[16]

In many respects, Macbeth is, right from the beginning, a poor candidate for the job of political assassin. For one thing, he is not really ambitious in the usual sense of the word. In

[14] Robert Heilman, " ' 'Twere Best Not Know Myself': Othello, Lear, Macbeth," in *Shakespeare 400*, ed. James McManaway (New York: Holt, 1964), p. 94: "When a protagonist 'knows' that his course is morally intolerable, but strains frantically against that knowledge lest it impair his obsessive pursuit of the course, the tension between knowing and willing may itself destroy him."

[15] William Rosen, in *Shakespeare and the Craft of Tragedy* (Cambridge, Mass.: Harvard Univ. Press, 1960), p. 68, notes that only in retrospect is the speech ironic.

[16] George Duthie, "Shakespeare's *Macbeth*: A Study in Tragic Absurdity," in *English Studies Today*, ed. G. A. Bonnard (Bern: Franke, 1961), pp. 121-128, analyzes the division in Macbeth's mind before and after the murder.

the scenes leading up to the murder, he scarcely mentions the crown; he has none of his wife's sanguine anticipation of a golden round or nights and days of solely sovereign sway and masterdom. Unlike Tamburlane, he does not find kingship a sort of apotheosis of the human condition, and, unlike Richard of Gloucester, he is not driven by a compulsive need to command, to check, and to o'erbear such as are of better person than himself. In conventionally ambitious men, anticipation of the fruits of crime blunts the sensibilities to the crime itself. But Macbeth is just the opposite of this; he scarcely gives a thought to the spoils that will proceed from the act and keeps his attention unwaveringly upon the act itself; and his attitude toward the object of his fixation is mixed attraction and repulsion. His repulsion springs from the deeply moral side of his nature. No other character is so acutely aware of himself as living in the eye of heaven. When he looks into himself and finds there inclinations that are anything but celestial, he is frightened and revolted, and he extends his abhorrence of his own instinct to heaven nature:

> Stars, hide your fires;
> Let not light see my black and deep desires.
> The eye wink at the hand.
>
> (I.iv.50-52)

Yet on the heels of this can come a reassertion of the impulse to terrible and forbidden action: "yet let that be / Which the eye fears, when it is done, to see" (52-53). It is the very fearfulness of the deed that seems to exert the strongest attraction for him, since it calls for a degree of resolution and daring quite beyond the slaying of rebels. For Macbeth, action is self-definition; he is revolted by the act, but tantalized by the possibility of doing exactly that which is most expressly forbidden by all laws, sacred and humane. He dares to kill his king not so much to become king himself as to become the man who dared to do it.[17]

[17] A. P. Rossiter, in *Angel With Horns and Other Shakespearean Lectures*, ed. Graham Storey (London: Longmans, 1961), pp. 210-

220

In such a frame of mind—revolted by his own inner promptings, but drawn to them nonetheless—he goes home to his wife. Much of the commentary on the play has centered upon how well Lady Macbeth knows her man, perfectly or not at all. The answer, I believe, is that she has an unfailing instinct for his weaknesses and fixes them precisely, though his strengths come as a complete surprise to her. Her misunderstanding of him is the reverse of her misunderstanding of herself: she has perfect confidence in her strengths; but her weaknesses, when they declare themselves, catch her defenseless and unaware. Throughout the play, she is most self-assured in those moments when Macbeth's nerve is failing, but her own nerve fails in those scenes where he is most independent and ruthless.

Macbeth and his lady have the makings of one murderer between them. She is capable of contemplating the crime with something that borders upon exaltation, but is not, it turns out, capable of dealing the fatal stroke herself. He is quite capable of doing that, but cannot even think of the moral quality of the act without horror and aversion. He would, no doubt, be capable of resisting the temptation to strike were it not for the devastating attack she launches against the foundation of his world-view, his concept of what it means to be a man.[18] Thus, the great confrontation between them in Act I, scene vii, presents the disconcerting picture of *two* people inciting each other to crime, for the presence of each makes crime possible for the other.

Macbeth's soliloquy at the opening of the scene gives us our first full view of the hero's subjective world; it is a world in which action is a continuum, an ongoing process of cause and effect, act and consequence, a world in which retributive

---

211, also rejects conventional ambition as Macbeth's motive. See also Stewart, *Character and Motive in Shakespeare*, p. 93.

[18] Both Charlton, in *Shakespearean Tragedy*, p. 147, and Eugene Waith, in "Manhood and Valor in Two Shakespearean Tragedies," *ELH*, 17 (1950), 265-266, discuss Macbeth's divided mind on the concept of manhood.

justice is not merely possible but certain. It is also a world of relatedness, a world in which duties and obligations are well defined and divinely sanctioned.[19] In such a world, vaulting ambition, far from being heroic self-assertion, is unconscionable overreaching, a violation of the sacrosanct bonds that define one's humanity. By the end of the soliloquy, Macbeth has decided to abandon all thoughts of regicide, for in such a world, to proceed would be not only appalling, but positively suicidal. When he announces his decision to his wife, the reason he gives, the "golden opinions" his valor has just won from all sorts of people, is an evasion. He cannot explain his real reasons—retribution from heaven, the sacred bonds of obligation—because she simply would not comprehend them, would, in fact, heap scorn upon them.[20] But his stated reason is a significant and characteristic evasion; the golden opinions epitomize his position as a valorous subject who is content to accept the status of subject and live as an honored member of the community.

Lady Macbeth is able to undermine his resolution so quickly not simply because she calls his virility into question, and not simply because she exerts enormous personal power over their relationship; Macbeth is quite capable of withstanding such pressures. She finally achieves her purposes by suggesting to him that his whole apprehension of reality is mistaken, that action is not an open-ended continuum, but is final and conclusive, and that the essence of humanity is not living within the limits of an assigned place, but daring to do anything. Her attack on Macbeth is the same as Goneril's attack upon Albany; because he is moral, he is a coward and a fool who deceives himself about the way the world really operates.[21] But her arguments are far more effective than

[19] L. C. Knights, in *Some Shakespearean Themes* (1959: rpt. Stanford: Stanford Univ. Press, 1960), p. 134, notes the special emphasis in this play upon words that name familial and social relationships (children, servant, cousin, etc.).

[20] Adams makes a similar point on p. 156 of his edition.

[21] The parallel is also drawn by D. W. Harding, "Women's Fantasy

Goneril's because she is not telling her husband anything new, but reiterating things he had already told himself. Like Hamlet and Othello, Macbeth has a divided mind about some of the most fundamental issues of existence; Lady Macbeth is the voice of one side of it.

However, she makes not one but two false beginnings, first taunting him with the "hope" he has of being king, and then trying to use love to blackmail him. These tactics elicit no reaction whatsoever; Macbeth usually stays out of trouble as long as he can keep his mouth shut. But then she puts her finger squarely on the central paradox of his present position:

> Wouldst thou have that
> Which thou esteem'st the ornament of life,
> And live a coward in thine own esteem,
> Letting 'I dare not' wait upon 'I would,'
> Like the poor cat i' th' adage?
>
> (I.vii.41-45)

The ornament of life, his present position as first peer of the realm, is contingent upon his willingness to accept one limitation, not to dare to rise up against his king. She tantalizes him with his own self-image as a man who dares anything, for whom no limits of any kind exist. This line of argument draws an immediate reaction, not because he cannot stand her taunts of cowardice, but because she has touched upon a deep ambivalence in his own mind about what it is to be a man. He counters with a reassertion of the idea that to be a man is to live within human limits, and she responds with an assertion of the opposite:

MACBETH: I dare do all that may become a man;
Who dares do more is none.

(46-47)

of Manhood: A Shakespearean Theme," *Shakespeare Quarterly*, 20 (1969), 250-251.

LADY: When you durst do it, then you were a man;
And to be more than what you were, you would
Be so much more the man.

(49-51)

But this pro and contra is getting nowhere. Clearly, she needs
something to break the deadlock, and her instinct leads her
surely to the clincher: her version of the world and of man
was once *his* version too. She undermines his confidence in
the vision of the soliloquy by pointing out that he does not
fully believe in it himself. At one time he had been more than
willing to kill the king if only the opportunity would present
itself. "If we should fail?" (59). This, Macbeth's last attempt
at resistance, has been widely misunderstood. As the soliloquy
showed, he is not in the least worried about the practical
possibility of executing the murder: if that were all there were
to it, he would proceed at once. But the failure Macbeth fears
is the long-range failure in a world of relatedness, where action is a continuum and justice is certain—to be cut off forever from the rest of humanity, to be hated and cursed by all
men, and finally to be hounded down by inexorable retribution. It is the long-range failure he had pictured in harrowing
detail, and it is, in fact, exactly what happens. Lady Macbeth,
however, misunderstands him completely; she thinks he is
worried about the practicability of getting away with the
crime in the short run, and so she reassures him that her plan
is foolproof. We come now to the most crucial moment of
the tragedy, when Macbeth changes his mind for the second
time and commits himself to murdering the king. He is not
really persuaded; rather, as at several other junctures in the
play, he wilfully disregards his own better judgment, pushing
to the back of his mind all his best perceptions and most
passionately held beliefs, and substitutes in their place the
shallow, faulty rationalizations for which his wife has been
spokesman.[22] First of all, he unequivocally accepts the idea
that the essence of manhood is unbounded action:

[22] Sanders discusses Macbeth's "manifest will to self-deception" on
p. 284 of *The Dramatist and the Received Idea.*

> Bring forth men-children only;
> For thy undaunted mettle should compose
> Nothing but males.
>
> (72-74)

There is gruesome irony in his praising her fitness to bear sons, since she has just declared that she would kill her own child without compunction were it necessary to vindicate her will. But far more important, Macbeth accepts the notion that action is final and conclusive, that accomplishment of the deed is tantamount to success, that the consequences of an action may be circumvented:

> Will it not be received,
> When we have marked with blood those sleepy two
> Of his own chamber and used their very daggers,
> That they have done't?
>
> (74-77)

Like Othello's "And yet, how nature erring from itself—," it is the point of no return, for it signals not simply a change of mind, but a movement from one world-view to another. The seeds of Macbeth's tragedy are planted here, not only because he dedicates himself to the first of many brutal crimes, but even more because he does not really *believe* in a world in which a man may dare anything, in which action is final and conclusive. He *wants* to believe in it, for such a world poses no impediments to action. His ruthless will scores a temporary victory over his own best perceptions.[23] But the shallowness and patent self-deception of this speech contrast sharply with the intense and passionate conviction of the soliloquy. From this point on, Macbeth is in the position of having to insist with all the vigor of his will upon the truth

---

[23] Francis Fergusson, "*Macbeth* as the Imitation of an Action," in *The Human Image in Dramatic Literature* (Garden City, N.Y.: Anchor, 1957), p. 117, has suggested: "It is the phrase 'to outrun the pauser reason,' which seems to me to describe the action, or motive, of the play as a whole." See also the same author's *Shakespeare, The Pattern in His Carpet*, pp. 241-242.

225

of something which, in his own mind, he does not really believe. His method of insistence will be action, and the result will be tragedy.

The undermining of the subjective world is different in Macbeth's case from the undermining of the world-views of the other three heroes. They all found, for one reason or another, that their most fundamental assumptions about the world and themselves were erroneous: he, on the other hand, finds himself irremediably estranged by his actions from his most fundamental beliefs, an estrangement which deepens until he finds the absolute bedrock of the final soliloquy.[24] For the remainder of the play, Macbeth sees himself as being in fundamental conflict with the world itself, with his indomitable will pitted against its moral order, its communal obligations, its immutable and inescapable ethical laws. Like all the Shakespearean tragic heroes, he sees his own actions in cosmic terms; but after the dreadful finality of "I am resolved," he is positively obsessed by the notion of being at the center of a universe which is fundamentally opposed to what he is doing. Like Hamlet, he declares total, all-out war upon the world of the play, but his attack is not against duplicity and corruption, but against humane feeling and divine justice.

In the famous dagger speech, Macbeth animates and vivifies the elements themselves, endowing them with a moral attitude toward his actions. Nature itself is atrophied by the enormity of what he is about to do; the darkest and most sinister powers have usurped the primacy of nature and, like himself, hover breathlessly on the brink of an abyss. The night seems full of sentient beings all watching what he is about to do, and the very stones of the earth are ready to cry out. It is the same vision he had seen in the first soliloquy, but now charged and animated, for the action is no longer hypothetical, but is about to become an actuality. Having

---

[24] Sanders has brilliantly analyzed Macbeth's estrangement from himself and the "construction of a new 'self' whose premise is murder" (p. 290).

226

thus projected his own emotional state onto the world, he turns from this harrowing vision and forces to the front of his mind the simple imperative of action; action and only action has value, action is the very substance of life itself: "Words to the heat of deeds too cold breath gives. / I go, and it is done" (ii.i.61-62).

Yet in the very commission of his act, he is still haunted by the conviction that the entire universe is opposed to his breech of nature, as, in the *Macbeth*-world, it clearly is. His hysteria after the crime reflects not merely fear of real and imagined horrors; the purport of all his speeches after the murder is a sense of incalculable loss, panic-stricken realization of his estrangement from all that had formerly constituted his life, from his subjective world itself. First of all, he is cut off from the metaphysical order that is one of the givens of the *Macbeth*-world:

> But wherefore could not I pronounce 'Amen'?
> I had most need of blessing, and 'Amen'
> Stuck in my throat.
>
> (ii.ii.30-32)

He is cut off from the normal, life-sustaining processes of nature:

> —the innocent sleep,
> Sleep that knits up the ravelled sleave of care,
> The death of each day's life, sore labor's bath,
> Balm of hurt minds, great nature's second course,
> Chief nourisher in life's feast.
>
> (35-39)

The self-delusion that action is final and conclusive crumbles before the realization that the consequences of his deed will last as long as his life: "Macbeth shall sleep no more" (42). He is fully aware that he can never by any means get back to the bank and shoal of time from which he has so precipitously leaped; nothing can change or mitigate the consequences of his act:

227

Will all great Neptune's ocean wash this blood
Clean from my hand? No, this my hand will rather
The multitudinous seas incarnadine,
Making the green one red.

(59-62)

But most of all, his crime destroys his capacity to respect or
even to tolerate himself. For the remainder of the play, the
vantage point from which he judges himself is the world-view
from which he is hopelessly estranged. His own hands are
unrecognizable to him, savage, hangman's hands that would
pluck out his eyes. But, in fact, they do not obliterate his
vision; he must continue staring at them and at the self they
epitomize. The primary purpose of his act had been to define
his manhood. Ironically, it does, but the definition is one he
cannot contemplate without horror and revulsion: "To know
my deed, 'twere best not know myself" (72). This line sets
the tone for the remainder of the tragedy. He *is* his deed in his
own eyes, and in his own eyes his deed is appalling. Hence,
he faces the characteristic problem of the Shakespearean
tragic hero, how to endure what is, for him, simply unendurable. I do not read *Macbeth* as a tragedy of ambition, nor as a
tragedy of fear. It is above all a tragedy of self-loathing, of
self-horror that leads to spiritual paralysis, the tragedy of a
man who comes to condemn all that is in him for being there.
Macbeth is indeed terror-stricken in this scene, but what
strikes him full of terror is not the deed itself, and still less
the fear of being caught, but rather a full realization of what
his action has done to him. He has cut himself off from the
world he believes in and has committed himself to its
antithesis, a world in which man is a predatory animal. The
commitment is irrevocable, and all he can do is follow it re-
morselessly to its conclusion. It is as if by insisting vehemently
enough on such a world-view, Macbeth believes he can validate it, can establish its reality by sheer force of will. It is
the desperate need to validate the world-view to which he is
committed, his determination to win a battle of wills with the

228

macrocosm itself, that plunges him into steadily deepening cruelty in Acts III and IV. Where before he had refused to return to the chamber and look upon what he had done, he now rushes in without hesitation, feigning astonishment and grief. Where before the stirring and muttering of the sleeping grooms had all but paralyzed him, he is now capable of killing them without compunction. But despite the increasing vigor and brutality of his actions, he is never able to rid himself of his former vision of a world of relatedness and justice; rather, it becomes a kind of waking nightmare, forcing him to contemplate what he has lost and what he has become. The tension between the two world-views is clearly evident in his next soliloquy.

Macbeth had known all along that the prophecies in which he places such confidence decreed that Banquo's issue would ultimately come to the throne. Indeed, just a few minutes before the murder, he had discussed the weird sisters with Banquo, but did not for an instant allow the fact that his own posterity would benefit nothing from his crime to deter him. Characteristically, he pushed it out of his mind and wilfully ignored it until after he had committed the act toward which he was so strongly impelled. His soliloquy now is animated not so much by fear of Banquo as by intense envy of him, for Banquo is incumbent in exactly the position Macbeth himself has lost, that of a loyal peer whose daring and valor are exercised within the prescribed, acceptable limits: [25]

> 'Tis much he dares;
> And to that dauntless temper of his mind
> He hath a wisdom that doth guide his valor
> To act in safety.
>
> (III.i.51-54)

Moreover, Macbeth, as in the scene immediately following the murder, is acutely aware of his own enormous loss: he has filed his mind, put rancors in the vessel of his peace,

[25] Kirschbaum, in *Character and Characterization*, p. 59, takes a similar view.

229

slain a gracious king, and delivered up his soul to eternal damnation. It is a terrible self-awareness with which to live, and the knowledge that he has sacrificed everything to gain "nothing" makes it intolerable. Macbeth's solution, as at every crisis in the play, is ruthless, unrestrained action, the action of self-assertion, action based upon a world-view which makes of man a predatory hunter. Many critics have observed that, in the scene with the murderers, Macbeth uses the same line of argument that Lady Macbeth had used upon him. This is not because he has been learning tactics from his wife, but because he is now speaking from the same point of vantage as she had spoken from previously, attempting to validate the idea of manhood that underlies all his crimes. The hired assassins are to prove that their station in the file is not in the worst rank of manhood by ambushing a lone man and a boy. "Your spirits shine through you," Macbeth lauds them as soon as they agree (III.i.128).

The next scene displays even more vividly Macbeth's determination to impose, by sheer force of will, the version of reality to which he is committed upon the macrocosm itself:

> But let the frame of things disjoint, both the
> worlds suffer,
> Ere we will eat our meal in fear, and sleep
> In the affliction of these terrible dreams
> That shake us nightly.
>
> (III.ii.16-19)

But the affliction and the fears, like his own judgment of himself, arise from that other world-view where his emotions are really engaged, a world which demands his destruction for having violated its most basic laws. "Treason has done his worst" Macbeth reflects, thinking of Duncan's peaceful sleep (24); there is a terrible self-indictment implied in the line. His image of his own mind as a rack upon which he lies being tortured is most apt and precise, for it is the torture of tension, of being torn between irreconcilable opposites. When Macbeth undertook his crime, he undertook living with its aftermath, and now the most abhorrent aspect of that aftermath is the need to be a hypocrite, to give mouth-honor to a man whom at that very moment he is causing to be treacherously struck down:[26]

> Unsafe the while, that we must lave
> Our honors in these flattering streams
> And make our faces vizards to our hearts,
> Disguising what they are.
>
> (32-35)

Like the other Shakespearean tragic heroes, Macbeth is constitutionally incapable of tolerating false appearances, especially evil masquerading as good. What his heart is is bad enough in his eyes, but the realization that he must mask it under false magnanimity elicits from him one of the most anguished outbursts in Shakespeare: "O, full of scorpions is my mind, dear wife!" (36). Yet is seems to me that this is the only point in the scene at which the two protagonists are in emotional touch with each other. Throughout the rest of the encounter, she is trying desperately to bridge the gulf between them and he is consciously trying to widen it. Just as she had not foreseen her own failure of nerve in the aftermath of the murder, so she had not foreseen the emergence of a ruthless and completely independent will in her husband. She can no longer pour her spirits in his ear or chastize him with the valor of her tongue, and this signals a complete breakdown of their relationship, a breakdown which is at least as responsible as pangs of conscience for her own psychic disintegration. Over half her famous sleepwalking scene will be addressed to him, and will recreate exactly those moments when she was sustaining him through a crisis. But at this

---

[26] Knight (p. 171) suggests that the need to play the hypocrite is the worst element in Macbeth's suffering. Cleanth Brooks, "The Naked Babe and the Cloak of Manliness," in *The Well Wrought Urn* (New York: Reynal and Hitchcock, 1947), p. 32, sees Macbeth's hatred of hypocrisy as central to the clothing imagery of the play.

present juncture, all she can do is stare in astonishment and apprehension at the man he has, at her urgent insistence, become: "Come on. / Gentle my lord, sleek o'er your rugged looks" (26-27). But his struggle is with himself; it has very little to do with her: "Thou marvell'st at my words, but hold thee still; / Things bad begun make strong themselves by ill" (54-55). The last line is significant in two senses: first, it reasserts Macbeth's determination to validate by force of will the world-view to which he is committed, and, second, it implies that having embarked upon his course, he can now steel *himself* to commit further crimes. He no longer needs her to do it for him.

Of course, this does not prove to be the case, at least not all the time. In the banquet scene, Macbeth completely loses his nerve, and, just as suddenly, she finds hers again. His weakness is an absolute prerequisite for her strength. In assuming that the murder of Banquo and Fleance would set his mind at rest, Macbeth was once again wilfully deluding himself, pretending that, if he insisted vehemently enough upon something, and put that insistence into act, then the thing would be true. But even if Fleance had shared his father's fate, it would be difficult to imagine a Macbeth who was not cabined, cribbed, and confined; his prison, his torture chamber, is not the macrocosm but the microcosm, and the death of one man or of thousands is incapable of setting things to rights there. But the escape of Fleance once again makes him see that the murder of Duncan was not a final or definitive act. It will go on through a continuum of cause and effect to produce consequences completely beyond his control. When he confronts the shade of Banquo (or the evil spirit sent by the witches in Banquo's shape, or the product of his own haunted imagination—there is no way of telling which, and no need to tell), he gives voice, even in his hysteria, to the basic rift in his own subjective world. On the one hand there is the world of infinite daring, but on the other there is the world of swift and terrible justice, in which dead victims rise again to push murderers from their

232

stools. On the one hand there is the primitive world of the olden time when blood was shed in perfect impunity without compunction, but there is also the later order, in which humane statute has purged the gentle weal. Lady Macbeth tries once again to shame him into manhood, but he will have none of it. The visible emblem of what he has done terrifies him more than any consequences he may have to face as a result of revealing his guilt.

In the aftermath of his great feast, Macbeth is more convinced than ever that he is living in a macrocosm which implacably requires his destruction:

> It will have blood, they say: blood will have blood.
> Stones have been known to move and trees to speak;
> Augures and understood relations have
> By maggot-pies and choughs and rooks brought forth
> The secret'st man of blood.
>
> (III.iv.122-126)

Yet, far from impeding him from further action, his conviction only impels him to ever more ruthless action; his insistence upon the world to which he is committed is now fired by desperation. In the face of his implacable will, all causes shall give way. His image of himself is not simply of a man with bloody, hangman's hands, but of a man inundated in blood, bathed in it from head to foot, literally into it over his head. But the total estrangement from all his previous values confers upon Macbeth, as it has upon other Shakespearean heroes, a terrible, lonely freedom. The man who has lost positively everything he cherishes is the freest of all possible men; he has nothing further to lose and nothing to worry about salvaging.

By the time he reaches the witches' abode, the naked force of his will has reached apocalyptic proportions reminiscent of the third act of *King Lear*. Macbeth thinks he has come to learn by the worst means the worst, for to know the worst is to lose a large part of fear of the worst. But the witches *want* Macbeth to struggle and hope, for they know that struggle is futile and hope groundless, and therefore torture.[27] Thus, they tell him what appears to be better news than he had expected to hear. He greets the prophecies so eagerly not primarily because they promise him apparent invulnerability, but more because they confirm him in his chosen course, urge him to become exactly the kind of man he has been trying desperately to become: "Be bloody, bold, and resolute! Laugh to scorn / The pow'r of man" (IV.i.79-80); "Be lion-mettled, proud, and take no care" (90). But if one side of Macbeth is impelled to mindless violence, another side knows that actions have consequences, and he must discover what the consequences of his initial crime will be. The parade of kings is far more than merely a salute to Shakespeare's royal patron, and productions that cut it err seriously; for the sight of Banquo's crowned progeny enjoying the fruits for which he himself has lost everything of real importance to him forces Macbeth to confront the futility of all his actions, past, present, and future. In the face of this, paradoxically, his will to act is increased to almost manic intensity:

> The flighty purpose never is o'ertook
> Unless the deed go with it. From this moment
> The very firstlings of my heart shall be
> The firstlings of my hand.
>
> (145-148)

The more aware he becomes of his estrangement from the real world, the more vehemently he must insist upon the validity of the world he has embraced—even when he does not believe in its validity himself. This conflict between vehement action and conviction of the futility of action rages through his mind for the rest of the play. In the great scenes at Dunsinane, boasting speeches of furious resolve alternate with the most soul-sick contemplations ever written.

[27] See Fergusson, *Shakespeare, The Pattern in His Carpet*, pp. 244-245.

By far the most usual interpretation of the last act is that Macbeth has completely lost his humanity, has become the monster he set out to be, and though we continue to have grudging admiration for his animal courage, we rejoice with the followers of Malcolm when the tyrant and his fiend-like queen are overthrown. Rather, it seems to me that we are so absorbed in Macbeth's private conflict that his death and the triumph of unimpressive right is almost incidental to the tragedy. Moreover, Macbeth does not lose his humanity because he *cannot* lose his humanity no matter how hard he tries; that is exactly what makes him a tragic hero.[28] His case is in one way analogous to Othello's: the Moor repeatedly resolves to cast away all love for Desdemona, but he simply cannot do it. His love remains, coexistent with his belief she has betrayed him, and the result is excruciating inner torture. Macbeth's humanity is vested in that world-view he unfolded in his first major soliloquy, and, though his most vigorous efforts throughout the play have been to rid himself of that vision, he has never even come close to doing so. It remains as a vantage point from which he must assess all that he has done, all that he has lost, all that he has become: "I am sick at heart, / When I behold—" (v.iii.19-20). The thought is left uncompleted, but clearly what Macbeth beholds all through these scenes is himself:

> I have lived long enough. My way of life
> Is fall'n into the sear, the yellow leaf,
> And that which should accompany old age,
> As honor, love, obedience, troops of friends,
> I must not look to have.

> (22-26)

Honor, love, obedience, and troops of friends are the values of the limited, structured world he had abandoned; in the predatory world he embraced, they should have no impor-

[28] R. A. Foakes also differs from the majority view about Macbeth's lost humanity, in "*Macbeth*," in *Stratford Papers on Shakespeare, 1962*, p. 161.

tance whatsoever. "To be tender-minded / Does not become a sword," Edmund had observed. But those values are terribly important to Macbeth, and only his loss of them has made him realize how important they are. Alfred Harbage has observed that "no voice in literature has sounded with greater sadness" than Macbeth's in the above speech.[29] To have a passionately held, demonstrably valid vision of the world, and yet to be cut off from it by one's own actions, to be hated and cursed by all humanity, to have to struggle against one's own most deeply felt emotions, and to be *aware* of all this with perfect, unblinking clarity, is surely the most harrowing vision of human isolation that has ever been realized in drama. It is perhaps the degree of his self-awareness that most differentiates him from other Shakespearean malefactors: he sees his own situation unflinchingly and refuses either to soften it or to be sentimental about himself. He drains the ingredients of his poisoned chalice to the last bitter dregs. Self-awareness is one of the hallmarks of the Shakespearean tragic hero, and in Macbeth's case, it is the very essence of his tragedy. Also, like the other three, he has a desperate need to have his actions in consonance with a broader scheme of reality, including the rest of humanity and the metaphysical order. But, as Macbeth fully realizes, such consonance is impossible for him because he is so utterly cut off from the only world he believes in or values. In self-recognition and self-horror he realizes he has lost even the capacity to feel fear, and a moment later he cannot feel normal human grief at the death of his wife. Above all, he realizes he has committed himself to action and yet he believes action to be futile, full of sound and fury, but signifying nothing.

That the vision of life offered in Macbeth's final soliloquy is not Shakespeare's ultimate or only significant pronouncement upon the human condition we need only our experience with the canon, including the other tragedies, to attest. Besides, *Macbeth* does not "make a statement" any more

[29] Ed., *Macbeth*, in *The Complete Pelican Shakespeare*, p. 1108.

than Lear did. What Shakespeare was dramatizing was a potentiality of the human condition, in this case a most grim potentiality, but as true in its context as any other embodied in his dramas. It is realized with exceptional conviction and power, and to shrug it off as the observation of a man who has lost his humanity may make the play easier to live with, but undermines its imaginative vigor and ruthless integrity. Macbeth's pronouncement is the only pronouncement on life in the *Macbeth*-world; nothing of comparable weight is there to counterbalance it, and it draws its power not only from the greatness of the verse but also from its dramatic context. And here, I think, is the center of the problem, for is not its context a world which finally is moral, surely the most thoroughly just world Shakespeare created for a tragedy? The *Macbeth*-world is a moral world founded upon a moral incongruity, for while evil seems to issue spontaneously and irrepressibly from its very core, its most basic law is that evil *is* evil and must be destroyed. The same incongruity is repeated in the microcosm; Macbeth is strongly impelled to evil, but he is no less strongly impelled to abhor evil. Hence, he comes to abhor himself. If the world is basically inclined to evil, as the *Macbeth*-world is, then justice becomes little more than a tragic necessity. Its pyrrhic victory is retributive but not redemptive.

The play, then, explores dialectically the complementary tension between proneness to evil and abhorrence of evil in both the macrocosm and the microcosm. Macbeth is not a tragic hero *in spite* of his criminality but *because* of his criminality. Had he been able to resist his own inclinations and the promptings of his wife, he would be of no more interest than any other successful general. Had he been able to kill without compunction, he would be simply one of our rarer monsters. But he is caught in the tension between his action and his reaction, the primary tension of the *Macbeth*-world, and in his struggle and his failure to reconcile irreconcilable conflicts, he assumes tragic dimensions.

237

SIX

CONCLUSION

In my opening chapter, I alluded to the feeling that Shakespeare's four mature tragedies are related to each other in ways they are not to his historical, early, and Roman tragedies, and that the four of them together, more than even the greatest of them (whichever that may be) alone, constitute Shakespeare's full realization of the tragic potentiality in life. Like most extensive examinations of these four tragedies, the present study has been in large measure a search for common denominators and illuminating differences, an attempt to define, however partially or imperfectly, the essence of their solidarity, the vision behind them that places them in a class by themselves. If the foregoing has accomplished anything, I hope it has established that, in each of these plays, the world-view of the title character disintegrates, his subjective world collapses, and he must come to some new relationship with the world around him, with the cosmos itself. Much of the power of these plays derives from the fact that the undermining of the microcosm is at the level of the most fundamental values, values that are absolutely essential to the sustenance of life, and the demolition of the subjective world is devastatingly complete. It is, I think, significant that, while the pattern is repeated in each of the four tragedies I have been discussing, it is *not* discernible in the Roman tragedies written during roughly the same period.[1] Brutus does not make a radical reappraisal of himself. It does not occur to him that the premises of his actions are false, that he is not the man he thought he was, or that his apprehension of the world has been totally wrong. No doubt he regrets some

[1] For an interesting comparison of the mature tragedies and the Roman plays see Stampfer, *The Tragic Engagement*, pp. 17-19.

238

tactical blunders and would do certain things differently if he had them to do again, but he dies as secure as ever in his righteousness. The most remarkable thing about Coriolanus is that he can pass through so much tumultuous experience and be changed so little by it. He may switch his political allegiance impulsively, but his allegiance to Coriolanus is unshakable, and the man whom the Volscians strike down in Act v is exactly the same man who stormed the gates of Corioli in Act I. Antony is a more complicated case because he several times comes close to the kind of dissolution I have been discussing, especially after his flight at Actium. But his conviction that his love outweighs all losses sustains him to the end, even after he realizes he has been duped into fatally wounding himself.

Moreover, while the viewpoint of the Roman plays is complementary, the issue involved is not an ordered, benevolent universe versus a violent, anarchic one. At the risk of making a gross oversimplification, one may say that the Roman tragedies all have as their central theme some aspect of the relationship between the individual and the state: *Julius Caesar* explores the problem of individual conscience and the state; *Coriolanus* explores the relation between heroic individualism and the state; *Antony and Cleopatra* weighs romantic love against the demands of the state. The mature tragedies, on the other hand, isolate the individual in the cosmos, destroy his assumptions about it, and throw him on his own resources to cope with it as he can. The Roman heroes do not universalize their situations, nor are they driven by a compelling need to act in consonance with a set of universal norms. Most significantly, none of them is vulnerable to having his private world undermined at the level of its most fundamental assumptions. Were Brutus to decide that in killing Caesar he had committed a heinous crime against his own humanity, had Coriolanus sacked Rome and had to live with himself afterward, had Antony concluded Cleopatra had to be destroyed, we would have a very different kind of drama, something closer to *Othello* or *Macbeth*. This is not in the least to suggest that Shakespeare should have written his Roman

239

plays differently, or that they are a less astonishing accomplishment than his tragedies. The point is that the same patterns which relate the four tragedies to each other separate them from the rest of the canon.

Looking quickly over the rest of Shakespeare's tragic plays, we find that, while the collapse of the hero's world is not central, something like it does occur—or almost occurs—in several of them. *Timon of Athens*, that fascinating botched job, certainly presents a radical reversal of world-views, but, like so much in this play, the transition is sketched in roughly rather than drawn. When Timon retires at the end of II.ii, he still has faith that his friends will help him, and when we next see him in III.iv, he is already the confirmed misanthrope he will remain for the rest of the play. Instant transition from one view to another is not the same as the struggle to reorder a demolished world. Moreover, as Rabkin has pointed out (p. 193), the complementary balance characteristic of Shakespeare's drama appears, for whatever reason, to have completely broken down in this play.

In *Romeo and Juliet* the issues are completely different from the preoccupations of the mature tragedies. Beauty and love are destroyed by a combination of adult malice, youthful impetuosity, and bad luck, but the values involved are always clear and unambiguous, and the lovers' struggle is with their circumstances, not with their views of themselves or the world. However, Shakespeare's other early tragedy, *Titus Andronicus*, does present us with a character stripped of all that had previously constituted reality for him, and does embody the kind of psychic dissolution that signals the collapse of the subjective world. But the problem, of course, is that it makes no sense to talk of Titus' subjective world because the character is not that elaborately drawn. Moreover, while the situation may suggest the most sweeping questions about the nature of the world and the wellsprings of human cruelty, the questions are never seriously taken up. Still, as has been frequently observed, the play, at least in retrospect, is a clear marker on the long road to *King Lear*.

240

Richard III experiences a failure of nerve on the eve of Bosworth, and he has momentary doubts about the wisdom of the course he has pursued. But one can hardly call his temporary breakdown the collapse of his world. His pangs of conscience are isolated and momentary, and not too awfully convincing. In any case, the next morning he has fully recovered and, like Claudius, goes about his expedient tasks with no sign that his soul is divided. *Richard II*, however, is another case entirely, and constitutes an important milestone in Shakespeare's development as a tragic poet. By the end of the play, Richard's assumptions about himself and the world have been undermined, and, to a limited extent, he does universalize his situation. His fall is clearly the prototype of what is to come in the mature tragedies, though less fully and forcefully realized. But *Richard II* is fundamentally different from the later tragedies because it is less concerned with questions of universal order than with questions of political order. The emphasis is not upon Richard's struggle or failure to come to terms with the macrocosm, but upon the problems raised by the presence of an utterly incompetent king. If he is left on the throne he will surely wreck the kingdom, but if he is removed primogeniture will break down and decades of civil war may follow. Richard's personal misfortune, though compellingly depicted, is always subordinate to the main concern of the play, and the main concern is what happens if the king is deposed, not what happens to the king who is deposed. Richard has (or comes to have) many of the qualities of the Shakespearean tragic hero, but his characterization is set in a play that has few of the hallmarks of mature Shakespearean tragedy.

In reviewing *Hamlet, Othello, King Lear*, and *Macbeth* (accepting that this is the order in which they were written), one is struck by the way they become progressively grimmer, the worlds they delineate more gruesome and less habitable. The *Lear*-world is terrible because the medieval Christian assurances have been removed, but the *Macbeth*-world is worse precisely because those assurances have been left intact and made the premises of tragedy. Moreover, as the worlds progressively darken, the fact of the hero's death becomes less central to the substance of the tragedy. *Hamlet* ends tragically because Hamlet dies; he has come to terms with the world, has accomplished his mission, and if he had lived would have proved most royal. Othello, however, can never come to terms with the world once he has killed Desdemona; to go on living would be impossible, and death is a way of evening the scales. For Lear, the tragedy is life; death is deliverance from the rack. By the time we reach *Macbeth*, death is almost incidental; Lady Macbeth and probably her husband both die off-stage, and their demise is announced after the fact. The tragedy is complete by the end of the hero's final soliloquy. Tragic suffering is mental suffering in Shakespeare, and the substance of tragedy is the way men live, not the hero's mortality.

At no point in this study has it been my intention to formulate a general theory of tragedy or of Shakespearean tragedy, but rather to examine one aspect—though a crucially important one—of tragic experience as rendered by Shakespeare at the height of his powers. The destruction of the subjective world does not occur in every play which critics are accustomed to discuss under the largely honorific term, "tragedy." Orestes' problems, for instance, are clearly with the Eumenides, not with his view of the Eumenides. The complete disorientation of the individual from his most basic assumptions about himself and the world around him is certainly not a definition of tragedy, but just as certainly, the collapse of the subjective world figures prominently in a conspicuous number of works that may be called tragic, in Sophocles' *Oedipus the King*, for example, or in Dostoyevsky's *Crime and Punishment*, or in such modern works as O'Neill's *The Iceman Cometh* or Miller's *Death of a Salesman*.

But ultimately the essence of tragedy, as well as its irresistible attraction, remain a mystery; the most we can attempt is analysis of its parts in the hope that understanding of the parts will contribute to our appreciation of the whole. One

242

of Shakespeare's most extraordinary gifts was the ability to grasp and depict the complex, intensely problematic nature of existence, a gift at least as important to his art as his theatrical craftsmanship or his astonishing powers of expression. Taken together, the four mature tragedies strike one as a coherent unit of expression, a single, protracted act of the imagination. One cannot define the vision behind them without simplifying it out of existence; but one can note that the common subject of all four plays is the struggle of an extraordinary individual to come to terms with a complex, uncertain, two-sided reality after all his basic assumptions and confidences have been destroyed. Shakespeare's emphasis is invariably upon the problems rather than the solutions, and the substance of his tragedy is not the outcome of the struggle, but the struggle itself.

"FALSE" RHETORIC IN *OTHELLO*

A NUMBER of influential critics have based their unfavorable appraisal of the Moor in part upon the very idiom in which he expresses himself:

> I do agnize
> A natural and prompt alacrity
> I find in hardness.
>
> (I.iii.231-233)

"Can you really take a fellow who talks like that seriously," the anti-Othello critics ask in effect. Yes.

G. Wilson Knight appears to have been the first to suggest that at certain times, especially in the speech beginning "O cursed, cursed slave," Othello's speech degenerates into "an exaggerated false rhetoric." Subsequent critics have descended upon the passage like the Huns and the Visigoths:

> Whip me, ye devils,
> From the possession of this heavenly sight!
> Blow me about in winds! roast me in sulphur!
> Wash me in steep-down gulfs of liquid fire!
> Oh Desdemon! dead Desdemon! dead! Oh! Oh!
>
> (v.ii.278-282)

Knight opines: "There is a sudden reversal of poetic beauty: these lines lack cogency because they exaggerate rather than concentrate the emotion. Place beside these violent eschatological images the passage from *Lear*: 'And my poor fool is hang'd!' " (p. 113). It is no accident that such objections to Othello's speech come from critics who approach the play mainly through its diction and imagery; the results in this case illustrate one limitation of the method. In the passage

245

from *Lear*, the dramatic situation is entirely different from that in *Othello*. The King is lamenting a heartbreaking loss imposed upon him from without, while Othello is confronting a brutal crime which he himself has committed. If it makes sense to compare the imagery of two speeches without reference to dramatic context, then why not substitute for Knight's passage from *Lear* a different speech from the storm scene?

> You sulph'rous and thought-executing fires,
> Vaunt-couriers of oak-cleaving thunderbolts,
> Singe my white head. And thou, all-shaking thunder,
> Strike flat the thick rotundity o' th' world,
> Crack Nature's moulds, all germains spill at once,
> That makes ingrateful man.
>
> (III.ii.4-9)

Surely throughout the storm scenes Lear is using images as "violent" and "eschatological" as anything in Othello's speech, but must we say then that Lear is "exaggerating" rather than "concentrating" his emotion? Such comparisons are utterly specious. Dramatic verse is "cogent" or "lacks cogency" insofar as it succeeds or fails in dramatizing the situation and emotion involved. The situation and emotion in Othello's case is nothing less than the literal howling of the damned, and, given the tension of the situation, it is hard to imagine how "violent eschatological images" exaggerate it, any more than they do Lear's battle with the elements.

Once the "false" rhetoric idea gained currency, however, subsequent critics, most notably Leavis and Heilman, expanded it, arguing that Othello's speech throughout the play is supposed to reflect self-deception, limitedness of feeling, and egotistical self-dramatization.[1] Now "false" and, by implication, "true" applied to rhetoric are very nebulous terms indeed. Presumably the assertion is that Othello's idiom is

[1] Leavis, "Diabolic Intellect and the Noble Hero," p. 143; Heilman, *Magic in the Web*, pp. 137-138. John Bayley effectively refutes Leavis in *Characters of Love*, pp. 155-157.

grandiloquent and orotund, but there is no concrete evidence of this in the text. Rather it seems to be a feeling which some critics have about the tone of Othello's verse, a feeling which, as the briefest glance at the rest of the canon shows, is in no way justified. Shakespeare frequently used heightened, stately, even artificial rhetoric without there being the slightest intimation that the character is a pompous self-dramatizer. I am particularly struck by the similarity in tone and technique between Othello's Senate speech and Burgundy's speech to the gathered belligerents in *Henry V* (v.ii.23-67). Both are formal addresses to persons of great rank; both are intended to mollify disputants and restore order to a turbulent and dangerous situation; both use embellished, stately, even-paced verse; both, though low-keyed, are primarily appeals to the emotions rather than the intellects of the auditors. Many of the same rhetorical devices appear in Burgundy's speech and in Othello's—elaborate physical description in vivid visual terms, long strings of mutually supporting adjectives ("the naked, poor, and mangled peace"), and similar strings of nouns ("Dear nurse of arts, plenties, and joyful births . . . hateful docks, rough thistles, kecksies, burrs . . . vinyards, fallows, meads, and hedges"), and a fondness for highflown words unusual in Shakespeare's idiom ("con-greet," "deracinate"). Now is this rhetoric "true" or "false"? Should all this elaborate formality and complex redundancy lead us to see Burgundy as a pompous bore, infatuated with the sound of his own voice—a kind of Elizabethan commencement orator? Clearly that is not the intention, since the speech is a turning point of the play, leading directly to the celebrative tone of the conclusion.

Of course, Burgundy's speech is a prepared address upon a most formal and solemn occasion, while Othello uses his "false" rhetoric in conversation and even in soliloquy. But so does John of Gaunt in his conversation with York in *Richard II*, culminating in his famous apostrophe to England beginning, "Methinks I am a prophet new inspired" (II.i.31-68). Gaunt's is very fancy rhetoric indeed, replete with redundant images and keen visual detail. Perhaps, however, it is not "true" but "false" rhetoric. Should we see in this scene an old man enjoying the staginess of his own death, "A lunatic lean-witted fool, / Presuming on an ague's privilege" (115-116), as Richard describes him? Is Shakespeare exposing for our modern edification the hysteria of chauvinism? Again, one can only appeal to the context, the purpose of the speech, the prevailing view of Gaunt among other characters, and common sense.

Shakespeare did, on occasion, use rhetorical excess to underscore the tendency of a character to dramatize himself, and the history play at hand provides the most spectacular example: "Down, down I come, like glist'ring Phaeton, / Wanting the manage of unruly jades" (III.iii.178-179). One can easily gather that Richard is striking a pose, but Shakespeare did not depend upon rhetoric alone to establish so crucial a point as Richard's self-dramatization. Both his friends and his enemies agree that he is too fond of histrionics and reproach him for it, and his shameless theatricality in the deposition scene puts even the laconic Bolingbroke out of patience. Now Othello is accused of a great many faults by other characters in the play, but no one, not even Iago who lets no weakness pass without comment, so much as hints that the Moor enjoys contemplating his own image or takes an attitude toward his own emotions.

The problem with the "Othello music" theory as expounded by Leavis and Heilman is that, being very nebulously conceived, it is tested against one case only. Once we remove this critical approach of differentiating between "true" and "false" rhetoric outside *Othello*, its amorphous nature becomes clear. If heightened, artificial, or musical rhetoric is an indication of something fishy about a character, might one not postulate "Cleopatra music" to show the shallowness and egotism of the Queen? And if one were to do so, how account for the fact that the most rhapsodic concert of such music issues from the mouth of the level-headed Enobarbus when he describes her arrival on her barge? Or should we hear in the "Prospero music" the sentimentalizing of a self-pitying old man who, to compensate for past misfortunes, has set himself up as a petty tyrant? The implications of such an approach would be appalling if one took them seriously. The "false" rhetoric theory is not simply wrong in its conclusions; the approach itself is utterly specious.

ESTMAR COLLEGE LIBRARY